Maurice Merleau-Ponty
Between Phenomenology and Structuralism

Theoretical Traditions in the Social Sciences

General Editor: ANTHONY GIDDENS

This series aims to create a forum for debate between different theoretical and philosophical traditions in the social sciences. The series will concentrate on the work of particular thinkers whose ideas have had a major impact on social science.

Maurice Merleau-Ponty

Between phenomenology and structuralism

James Schmidt

Boston University

St. Martin's Press   New York

St. Martin's Press, Inc., 175 Fifth Avenue, New York, NY 10010
Printed in Hong Kong
Published in the United Kingdom by Macmillan Publishers Ltd.
First published in the United States of America in 1985

ISBN 0-312-52309-2
ISBN 0-312-52310-6 (pbk.)

Library of Congress Cataloging in Publication Data
Schmidt, James.
Maurice Merleau-Ponty: between phenomenology and
structuralism.
Bibliography: p.
Includes index.
1. Merleau-Ponty, Maurice, 1908-1961. I. Title.
B2430.M3764S36   1985   194   84-24829
ISBN 0-312-52309-2
ISBN 0-312-52310-6 (pbk.)

For J. E. M.

Contents

Acknowledgements

My thanks go first of all to Anthony Giddens, Steven Kennedy, and John Winckler for their encouragement at the start and their patience in waiting for the finish.

The finish was made easier by Gretchen Arnold (who processed these words), Jane MacDonald (who proofed them), and Carole Chandler (who persuaded a somewhat recalcitrant machine to give them back). A grant from the Graduate School of Boston University helped to defray the cost of preparing the manuscript.

I owe my introduction to Merleau-Ponty's work (and a good deal more) to four teachers: Christopher Schaefer, Hayward Alker, W. E. Griffith, and Kurt H. Wolff. I am also obliged to John O'Neill for suggesting some of the themes which eventually found a home in the third chapter. My first extended foray into Merleau-Ponty's writings took place at the Research Insitute on International Change (Columbia University); its director, Seweryn Bialer, deserves long-overdue thanks. Erazim Kohák, Jeffery Mehlman, and George Psathas, my colleagues at Boston University, helped on a number of points, both bibliographic and conceptual.

The manuscript profited greatly from Tom McCarthy's comments; its author has gained even more from his encouragement and support. Tim Allen saved me from a number of false steps, provided a steady stream of helpful references, aided with the index, and suggested some fruitful lines of inquiry. And Jim Miller helped beyond measure. We first met on a sweltering summer evening a decade ago over under-cooked chicken, Barry White, and Alban Berg and talked about Merleau-Ponty. We have talked a good deal since then, and I hope that some of what I have gained from our friendship has made its way into these pages.

James Schmidt

The author and publishers would like to thank Northwestern University Press for permission to reproduce extracts from Maurice Merleau-Ponty, *Adventures of the Dialectic*, translated by Joseph Bien (1973), and Maurice Merleau-Ponty, *The Visible and the Invisible*, translated by Alphonso Lingis (1968) and Routledge & Kegan Paul and Humanities Press Inc. for permission to reproduce extracts from Maurice Merleau-Ponty, *Phenomenology of Perception*, translated by Colin Smith (1962).

Note on Abbreviations and Translations

Abbreviations in the Notes and References refer to the following of Merleau-Ponty's works. Although I have always cited English translations, I have made a number of minor changes in the interest of consistency and clarity.

AD   *Adventures of the Dialectic*, trans. Joseph Bien (Evanston: Northwestern University Press, 1973)

CAL   *Consciousness and the Acquisition of Language*, trans. Hugh J. Silverman (Evanston: Northwestern University Press, 1973)

H&T   *Humanism and Terror*, trans. John O'Neill (Boston: Beacon Press, 1969)

IPP   *In Praise of Philosophy*, trans. John Wild and James M. Edie (Evanston: Northwestern University Press, 1963)

PP   *Phenomenology of Perception*, trans. Colin Smith (London: Routledge & Kegan Paul, 1962)

PrP   *The Primacy of Perception and Other Essays*, edited by James M. Edie (Evanston: Northwestern University Press, 1964)

PW   *The Prose of the World*, trans. John O'Neill (Evanston: Northwestern University Press, 1973)

S   *Signs*, trans. Richard C. McCleary (Evanston: Northwestern University Press, 1964)

SB   *The Structure of Behaviour*, trans. Alden L. Fisher (Boston: Beacon Press, 1963)

SNS   *Sense and Non-Sense*, trans. Hubert L. Dreyfus and Patricia Allen Dreyfus (Evanston: Northwestern University Press, 1964)

TFL   *Themes from the Lectures at the Collège de France 1952–1960*, trans. John O'Neill (Evanston: Northwestern University Press, 1970)

VI   *The Visible and the Invisible*, trans. Alphonso Lingis (Evanston: Northwestern University Press, 1968)

1

Introduction: Merleau-Ponty and Social Thought

This is a study of Maurice Merleau-Ponty's social thought, its often troubled relations with Edmund Husserl's phenomenological philosophy, and its equally ambivalent stance toward those approaches in the human sciences which take Ferdinand de Saussure's structural linguistics as their point of departure. It seeks to do justice to one of the more complex and elusive figures in contemporary philosophy and social theory. By the time of his death, Merleau-Ponty was regarded as 'the greatest of French phenomenologists'; yet his last writings questioned the very coherence of Husserl's project.[1] He built a case for Marx's philosophy of history which is among the most subtle in the Marxian tradition; and he produced one of the most powerful and merciless critiques Marxism has ever received.[2] He was the first French philosopher to appreciate the importance of Saussure's linguistics; but even his admirers admit that the things he purported to find in Saussure are simply not there to be found.[3] He was the author of a corpus of works whose relevance for contemporary social theory has been matched only by the striking indifference which they all too often have received.[4] He was and remains an enigmatic and compelling thinker. As one of his most able readers once confessed, 'Thinking about him produces a kind of verbal vertigo.'[5]

The life and the reputation

He was born in 1908 and, despite the loss of his father in the First World War, enjoyed what he later described to Jean-Paul Sartre as 'an incomparable childhood'.[6] He attended the Parisian lycées Janson-de-Sailly and Louis-le-Grande and in 1930 graduated from the École Normale Supérieure. It was there that he first met Sartre, whose work would both inspire and annoy him for the rest of his life. While teaching philosophy at various lycées in the 1930s he made the acquaintance of Claude Lévi-Strauss and Simone de Beauvoir, entered into a brief association with the group around the Catholic left journal *Esprit*, and attended – along with Raymond Aron, Georges Bataille, Raymond Queneau, Jacques Lacan, Eric Weill, and (occasionally) André Breton – Alexandre Kojève's historic lectures on Hegel's *Phenomenology of Spirit* at the École Practique des Hautes Études. By the end of the decade he had become interested in the phenomenology of Edmund Husserl, whose efforts to provide 'an inventory of consciousness as milieu of the universe' would remain a lifelong point of reference for his own work.[7] His *thèse complementaire*, *The Structure of Behaviour*, was completed in 1938 and published four years later.

He served in the infantry between 1939 and 1940. During the Occupation he resumed contact with Sartre through the Resistance group 'Socialism and Liberty', the two discovering that by different paths they had come to a common interest in Husserl and Heidegger. He completed his major work, *Phenomenology of Perception* (1945), shortly before the end of the war, drawing in part on a collection of Husserl's unpublished manuscripts which had been transported from Louvain to Paris in 1944.[8] After the Liberation, he collaborated with Sartre in the publication of the review *Les Temps Modernes*, serving as political editor and publishing essays on philosophy, politics, and the arts which were subsequently reprinted as *Sense and Non-Sense* (1948). A series of articles on Arthur Koestler's novel *Darkness at Noon* became the basis for his controversial study of the Moscow trials, *Humanism and Terror* (1947).

Having received his doctorate on the strength of his first two books, Merleau-Ponty taught at the University of Lyon and the École Normale, offering courses on the philosophy of language, psychoanalysis, *Gestalt* psychology and the social theory of Durkheim, Mill, and Weber. In 1949 he was named to a position at the Sorbonne in 'Child Psychology and Pedagogy'. There he taught a sequence of courses on the linguistic and cognitive development of the child, the relations of the child with adults, and – on a more theoretical plane – the relationship between phenomenology and the human sciences.[9]

As a consequence of longstanding political differences exacerbated by the Korean War, Merleau-Ponty broke with Sartre and resigned from the editorial board of *Les Temps Modernes* in 1952.[10] In the same year he was appointed to the chair of philosophy at the Collège de France, a position which had been held a generation earlier by Henri Bergson. His inaugural lecture, *In Praise of Philosophy* (1953), was dedicated to the memory of his mother, with whom he had remained very close. She had died in the same year as his appointment and his dispute with Sartre.

His courses at the Collège de France and his writings throughout the 1950s spoke to his desire to complete the analysis begun in *Phenomenology of Perception* with an account of expression and a philosophy of history. *Adventures of the Dialectic* (1955), over half of which was consumed by a detailed and bitter critique of Sartre's philosophy and politics, explored the promise and the shortcomings of the Marxian philosophy of history. A series of masterful essays, subsequently republished as *Signs* (1960) – a work whose elegiac introduction recorded the healing of the breach with Sartre – probed the nature of expression in philosophy, art, and politics. In the latter half of the 1950s he became increasingly critical of Husserl's standpoint and increasingly receptive to certain aspects of Martin Heidegger's work. He now felt it was necessary to elaborate a 'new ontology' which would be presented 'without any compromise with *humanism*, nor moreover with *naturalism*, nor finally with theology'.[11]

He died suddenly on 3 May 1961. At the time he was working on a manuscript posthumously published as *The Visible and the Invisible* (1964). Another unfinished manuscript, begun before his appointment to the Collège de France and abandoned sometime around 1952, was eventually published under the title *The Prose of he World* (1969).

, His career as a writer thus began in the wake of Sartre's existentialism and ended on the eve of the counter-offensive Lévi-Strauss would launch, in *The Savage Mind* (a book dedicated to Merleau-Ponty's memory), against Sartre, phenomenology, and the *cogito*.[12] Throughout the 1950s Merleau-Ponty had sought to distance his understanding of phenomenology from that of Sartre by marshalling the very authorities which, as Vincent Descombes has noted, 'would be invoked against all forms of phenomenology after 1960':

During the fifties, Saussurian linguistics and the structural anthropology of Lévi-Strauss were his allies. It is as if these allies in the resistance to Sartrian activism transformed themselves, after Merleau-Ponty's death in 1961, into opponents of phenomenology in general, forming the heteroclite camp which was christened 'structuralism'.[13]

Once those lines had been drawn, it was clear to the structuralists where Merleau-Ponty belonged: on the other side of the divide which separated them from phenomenology. His critique of Sartre, however bitter, appeared in retrospect to have been but a family squabble. Gilles Deleuze, reviewing Michel Foucault, expressed as succinctly as anyone the concerns that had come to the fore with the new decade:

A cold and concerted destruction of the subject, a lively distaste for the notion of origin, of lost origin, of recovered origin, a dismantling of the unifying pseudo-synthesis of consciousness, a denunciation of all the mystifications of history performed in the name of progress, of consciousness, and of the future of reason.[14]

Michel Foucault, reviewing Gilles Deleuze, pressed home how different all of this was from Merleau-Ponty:

Logique du sense [Deleuze's book of 1969] can be read as the most alien book imaginable from *The Phenomenology of Perception*. In this latter text, the body-organism is linked to the world through a network of primal significations, which arise from the perception of things, while, according to Deleuze, phantasms form the impenetrable and incorporeal surface of bodies; and from this process, simultaneously topological and cruel, something is shaped that falsely presents itself as a centred organism and that distributes at its periphery the increasing remoteness of things.[15]

Where Merleau-Ponty remained faithful to Husserl's call for a return to the 'things themselves' and sought access, in the world of perception, to the 'origin of truth', the most influential thinkers of the 1960s were suspicious of the entire vocabulary which spoke of origins, of returns, and even of truth. Where Merleau-Ponty sought 'foundations' and 'grounds', they found only 'ruptures' and 'displacements'. And thus he came to suffer the cruellest of fates which can befall a French thinker: he became unfashionable.[16]

Such a reading of his work, however, is a bit too neat. His structuralist critics were as blind to the ambivalences which wracked his writings as his phenomenological disciples. Both defined his achievement almost exclusively in terms of the *Phenomenology of Perception* – structuralists to criticise it, phenomenologists to embrace it. But while the *Phenomenology of Perception* may be his most impressive work, his philosophical development did not end in 1945. He saw the need to address problems which it had barely mentioned. And in addressing these problems he came to see that it was necessary to rethink the grounds on which the *Phenomenology of Perception* rested.

The works and the lacunae

The itinerary Merleau-Ponty intended to pursue is sketched clearly enough in a prospectus he drew up at the time of his candidacy to the Collège de France. In it, Merleau-Ponty saw his work as falling into two distinct phases: (i) an attempt 'to restore the world of perception' and (ii) an attempt 'to show how communication with others, and thought, take up and go beyond the realms of perception which initiated us to the truth'.[17] The first stage, consisting of *The Structure of Behaviour* and *Phenomenology of Perception*, had been completed by 1945. The second phase, which would trace the 'sublimation' of the perceptual world, had been anticipated in a few of his post-war essays – Merleau-Ponty specifically pointed to *Humanism and Terror* and to essays on Cézanne and Simone de Beauvoir's novel *L'Invitée*, both of which had been collected in *Sense and Non-Sense*. But, he noted, 'the philosophical foundations of these essays are still to be rigorously elaborated'.[18] This was the task reserved for a work tentatively titled *The Origin of Truth*. As a prologue to this book, Merleau-Ponty planned to write a study of literary expression, to be called *The Prose of the World*. It would approach 'less directly' the process by which the world of perception was sublimated into a world of symbols which were, in turn, shaped in history, and would focus on how writers such as Montaigne, Stendhal, Proust, Breton, Arbaud, and Valéry took up existing conventions of speech and employed them in new ways.[19]

While Merleau-Ponty seems initially to have conceived *The Prose of the World* as 'a sort of *What is Literature?*'[20] – here, as elsewhere, Sartre would serve as a spur for his own studies – the implications of the book reach beyond the fields of aesthetics or poetics. In his prospectus, Merleau-Ponty expressed the desire to 'elaborate the category of prose beyond the confines of literature and give it a sociological meaning'.[21] He seems to have wanted to employ the analyses developed in *The Prose of the World* as prototypes for his inquiries into the domain of social theory proper:

> The linguistic relations among men should help us understand the more general order of symbolic relations and of institutions, which assure the exchange not only of thoughts but of all types of values, the co-existence of men within a culture and, beyond it, within a single history.[22]

Such an approach to history, he argued in his inaugural lecture at the Collège de France, could overcome the shortcomings of Hegelian and Marxist philosophies of history by showing a way beyond the fruitless opposition of '*things* versus *consciousness*'.[23]

His hopes, however, never bore fruit. *The Prose of the World* was abandoned sometime around 1952 and while certain of the implications of the inaugural lecture were pursued in courses on language, literature, and history conducted at the Collège de France between 1952 and 1955,[24] the next work he published was not the promised elaboration of a sociologically relevant account of prose. Instead, drawing on discussions of Weber and Lukács from his 1953–4 course 'Materials for a Theory of History' and coupling them with a blistering critique of Sartre's 1952 articles 'The Communists and Peace', he produced *Adventures of the Dialectic*, a work which he described in its preface as a set of 'samplings, probings, philosophical anecdotes, the beginnings of analyses'.[25]

The reader who searches for a sequel to the *Phenomenology of Perception* which would show how the 'bad ambiguity' of perceptual life gives birth to the 'good ambiguity' of expression is thus brought up short. Had Merleau-Ponty died in 1953, leaving *The Prose of the World* unfinished, one could try to flesh out the argument by turning to the essays which immediately preceded it and, when necessary, making recourse to *Phenomenology of Perception* in hopes of ferreting out the more general presuppositions on which the entire enterprise rested. But Merleau-Ponty died in 1961, not 1953, and *The Prose of the World* was not interrupted; it was abandoned. It may very well be not simply an *unfinished* book; it is quite possibly a book which Merleau-Ponty found to be *unfinishable*.

The difficulties facing a reader who desires to complete what Claude Lefort once termed Merleau-Ponty's 'unfinished thought'[26] do not, however, end here. With his attempt to show how expression took up and transcended the world of perception now abandoned, Merleau-Ponty went on to call into question the conclusions he had reached in the first phase of his career. It is not simply *The Prose of the World* which became problematic for him; he also came to regard *The Structure of Behaviour* and the *Phenomenology of Perception* with ever-greater suspicion.

Throughout the 1950s Merleau-Ponty was working on a manuscript which was tentatively titled, at one time or another, *Being and Meaning*, *Genealogy of the True*, *The Origin of Truth*, and finally *The Visible and the Invisible*.[27] In the 'working notes' Lefort appended to the unfinished text of *The Visible and the Invisible*, Merleau-Ponty stressed the need for a study which 'takes up again, deepens and refines my first two books' and which would thus bring the results of the *Phenomenology of Perception* to 'ontological specification'.[28] He felt that it was necessary 'to show that what one might consider "psychology" (*Phenomenology of Perception*) is in fact ontology' and considered one of the central tasks of this ontology to be 'the elaboration of the notions that have to replace that of transcendental subjectivity, those of subject, object, meaning'.[29] The purpose of *The Visible and the Invisible*, at first glance, would thus appear to be that of showing that the discussions of incarnate subjectivity in the *Phenomenology of Perception* were not to be taken simply as a contribution to the understanding of the subject; they were, more importantly, an entrée to an account of the structure of being.[30]

But it is apparent from some of the working notes that more was afoot here than a simple clarification of what the *Phenomenology of Perception* had presumed; Merleau-Ponty also stressed that certain of the accounts offered in the earlier book were in crucial ways deficient 'due to the fact that in part I retained the philosophy of "consciousness" '.[31] The problems posed in the *Phenomenology of*

Perception, he wrote, 'are insoluble because I start there from the "consciousness"–"object" distinction'.[32] It was not enough, then, simply to clarify the argument of the *Phenomenology of Perception*. Increasingly, Merleau-Ponty seems to have felt that it was necessary to reformulate the arguments attempted there from a standpoint other than that of the reflecting subject. A note written a little over a year before his death indicates the magnitude of the revisions he had in mind:

> Replace the notions of concept, idea, representation with the notions of *dimensions*, articulation, level, hinges, pivots, configuration – – The point of departure = the critique of the usual conception of the *thing* and its *properties* → critique of the logical notion of the subject, and of logical inherence → critique of the *positive* signification (differences between significations), signification as a separation [*écart*], theory of predication – founded on this diacritical conception.[33]

A set of terms deriving from the 'philosophy of consciousness' (concept, idea, mind, representations) is to be replaced with a new set of terms (dimensions, articulations, levels, hinges, pivots, configurations) which neither give primacy to the standpoint of consciousness nor rest on a distinction between subject and object.

Even before this explicit recognition that the vocabulary of the 'philosophy of consciousness' had to be rejected, a peculiar new argot begins to make its way into Merleau-Ponty's published writings. 'Vision' replaces 'perception', 'carnal existence' is used instead of 'corporeal existence', 'Earth' is used in place of Merleau-Ponty's more usual 'world', 'being' begins to be written with a capital letter, and 'flesh', perhaps the most important of these new categories, gradually comes into prominence.[34] At roughly the same time a curious shift of agency begins to occur at decisive moments in some of Merleau-Ponty's writings. In his last essay, 'The Eye and the Mind', we are told that painters sometimes find the relationship between themselves and the things they paint reversed and sense 'that things are looking at them', while the notes to *The Visible and the Invisible* stress the necessity of saying 'that things have us, it is not we who have things . . . language has us . . . it is not we who have language . . . it is being that speaks within us and not we who speak of being'.[35]

It is by no means clear what the ultimate goal of these changes in terminology, expression, and voicing might have been. Commentators on *The Visible and the Invisible* have found in it a shift 'from phenomenology to metaphysics',[36] a replacement of 'time' by 'Being' as the central analytic category,[37] an abandonment of Husserl's notion of intentionality as a point of departure,[38] a recognition of the degree to which 'philosophies of consciousness' must draw on the illusion of non-linguistic signification to support the *cogito*,[39] a 'displacement of the place of thought',[40] a 'defenestration' of the philosophy of the *cogito*,[41] and a 'ritual killing of the father' – Husserl – that was both 'pious and pitiless'.[42] Indeed, as Marjorie Grene has observed, perhaps the only thing that is 'wholly clear' in this 'enigmatic document' is that Merleau-Ponty saw the need to develop 'a new, or renewed, ontology'.[43]

This is a study of Merleau-Ponty's social thought and not an account of his ontology. But while I shall make no attempt to decode all the riddles of Merleau-Ponty's last writings, the fact that Merleau-Ponty was engaged, in the last years of his life, on a project which called into question certain aspects of his earlier work cannot be ignored. Merleau-Ponty attempted to elaborate an account of expression and history which presumed the validity of certain arguments he had articulated in the *Phenomenology of Perception*. He could not do it and, after abandoning *The Prose of the World*, he began to outline an argument which culminated in a work which differs markedly from the *Phenomenology of Perception*. While it is unreasonable to argue that the failure of his philosophy of expression and history was the sole cause of his decision to take up again the questions which the *Phenomenology of Perception* presumably settled, it is equally unreasonable to assume that his failed attempt at an account of expression and history and his critique of his earlier work have nothing to do with one another. *What* they might have to do with one another is one of the questions I have sought to investigate in this book.

An overview and some caveats

My concern, then, will be with the way Merleau-Ponty's efforts at articulating the social dimension of his phenomenological account of perception led him to adopt a stance towards his initial standpoint which, while paralleling in certain respects the critique of phenomenology which developed in France in the decade after his death, nevertheless remained in a productive tension with central elements of Husserl's project. The argument will be elaborated by examining the evolution of Merleau-Ponty's thinking on three issues: (i) the relationship of philosophy and the human sciences (Chapter 2); (ii) the nature of intersubjectivity and the problem of our knowledge of others (Chapter 3); and (iii) the character of expression and of historical meaning (Chapter 4). These three problems not only illuminate different aspects of Merleau-Ponty's social theory, they also show how his thought developed as a consequence of a dialogue with a few key thinkers. Thus, Chapter 2 examines Merleau-Ponty's stance towards Husserl and Lévi-Strauss, Chapter 3 is concerned with his stormy relationship with Sartre and, to a lesser extent, his debts to the work of Jacques Lacan, and Chapter 4 explores his use of Saussure and its significance in his interpretation of Marx, Weber, and Georg Lukács. In a concluding chapter I have attempted, in a somewhat more cursory fashion, to locate Merleau-Ponty's final position with regard to Husserlian phenomenology and structuralist analyses.

The perspective I have sought to open on Merleau-Ponty's work differs from that of other studies. I have been concerned with keeping his most general notions about the nature of society and his understanding of the proper concerns and character of the human sciences at the centre of this account. Such a focus necessarily implies certain choices about what is to be highlighted and what is to be neglected. I have ventured into his more strictly philosophical works – *The Structure of Behaviour*, the *Phenomenology of Perception*, and *The Visible and the Invisible* – only in so far as they cast light on the way in which he conceived the relationship between philosophy and the human sciences, on his account of the 'Other', or on his account of expression and history.[44] Likewise, I have discussed his more exclusively political works – I am thinking here primarily of some of the essays in *Sense and Non-Sense* and *Signs* as well as *Humanism and Terror* – only in so far as they illuminate the motives behind his turn from Marx to Saussure.[45] I have forgone an examination of his critique of contemporary psychology in order to devote more attention to his discussion of developments within ethnology, sociology, and linguistics.[46] Perhaps most important, the account I have given of the development of his critique of

Husserlian phenomenology has focused on the impetus given by his failed attempt at elaborating a philosophy of expression and history and thus has not been able to consider other possible motivations for his critique of Husserl. This is, of course, not to deny that there were other influences at work. Certainly his renewed interest in Heidegger in the last years of his life goes a long way towards explaining at least some of the motivations behind the argument of *The Visible and the Invisible*; but I will have less to say about Heidegger here than about Lévi-Strauss, Lacan, Marcel Mauss, and Max Weber. This is a study of Merleau-Ponty's views on society and the social sciences, and whatever Heidegger (or Bergson, or Scheler) might have contributed to the development of his ontology, he had little to say to Merleau-Ponty's social thought.[47]

I should also note that I have tried to be more forthright than has sometimes been the case in the secondary literature about the peculiarities of Merleau-Ponty's interpretations of other thinkers. Much in them seems to involve either serious misunderstandings or wanton misrepresentations. His reading of Husserl, for example, is quite suspect; his discussion of Saussure, more often than not, is simply wrong. There seems little reason to ignore his somewhat wayward exegeses of other thinkers' works, especially when an understanding of the degree to which he misread other thinkers may be one of the best guides we have to understanding his own peculiar concerns and emphases. I need to stress as well that it is not at all clear that Merleau-Ponty was able to bring many of the problems discussed here to anything even remotely resembling a convincing or even an unequivocal conclusion. But it must also be stressed that in almost every case I would rather have Merleau-Ponty's misreadings and equivocations than the scrupulous but tedious exegeses of more responsible, but less provocative, commentators or the clear but implausible or inconsequential conclusions of more single-minded, but less gifted, theorists. Merleau-Ponty may have been a staggeringly inaccurate reader of Saussure, but what he forced Saussure to say is as important as anything Saussure actually said. Merleau-Ponty may have been maddeningly obscure as to what his final conclusions were with regard to the problems with which he wrestled; but the problems he faced were real problems, and if he did not manage to solve them, at least he noticed them.

That, in the end, is what matters about Merleau-Ponty. He did not answer all of the questions he asked, but the questions he posed more often then not still lie at the heart of contemporary social theory. Nearly a quarter of a century after his death he remains current. His problems are ours, and if a reading of his work does not make them vanish, it at least allows us to understand a bit more clearly what is at stake.

2
Phenomenology, Structuralism, and the Human Sciences

Descartes's ghost

Explaining phenomenology at the Sorbonne in February, 1929, Edmund Husserl began:

> No philosopher of the past has affected the sense of phenomenology as decisively as René Descartes ... Phenomenology must honor him as its genuine patriarch ... The study of Descartes' *Meditations* has influenced directly the formation of the developing phenomenology ... to such an extent that phenomenology might almost be called a new, twentieth century, Cartesianism.[1]

Descartes had shown phenomenology the path it must follow: 'Anyone who seriously considers becoming a philosopher must once in his life withdraw into himself and then, from within, attempt to destroy and rebuild all previous learning.'[2]

Three decades later, in Geneva, Claude Lévi-Strauss called on the city's native son for aid in exorcising the spell the patriarch of phenomenology had cast over the human sciences:

> To attain acceptance of oneself in others (the goal assigned to human knowledge by the ethnologist), one must first deny the self in oneself. To Rousseau we owe the discovery of this principle, the only one on which to base the sciences of man. Yet it was to remain inaccessible and incomprehensible as long as there reigned a philosophy which, taking the *cogito* as its point of departure, was imprisoned by the hypothetical evidences of the self.[3]

Descartes believed that one could proceed directly 'from a man's interiority to the exteriority of the world'; he forgot that 'societies, civilizations – in other words, worlds of men – place themselves between these two extremes'.[4]

For Husserl, Descartes was the model that philosophy must emulate; for Lévi-Strauss, he was a symbol of everything the human sciences must reject. And for Merleau-Ponty, he was the last to know that 'secret of equilibrium' between philosophy and science which subsequent generations could neither completely recover nor totally forget. Science, philosophy, and theology could mutually support one another in his system only because 'the mental universe was not torn apart' and 'men remained at the entrance to the three paths'.[5] The equilibrium had been 'lost for good', but its memory continued to haunt philosophy and the human sciences: 'Our science and our philosophy are two faithful and unfaithful consequences of Cartesianism, two monsters born from its dismemberment.'[6]

Virtually all of Merleau-Ponty's works can be read as attempts to reunite parties which, since Descartes, had increasingly come to face one another as antagonists. His first two books displayed a mastery of the relevant empirical research in behavioural and *Gestalt* psychology. His courses at the Sorbonne surveyed a broad spectrum of work in developmental psychology and linguistics. He studied the works of Emile Durkheim and Marcel Mauss and was an enthusiastic commentator on the writings of Claude Lévi-Strauss. Even as he moved closer to the work of Martin Heidegger in the last years of his life, he chided Heidegger for condemning philosophy to silence too quickly by ignoring the light which developments in the natural sciences cast on fundamental issues in ontology.[7]

Merleau-Ponty found in phenomenology a philosophy which seemed uniquely open to the contributions of the empirical sciences. Yet Lévi-Strauss, one of the 'non-philosophers' on whom he drew for philosophical insights,[8] argued that the development of his discipline had been thwarted for too long by that 'philosophy of the *cogito*' which Husserl had sought to perpetuate. Our examination of Merleau-Ponty's social thought can take its start from these diverging evaluations of the relevance of Husserlian phenomenology for the human sciences.

In the Turkish bath

Merleau-Ponty and Lévi-Strauss were exact contemporaries, born in 1908 – a fact that occasioned a set of arcane references to the number eight at the start of Lévi-Strauss's inaugural lecture at the Collège de France.[9] They first met in 1930 when, along with Simone de Beauvoir, they were brought together at the Lycée Janson-de-Sailly to complete the training which led to the *'agrégation'*, the examination which certifies would-be teachers as competent to teach in lycées.[10]

Like Simone de Beauvoir's slightly older friend, Jean-Paul Sartre, Merleau-Ponty and Lévi-Strauss were repelled by the academic philosophy in which they were trained. Sartre found the lectures in the *'cours magistral'* to be 'idiotic' and 'abstained from ever going to the Sorbonne'.[11] The questions which had driven him to philosophy – 'Why do we lead a life which is disqualified by its absences? And what does it mean to live?' – found no answers in the lecture hall:

> Futile and serious, our teachers were ignorant of History. They replied that these were questions which shouldn't be asked, or that were badly expressed, or (and this was a tic of every teacher at the time) that 'the answers were to be found in the questions'. To think is to weigh, said one of them, who did neither.[12]

Lévi-Strauss was no kinder toward his reputedly 'advanced' teacher, Gustave Rodrigues:

> He was, it is true, a militant member of the S.F.I.O. [the French Socialist Party]: but on the philosophical level all he had to offer was a mixture of Bergsonism and Neo-Kantianism ... He expounded his dry dogmatic views with great fervour and gesticulated passionately throughout his lessons. I have never known so much naive conviction allied to greater intellectual poverty.[13]

Merleau-Ponty's reaction was much the same. He characterised the curriculum in which he was trained as 'a march to the Kant of the Three Critiques'. It ignored such concerns as art, the problem of the other, and history; it reduced speech to an 'exterior accompaniment' of the thoughts of a 'pure consciousness'.[14] All these issues, typically consigned to the disciplines of empirical psychology and sociology, demanded a philosophy far more willing to confront the ambiguities of existence than that rationalism which, with the eruption of the Second World War, was 'collapsing before our eyes'.[15]

The tradition that Sartre, Lévi-Strauss, and Merleau-Ponty were rejecting was epitomised by Léon Brunschvicg, the dominant influence in philosophy at the Sorbonne from 1909 until the German occupation in 1940. Paul Nizan, Sartre's friend and classmate, sketched a nasty portrait of the man in his 1931 novel, *Aden, Arabie*:

> This little retailer of sophisms had the physical appearance of an old maitre d'hotel who late in life had been permitted to grow stout and wear a beard . . . Winking, letting fly his witicisms as though they were decrees of reason, suggesting in every speech: leave it to me, everything is going to be all right, I can fix everything, both in souls and in the sciences.[16]

Brunschvicg's thought, as Merleau-Ponty characterised it in a more temperate recollection from 1959, 'consisted primarily of an effort of reflection, of a return to the self' which took Kant and Descartes as its models.[17] He viewed the existence of objects of knowledge as relative to the act of judgement which creates them; the copula 'is' had no force of existence for him – an argument which greatly annoyed Gabriel Marcel, an early influence on Merleau-Ponty – it merely expressed the synthesis which consciousness had effected through its own activity.[18] Consciousness, however, was not a static category for Brunschvicg. The history of western thought could be viewed as a progress, at times interrupted, from the individual *cogito* to that universal *cogito* which found its purest expression in science, mathematics, and philosophical reflection. This was what Nizan, Sartre, Lévi-Strauss, and Merleau-Ponty could not accept. Empirical history bore scant resemblance to Brunschvicg's '*progrès de la conscience*' and his focus on the activities of scientific consciousness said nothing about the life of concrete individuals.[19]

What did? Lévi-Strauss found his answer when he chanced upon Robert H. Lowie's *Primitive Society* and at last made his escape from 'the claustrophobic, Turkish bath atmosphere' of philosophy by turning in 1934 to the field of ethnology.[20] Nizan reached his conclusion even earlier. By the mid-1920s he was associated with the *'Philosophies'* group, a circle of young radical intellectuals (including Georges Politzer, Henri Lefebvre, and Norbert Gutermann) who on occasion formed alliances with André Breton's surrealists in a common front against contemporary French philosophy.[21] Merleau-Ponty found an approach to philosophy that was 'a good deal more concrete, a good deal less reflexive' than that of Brunschvicg in the writings of Henri Bergson.[22] Jean Wahl's 1932 study of William James, Alfred North Whitehead, and Gabriel Marcel, *Vers le concret*, struck a common chord in both Sartre and Merleau-Ponty.[23] And Alexandre Kojève's lectures on Hegel's *Phenomenology of Spirit*, with their radically secular and anthropological interpretation of Hegel's work, had a decisive impact on Merleau-Ponty.[24] But the thinker who would prove to be most crucial for both Merleau-Ponty and Sartre was Edmund Husserl.

Waiting for phenomenology

Phenomenology, Merleau-Ponty wrote in 1945, 'existed as a movement' before it came to full consciousness of itself as a philosophy:

> It has been long on the way, and its adherents have discovered it in every quarter, certainly in Hegel and Kierkegaard, but equally in Marx, Nietzsche, and Freud.

Readers who encountered Husserl or Heidegger for the first time had the impression 'not so much of encountering a new philosophy as of recognizing what they had been waiting for'.[25]

So it seems in the case of Sartre, who first encountered what he had been waiting for at that fateful meeting with Raymond Aron and an apricot cocktail which Simone de Beauvoir preserved for posterity:

> We spent an evening together at the Bec de Gaz in the Rue Montparnasse. We ordered the speciality of the house, apricot cocktails; Aron said, pointing to his glass: 'You see, my dear fellow, if you are a phenomenologist, you can talk about this cocktail and make philosophy out of it!' Sartre turned pale with

emotion at this. Here was just the thing he had been longing to achieve for years – to describe objects just as he saw and touched them, and extract philosophy from the process.[26]

Husserl provided Sartre with the escape route Lévi-Strauss had found in ethnology. 'We have all read Brunschvicg, Lalande, Meyerson,' he wrote in 1939, 'we have all believed that the spidery mind trapped things in its web, covered them with a white spit and slowly swallowed them, reducing them to its own substance.'[27] Phenomenology was the emetic he needed to counter this 'digestive philosophy':

> To know is to 'burst toward', to tear oneself out of the moist gastric intimacy, veering out there beyond oneself, out there near the tree and yet beyond it, for the tree escapes me and repulses me, and I can no more lose myself in the tree than it can dissolve itself in me.[28]

Heady stuff, this phenomenology. It allowed Sartre to maintain the standpoint of the *cogito* without dissolving all reality into consciousness.

Merleau-Ponty's first encounter with Husserl's work was a good deal less colourful, and its impact was considerably weaker. He attended Husserl's lectures at the Sorbonne, although he understood little of what was being said; Husserl lectured in German, and at this point Merleau-Ponty did not know the language.[29] By 1933 he had drawn up a proposal for a thesis, 'On the Nature of Perception', which sought to demonstrate – against Brunschvicg – that the 'sensible and the concrete' are 'ireducible to intellectual relations' and that the 'universe of perception is not assimilable to the universe of science'.[30] But to demonstrate this, he turned not to Husserl (who is never mentioned in the initial proposal) but to *Gestalt* psychology and 'Anglo-American realist philosophies'.[31] He first became acquainted with Husserl's work in 1934, when Sartre returned from Berlin with a copy of Husserl's *Ideas Towards a Pure Phenomenology and Phenomenological Philosophy*. After studying the book, he read – with less interest – Husserl's *Logical Investigations* and then took up the *Cartesian Meditations* and the *Formal and Transcendental Logic*.[32] But he did not seem to find what *he* 'had been waiting for' in phenomenology until he turned to

Husserl's *Crisis of the European Sciences and Transcendental Phenomenology* (the first two parts of which appeared in the journal *Philosophia* in 1936), the essay 'The Origin of Geometry' (which appeared posthumously in the 1939 memorial issue of the *Revue international de philosophie*), and the unpublished second book of the *Ideas* (which Merleau-Ponty read, along with the unpublished third part of the *Crisis*, the virtually unobtainable posthumously published *Experience and Judgement*, and a 1934 manuscript entitled 'Overthrow of the Copernican Doctrine' during a 1939 visit to the newly established Husserl archives in Louvain).[33] In these works he found a Husserl who, in his eyes, had rejected the standpoint of the 'estranged spectator' of the Cartesian rationalism and instead had taken up a study of concrete, individual existence that coincided perfectly with the position Merleau-Ponty himself had reached – in part under the influence of Gabriel Marcel, Max Scheler, Emmanuel Mounier, and Kojève's Hegel – in *The Structure of Behaviour*.[34]

Exits

Four escapes from the Turkish bath of French philosophy: Lévi-Strauss to Brazil and Anglo-American ethnology, Nizan to Aden and Marx, and Sartre and Merleau-Ponty to Husserl – the former spending a year at the French institute in Berlin (1933–4), the latter staying in Paris, except for his brief trip to the Husserl archives. On the face of it, the route chosen by Sartre and Merleau-Ponty kept them closer – theoretically as well as geographically – to everything from which Lévi-Strauss and Nizan were fleeing. Had not Husserl himself, in his lectures at the Sorbonne, stressed the continuity of his work with the project of Descartes? Could not the audience at the Sorbonne, whether more sympathetic to Brunschvicg or to Bergson, find resonances in Husserl's thought? Husserl, after all, shared Brunschvicg's conviction that philosophy had to be a rigorously scientific examination of the categories through which we give meaning to the world and, like Bergson, had a passion for the detailed description of the immediate data of consciousness and a conviction that 'intuition' was central to the practice of philosophy.[35] How could Merleau-Ponty escape from the prison of the *cogito* by turning to a thinker who closed his Sorbonne lectures with

Augustine's '*Noli foras ire, in te redi, in interiore homine habitat veritas*'?[36]

The answer must be sought in the ambivalent relationship between Merleau-Ponty and Husserl. Merleau-Ponty's reading of Husserl was not Lévi-Strauss's. For Merleau-Ponty, phenomenology was not simply another 'philosophy of the *cogito*'; it was a philosophy which recognised the claims of the empirical sciences and put the *cogito* back in the world. He read Husserl in a notoriously 'creative' way, appropriating what he needed, rewriting what he could, overlooking what was irrelevant or antithetical to the project he had sketched for himself. He read Husserl this way at least in part because he had learned the tricks from Husserl himself, who had read Descartes in much the same way. So before we examine Merleau-Ponty's reading of Husserl, we must acquaint ourselves with his paradigm: Husserl's reading of Descartes.

Husserl's Descartes

At the Sorbonne, Husserl had termed phenomenology a 'new, twentieth century Cartesianism'. When he expanded these lectures into his *Cartesian Meditations* (1931) he again called phenomenology a 'neo-Cartesianism' but immediately added that 'precisely by its radical development of Cartesian motifs', phenomenology had been forced 'to reject nearly all the well-known doctrinal content of the Cartesian philosophy'.[37] For Husserl, the Cartesian project was thus a complex of vital but muddled intentions which had uncovered a set of suggestive but misunderstood themes.[38] He shared with Descartes a conviction that philosophy alone could give the various empirical sciences the foundation which they now lacked. He was likewise convinced that the type of reflection which Descartes had introduced was the privileged path to this foundation. But he nevertheless felt that Descartes had misunderstood what it meant for philosophy to be rigorous and scientific, had employed his radical doubt in a fashion that was fundamentally misguided, and had an understanding of the *cogito* which was fatally flawed.

The ideal of science

Like Descartes, Husserl saw the goal of philosophy to be that 'conceptual distinctness and clarity' which is the hallmark of science, rather than that 'profoundity' which is 'an affair of wisdom'.[39] He felt, however, that Descartes had been misled by a 'fatal prejudice' which took the goal of *one* class of sciences – 'the ideal approximated by geometry and mathematical natural sciences' – as the proper goal of *any* scientific philosophy.[40] What was 'fatal' here was the belief that a scientific account must terminate in a reference to 'a universal and absolutely pure world of physical bodies', a belief which ultimately rests on the assumption that sensory experience will not deceive us if we carefully purge our perceptions of all subjective distortions. In assuming that the essence of science consists of such a reference to a world of things which exist independently of the subject, Descartes had equated scientificity in general with one particular example: Galilean science.[41]

In Husserl's view, 'science' is by no means exhausted by what he terms the 'objective sciences'.[42] The 'genuine concept of science' cannot be grasped 'by a process of abstraction based on comparing of the *de facto* sciences'.[43] Rather, one must analyse the *intentions* which sustain any conceivable scientific endeavour. If this is done, science will be seen to be a search for 'truths which are valid, and so, *once for all* and *for everyone*'.[44] Science is thus ultimately understood as 'an order of cognition, proceeding from intrinsically earlier to intrinsically later cognitions' which at each point rests on the determination to derive each judgement from evidence which is certain.[45] Understood in this way, the practice of science is agnostic towards ontology. It does not need to commit itself to any notion of what or how reality 'is'. It defines itself solely by its *use* of evidence, not by the alleged characteristics of this evidence.

What is afoot here, as Eugen Fink noted in the Husserl-endorsed defence of phenomenology he wrote for *Kant-Studien* in 1933 (an essay which exercised a considerable influence on Merleau-Ponty's reading of Husserl), is a 'transformation of the idea of science' which, starting from the traditional conception of science as 'world-immanent' knowledge, ' "extends" the concept of science by developing a knowing which is "world-transcendent" '.[46] Under the aegis of phenomenology, philosophy can no longer be viewed as one science among others. Rather, it is 'in a definite sense prior to all worldly knowledge'.[47]

The use of doubt

To appreciate the peculiar notion of science to which Fink was alluding, we must turn to the second of Husserl's differences with Descartes: his reformulation of Descartes's method of radical doubt. Descartes had employed doubt in hopes of finding, like Archimedes, 'one point, fixed and immovable, to serve in leverage'.[48] Husserl, in contrast, stressed that the goal of the suspension of the thesis of the natural standpoint – the constantly present but never explicitly articulated conviction that a self-subsisting world of facts exists 'out there beyond the subject' – was not to try to rescue 'a little tag-end of the world' from which the project of restoring the once-doubted world might proceed.[49] The phenomenological *epoché* or phenomenological reduction was for Husserl a methodological device which allowed him to illuminate a range of phenomena which might otherwise escape attention.[50] It is not an attempt to replace the thesis of the natural standpoint with an antithesis; it is, rather, an attempt to 'shut off', 'disconnect' or 'bracket' the thesis so that its functioning may be more carefully examined.[51]

This difference is worth underlining, for Merleau-Ponty made much of it. Recall how Descartes began the third of his *Meditations*:

> I shall now close my eyes, stop my ears, withdraw all my sense, I shall even efface from my thinking all images of corporeal things; or since that can hardly be done, I shall at least view them as empty and false.[52]

Doubt appears here as a substitute for an operation which 'can hardly be done': the annihilation of the world. For Husserl it is precisely the *persistance* of the world – the inability of doubt alone to close our eyes, stop our ears, withdraw our sense, and purge our minds of images – which is crucial. The phenomenological *epoché* does not annihilate the world; nor is that its intent. When we abandon the natural standpoint the world does not vanish; we are not left with nothing. Rather we are presented with a domain which we must now investigate on terms other than those which are suggested by the thesis of the natural standpoint.[53]

The status of the cogito

The most explicit and in many ways most basic of Husserl's differences with Descartes follows directly from his reformulation of the method of radical doubt. Since the world does not vanish, leaving the solitary thinking ego alone to contemplate its own existence, the *cogito* itself stands in need of reformulation:

> The transcendental heading, *ego cogito*, must . . . be broadened by adding one more member. Each *cogito*, each conscious process . . . *"means"* something or other and bears in itself, in this manner peculiar to the *meant*, its particular *cogitatum*.[54]

The ego does not simply think, it must think *about* something. Consciousness is not simply conscious; it is consciousness *of* something. The world which Descartes had tried to shut out returns at the heart of the *cogito* as *cogitatum*.[55]

This reformulation brings us to one of the better-known themes of Husserl's phenomenology: the so-called 'intentionality of consciousness'. Husserl owed the term itself to Franz Brentano who, in turn, had taken up the Scholastic notion of 'intentional inexistence' in his *Psychology from an Empirical Standpoint* (1874) as a way of denoting that 'reference to content', 'direction upon an object' and 'immanent objectivity' which characterises mental, as opposed to physical, phenomena.[56] Husserl, however, had doubts about the soundness of 'the use of the word "psychical" as the equivalent of intentionality'.[57] In the *Cartesian Meditations* he gave the term a carefully delimited meaning:

> The word intentionality signifies nothing else than this universal fundamental property of consciousness: to be consciousness *of* something; as a *cogito*, to bear within itself its *cogitatum*.[58]

Defined in this way, the term says nothing about the ontological status of consciousness and does not provide, as it did for Brentano, an index by which the 'being of consciousness' could be set off against the 'being of objects'.[59]

Intentionality, as Husserl understood it, made no contribution to our understanding of human psychology. Still less did it force us to see ourselves, in Sartre's words, 'on the road, in the town, in the midst of the crowd, a thing among things, a man among men'.[60] The ego to which Husserl made reference was not the object of empirical psychology. Brentano and Sartre were, in effect, making what, for Husserl, had been Descartes's fatal error:

> For Descartes, the *Meditations* work themselves out in the portentous form of a substitution of one's own psychic ego for the absolute ego, of psychological immanence for egological immanence, of the evidence of psychic, "inner", or "self-perception" for egological self-perception; and this is also their continuing historical effect up to the present day.[61]

To make these substitutions was to comprise one's analysis with a language which imported all of the prejudices of the natural standpoint into the description of the field which had been opened by its alleged suspension. To speak as if one were analysing 'an' ego (among other egos), to talk about a world 'outside' this ego, or to make use of the 'dangerous first person singular' in describing the activities of this ego, would be to take for granted a set of distinctions – ego and alter ego, ego and world, I and you – which must be systematically constructed rather than simply invoked.[62]

Husserl argued that the entire Cartesian project had shipwrecked here, with

> the apparently insignificant but actually fateful change whereby the ego becomes a *substantia cogitans*, a separate human *'mens sive animus'*, and a point of departure for inference according to the principle of causality.[63]

Descartes, certain that he exists as long as he thinks, but uncertain as to what it is that he is when he is thinking, surveyed a number of possible descriptions and concluded:

> I am therefore only a thinking thing, that is to say, a mind, an understanding or reason – terms the significance of which has hitherto been unknown to me. I am, then, a real thing, and really existent. What thing? I have said it, a thinking thing.[64]

This, for Husserl, was the fatal slip. With it, Descartes fathered not a 'pure' phenomenology but rather a bastard mixture of philosophy and psychology:

> There begins with Descartes a completely new manner of philosophizing which seeks its ultimate foundations in the subjective. That Descartes, however, persists in pure objectivism in spite of its subjective grounding was possible only through the fact that the *mens*, which at first stood by itself in the *epoché* and functioned as the absolute ground of knowledge, grounding the objective science . . . appeared at the same time to *be* grounded along with everything else as a legitimate subject matter *within* the sciences, i.e., in psychology.[65]

There is, then, at the heart of the Cartesian project, a fundamental confusion. On the one hand, the ego is the ultimate basis on which all knowledge must rest, the foundation which gives rise to all concepts, the source from which all distinctions must be derived. But, at the same time, the ego is also an object in the world, defined by the same categories that apply to physical objects, and capable of being studied in the same way as all other physical objects: through causal analysis. A presuppositionless account of the functioning of the ego – that 'first philosophy' which has the responsibility of grounding all other forms of inquiry – is thus transformed into an empirical psychology which battles onward with a host of unclarified presuppositions.

Phenomenology and psychology

The sins of the father, however, had once been the practices of the son. The same mingling of the transcendental and empirical subjects which Husserl bemoaned in Descartes lay at the basis of his own attempt, in the first (and only) volume of his *Philosophy of Arithmetic* (1891), at a psychological analysis of such concepts as plurality, unity, and number. The relationship between phenomenology and psychology thus merits closer scrutiny. It implies nothing less, as one commentator has suggested, than 'the whole progress of Husserl's philosophy'.[66]

Against 'psychologism'

The psychological inquiries begun in the first volume of the *Philosophy of Arithmetic* were to be extended, in the projected second volume, to the general logic of symbolic methods (in Husserl's terminology, 'semiotics'). But this proved far more difficult than Husserl had initially conceived and the severe criticism Frege directed against the first volume gave Husserl an addition impetus to rethink his approach.[67] In lectures dating from as early as 1895, Husserl began the critique of psychological analyses of logical categories that would become the 'Prolegomena to Pure Logic', the first volume of his *Logical Investigations* (1900).

The book won him an early reputation, in France and elsewhere, as a thinker squarely within the tradition of Frege, Bertrand Russell, and Anton Cournot.[68] But, in the six investigations which made up the second volume (1901), Husserl appeared to many critics to have lapsed back into his old ways.[69] While Husserl denied that psychology could clarify the *origins* of logical categories, he still maintained that epistemological criticism had to consist of a 'descriptive examination of . . . knowledge-experiences'. As he explained in the introduction to the second volume of the *Logical Investigations*:

> It is *not the full science of psychology that serves as a foundation for pure logic*, but certain classes of descriptions which are the step preparatory to the theoretical researches of psychology. These, in so far as they describe empirical objects whose genetic connections the science wishes to pursue, also form the substrate for those fundamental abstractions in which logic seizes the essence of its ideal objects and connections with inward evidence.[70]

Descriptive psychology could thus serve two masters. It could be a preparatory stage for an account of the *genesis* of psychological categories, and as such was a prolegomena to empirical psychology, or – in so far as it remained purely descriptive – it could also serve as the foundation of logic. It is this latter use of psychological description which Husserl called 'phenomenology'.

This satisfied no one – least of all Husserl himself. In a review essay of recent writings on logic published in 1903 and incorporated into the part of the revised introduction to the second volume of the *Logical Investigations* which, from the second edition (1913) onward, replaced his initial equating of phenomenology with descriptive psychology, Husserl argued that the descriptions offered by phenomenology were completely removed from the orbit of psychology since they dealt with neither 'lived experiences' nor 'empirical persons'.[71] Phenomenology does not speak of the perceptions, judgements, for feelings of any specific person, but rather is concerned with 'perceptions, judgements, feelings, as such'.[72] It moved, not within the world of facts, but rather within the domain of essences.

Toward a *'phenomenological psychology'*

The question of the relationship between phenomenology and psychology was not, however, put to rest with this apparently decisive segregation of the two disciplines. Husserl returned to the problem again and again throughout his career, making – at one time or another – at least three distinguishable claims:

(1) an insistence, which spans all his writings, that transcendental phenomenology is in no way reducible to psychology;

(2) an argument, emerging most forcefully in his work in the 1920s that phenomenology nevertheless carries in its wake a new sort of psychology: an 'eidetic' or 'phenomenological' psychology.

(3) a claim, which likewise became of increasing importance in his last writings, that because the concerns of phenomenological psychology and pure phenomenology parallel one another, phenomenological psychology can serve as a particularly important path to pure, transcendental phenomenology.

Let us examine each of these points briefly.

(1) From 1903 onward, Husserl insisted that phenomenology could in no way be equated with psychology, even if psychology was understood as a purely descriptive study of consciousness.[73] This was what had eluded Descartes, the recognition that with a correct understanding of the *cogito*, 'We abandon finally the standpoint of psychology, even descriptive psychology.'[74] Husserl would never retreat from the conviction that Descartes's project had ship-wrecked on a confusion of transcendental philosophy and psychol-

ogy.[75] The distinction between psychology and phenomenology can be made on three levels:

(i) Psychology is a science of facts which seeks either to frame general laws or to provide rigorous descriptions. Phenomenology is an eidetic science which is concerned with obtaining an insight into those essential characteristics which define a certain class of phenomena.[76] Thus, while psychology might investigate the factors which cause perceptual disturbances or describe what it was like to experience such disturbances, phenomenology would be concerned with the question of what is essential to a perception's being an act of perception rather than an act of remembering, imagining, or hallucinating.[77]

(ii) Psychology is a study of empirical consciousness, of consciousness as it appears as a part of nature, as an attribute of an embodied subject. Phenomenology places to the side all questions of material genesis, corporeal embodiment, or empirical situation, and studies 'purified' or 'transcendental' consciousness.[78]

(iii) Following from this last point, psychology is a 'worldly' or 'mundane' science which never questions the 'natural standpoint' and, at all times, presupposes the existence of the world. Phenomenology, in contrast, is an 'unworldly' science which brackets the natural standpoint in order to pose the more fundamental question of how this taken-for-granted world comes to be constituted.[79]

(2) While Husserl never retracted this contrast between psychology (empirical or descriptive) and transcendental phenomenology, he did eventually pose a more ambiguous relationship between phenomenology and something he called 'phenomenological psychology'. In the 1927 article on phenomenology written for the *Encyclopedia Britannica*, Husserl went so far as to suggest that the confusion of phenomenology with descriptive psychology in the first edition of the *Logical Investigations* was almost inevitable:

The term 'phenomenology' designates two things: a new kind of descriptive method which made a breakthrough in philosophy at the turn of the century, and an *a priori* science derived from it; a science which is intended to supply the basic instrument (*Orga-*

non) and, in its consequent application, to make possible a methodological reform of all the sciences. Together with this philosophical phenomenology, but not yet separated from it, however, there also came into being a new psychological discipline parallel to it in method and content: the *a priori* pure or 'phenomenological' psychology, which raises the reformational claim to being the basic methodological foundation on which alone a scientifically rigorous empirical psychology can be established.[80]

Transcendental phenomenology and phenomenological psychology were like twins born together, frequently taken for one another, distinguishable in fact but certainly related.

In Husserl's most sustained discussions of these disciplines, the following division of labour emerges. Phenomenological psychology is an *a priori* science of the psyche and as such stands in the same relation to empirical psychology as geometry does to physics. Just as geometry, in Husserl's view, is an *a priori* analysis of idealised forms of space which lays the foundations for an exact and rigorous empirical study of nature, so too phenomenological psychology provides empirical psychology with that exactness which 'lies in its being founded on an *a priori* form system'.[81] Phenomenological psychology, however, must not be equated with transcendental phenomenology since, like geometry, 'rational mechanics' and all the other *a priori* sciences, it is incapable of providing 'a theory of knowledge, a clarification and subjective grounding from the point of view of the critique of reason'.[82] This critical task is reserved for phenomenology proper, a transcendental discipline which stands outside the class of all 'objective sciences' – be they empirical, descriptive, or eidetic.[83]

Phenomenological psychology thus makes use of the 'phenomenological reduction' – it turns its attention away from objects in the world and focuses instead on the subject whose activities reveal this world. It also employs the 'eidetic reduction' – it concerns itself with essential structures rather than individual facts. But it does not carry out the 'transcendental reduction' – the subject which it studies is still a psychological subject, a person engaged in activities which address a world whose existence remains unproblematic and unquestioned.[84]

(3) Had Husserl simply treated phenomenological psychology as

one *a priori* science among others, it would have occupied a clearly circumscribed place within his philosophy. It would have clarified the concepts employed in empirical psychology, but it would have been dependent in turn on transcendental phenomenology for its own grounding. The hierarchy of disciplines would be clear and irreversible.

Matters, unfortunately, are not that simple. Phenomenological psychology does not remain merely one *a priori* discipline among others. It comes to play a more important role in Husserl's late philosophy, at least in part because Husserl came to feel that his own development could serve as a paradigm for the path to transcendental phenomenology. In a passage added to the second (and unpublished) book of his *Ideas*, sometime between 1924 and 1928 he wrote:

> Descriptive psychology serves as a proper and natural point of departure for the development of the idea of phenomenology. In fact it was this path that led me to phenomenology.[85]

The *Britannica* article amplified the point, explaining that, because it stood closer to 'our natural thinking', phenomenological psychology 'is well suited to serve as a preliminary step that will lead up to an understanding of philosophical phenomenology'.[86]

Phenomenological psychology could play the double role of both an *a priori* science dependent on transcendental phenomenology for its ultimate justification and a privileged point of departure for transcendental phenomenology, because both disciplines studied forms of consciousness. However hesitant Husserl might have been about importing terminology from the sphere of empirical consciousness into the analysis of transcendental consciousness, he was convinced that the psychological subject and the transcendental subject shared one crucial attribute: intentionality. He came to feel that his polemic against psychologism had gone too far. In the unpublished third book of his *Ideas* (1912), he stressed the need to abandon 'the old mistrust (still controlling even the author of the *Logical Investigations*) of psychic and egological reality'. This done, one could examine

> the remarkable relationship between phenomenological and psychological ontology which permits the former to find its place

in the latter and again, in a certain manner also permits the latter, like all ontological disciplines, to find a place in the former.[87]

Phenomenology and psychology are thus bound into what Merleau-Ponty, drawing on a term from classical rhetoric, would call a 'chiasmus'.[88] Phenomenology finds its place in psychology, just as psychology can find a place in phenomenology. Thus, as early as the first book of the *Ideas*, Husserl argued that

> Every phenomenological position concerning absolute consciousness can be reinterpreted in terms of eidetic psychology (which, strictly considered, is itself in no sense phenomenological).[89]

Nearly two decades later, in a preface written for the English translation of the book, he noted once again the

> thoroughgoing parallelism between a (properly elaborated) phenomenological psychology and a transcendental phenomenology. To each eidetic or empirical determinate on the one side there must correspond a parallel feature in the other.[90]

But what divides these two 'sides'? What separates these two parallel lines of inquiry? Everything appears to hinge on a 'mere change of attitude'. Phenomenological psychology 'still has the accessibility which is possessed by all positive sciences', but transcendental phenomenology requires 'an alteration of focus from one's entire form of life-style, one which goes so completely beyond all previous experiencing of life, that it must, in virtue of its absolute strangeness, needs be difficult to understand'.[91] It is on this strange and unprecedented shift in attitude – which the *Cartesian Meditations* described as a 'Copernican conversion' and which the *Crisis* likened to 'a religious conversion'[92] – that the separation of phenomenological psychology and transcendental phenomenology ultimately rests.

Straying from the 'Cartesian way'

In November of 1935, Husserl delivered a series of lectures in

Prague on 'Psychology and the Crisis of the Sciences'. These talks, which outlined the history of philosophy from Descartes to Kant before turning to a critique of modern psychology from Hobbes to Brentano, were the basis for *The Crisis of the European Sciences and Transcendental Phenomenology*, that last 'introduction' to phenomenology which Husserl wrestled with between 1934 and the onset of his terminal illness in the summer of 1937.[93] In reworking the Prague lectures, Husserl made two substantial additions. A long discussion of Galileo, who in the lectures had been treated only in passing as a precursor of Descartes, was added to the discussion, in Part I, of the 'Origins of the Modern Opposition Between Physicalistic Objectivism and Transcendental Subjectivism'.[94] An entirely new subsection, 'The Way into Phenomenological Transcendental Philosophy by Inquiry back from the Pregiven Lifeworld', was added to Part III, preceding the discussion, taken over from the lectures, of 'The Way into Phenomenological Transcendental Philosophy from Psychology'.[95] With these two modifications, a new theme – the 'life-world' (*Lebenswelt*) – forced its way to the centre of Husserl's analysis, and with the coupling of this theme to the peculiar mode of historical presentation adopted in the lectures, Husserl's Cartesian meditations were disrupted by ruminations of a rather different sort.

Galileo, Descartes, and the history of philosophy

At the Sorbonne, Husserl regarded Descartes's *Meditations* as the 'necessary prototype for the meditations of any beginning philosopher whatsoever'.[96] In the *Crisis*, the *Meditations* were no less central, but his approach to them differs markedly. Descartes's procedure was no longer a prototype to be followed. Rather, if the implications of Descartes's project are to be understood – and, even more crucial, brought to fruition – Descartes must be situated within what Husserl terms 'a teleological-historical reflection upon the origins of our critical scientific situation'.[97] Descartes can no longer be Husserl's sole concern. Before him stands Galileo, that 'discovering and concealing genius' whose oversights and presuppositions were uncritically taken up by Descartes.[98] After him stand Kant and Hume, the culmination of the two traditions, rationalism and empiricism, which took their start from Descartes's failure to overcome the prejudice of 'objectivism' – that neglect of the active subject which was the legacy of Galileo's mathematisation of nature.[99] And beyond all of these thinkers stands Husserl himself. The burden of the *Crisis* is 'to establish the unavoidable necessity of a transcendental-phenomenological reorientation of philosophy'.[100] Through its account of the history of philosophy, the *Crisis* was to demonstrate how phenomenology redeems Descarte's missed opportunity of reasserting the role of the subject in the face of Galileo's objectivism. Phenomenology learns what it must do as a result of this 'teleological-historical reflection' and at long last consummates the critique of 'physicalistic objectivism' that Descartes and the later heirs of the tradition of 'transcendental subjectivism' had never carried through successfully.

In this reading of history there is a hubris worthy of Hegel – or, to stay with an example more obviously objectionable to Merleau-Ponty, Brunschvicg. It constantly runs the risk of reducing earlier philosophies to the final Philosophy, or – in that distinction of Paul Ricoeur's which played a major role in Merleau-Ponty's own reflections on the history of philosophy – of constantly reducing individual, specific *events* to the continuing *advent* of an un-equivocal meaning.[101] For example, in the analysis of Descartes undertaken in the *Crisis*, Husserl is not concerned with Descartes's *own* understanding of his work. Rather, what matters is that 'hidden unity of intentional inwardness', which eludes the self-interpretation of individual thinkers, but which nevertheless 'con-stitutes the unity of history'.[102] The principal motif in this history, the perpetual struggle between 'objectivistic and transcendental philosophy', is never clearly articulated by any of the individual philosophers discussed. Nor, of course, could any of them under-stand where this all was leading. It is the unique achievement of the *Crisis* to articulate – and thus bring to completion – the movement which Husserl detects in this history 'toward a *final form* of transcendental philosophy ... phenomenology', a form of trans-cendental philosophy which 'contains, as a suspended moment, the *final form of psychology*'.[103]

The life-world and the 'new way' to the transcendental reduction

Phenomenology can view the history of philosopohy from this

privileged standpoint because it does not, like all philosophy since
Galileo, take his mathematised nature as the end-point for its
reflections.[104] Rather, it subjects the hitherto unquestioned equa-
tion of mathematised nature with 'the world' to rigorous scrutiny
and discovers, behind this idealised nature, that pre-theoretical
'realm of original self-evidence' which Husserl terms the 'life-
world'.[105] On first glance, there would appear to be little new in the
argument of the *Crisis*. The novelty of phenomenology as a science
which poses the problem of how we have a world had, since at least
the first book of the *Ideas*, been a persisting theme in Husserl's
work.[106] But the new meaning which Husserl gave to the term
'life-world' – in its few previous usages it was roughly synonymous
to 'cultural world'[107] – brought with it a major transformation in the
way in which the path that led to the transcendental reduction is
conceived. We must now proceed, he wrote, 'in an order opposite
that suggested by the Cartesian approach'.[108]

This new path to transcendental philosophy was schematised in
Experience and Judgement (1937) as consisting of two stages:

1. *In the retrogression from the pregiven world* with all of its
sedimentations of sense, with its science and scientific disciplines,
to the original life-world.
2. *In the regressive inquiry which goes from the life-world to the
subjective operations from which it itself arises.*[109]

While Descartes had turned away from the world in hopes of
finding, in himself, that Archimedean point from which this
now-doubted world could be restored, Husserl argued that we must
turn away from the 'garb of ideas' in which post-Cartesian science
and philosophy had clothed the world in order to recover the world
as it is lived prior to theory and prior to science.[110] An account of the
structure of this world, Husserl now argued, could lay the ground-
work and provide the orienting themes for an analysis of transcendental subjectivity.[111]

We see here a 'new way to the reduction, as contrasted with the
"Cartesian way" '. The 'shorter way' which had been employed in
the *Ideas*

has a great shortcoming: while it leads to the transcendental ego
in one leap, as it were, it brings this ego into view as apparently

empty of content, since there can be no preparatory explication; so one is at a loss, at first, to know what has been gained by it, much less how, starting with this, a completely new sort of science, decisive for philosophy, has been attained.[112]

The 'Cartesian way' had demanded too much and provided too little in return. The analysis of the life-world, by beginning with the mundane sphere of everyday life, was less demanding. And, by virtue of the richness and diversity of the themes it found in the life-world awaiting elaboration, it was far more promising as a topic of investigation than that apparently empty ego that lay at the end of the Cartesian way.

Merleau-Ponty's Husserl

Husserl was, for Merleau-Ponty, above all else this non-Cartesian Husserl. In the *Crisis*, the second book of the *Ideas*, and in the other unpublished writings he studied – first in Louvain and then, after 1944, in Paris[113] – Merleau-Ponty encountered a Husserl whose focus had shifted from the questions of meaning and signification which had been the point of departure for the *Logical Investigations*, to those problems of perception, embodiment, and life-world which would become the central themes of what has come to be called 'existential phenomenology'.[114] In these works, Merleau-Ponty discovered a radically different phenomenology from the one he found in Husserl's published works. The tension that the juxtaposition of these two visions of phenomenology must have produced in him was echoed in the famous preface to the *Phenomenology of Perception*:

Phenomenology is the study of essences . . . But phenomenology is also a philosophy which puts essences back into existence . . . It is a transcendental philosophy which places in abeyance the assertions arising out of the natural attitude . . . but it is also a philosophy for which the world is always 'already there' before reflection begins – as an inalienable presence . . . It is the search for a philosophy which shall be a 'rigorous science', but it also offers an account of space, time, and the world as we 'live' them. It tries to give a direct description of our experience as it is, without taking account of its psychological origin and the causal explanations which the scientist, the historian or the sociologist may be able to provide. Yet Husserl in his last works mentions a 'genetic phenomenology', and even a 'constructive phenomenology'. One may try to do away with these contradictions by making a distinction between Husserl's and Heidegger's phenomenologies; yet the whole of *Sein und Zeit* . . . amounts to no more than an explicit account of the *'natürliche Weltbegriff'* or the *'Lebenswelt'* which Husserl, towards the end of his life, identified as the central theme of phenomenology.[115]

It was with this other phenomenology, the phenomenology towards which Husserl moved as he advanced from 'the eidetic method or logicism of his earlier stage to the existentialism of the last period',[116] that Merleau-Ponty cast his lot.

Pushing Husserl

This 'existentialist' Husserl was a curious creature, as much a consequence of Merleau-Ponty's way of reading as of anything Husserl actually wrote. Husserl had not abandoned the goal of transcendental phenomenology in the *Crisis*; he had only questioned the path outlined in the *Cartesian Meditations*. Likewise, Husserl did not regard *Being and Time* as merely an 'explicit account' of the natural concept of the world; for him, it was a wrong-headed presentation of phenomenological reflection that remained stuck in the natural attitude and rested on a questionable anthropologism.[117] Whatever the virtues of Merleau-Ponty's account of phenomenology, it has long been apparent that fidelity to the letter of Husserl's argument is not one of them.[118]

But then he never claimed it was. He said that at times he was 'pushing Husserl further than he wished to go'.[119] His intent was 'to resume, instead of his theses, the very movement of his thought'.[120] Like Husserl's own approach to the history of philosophy in the *Crisis*, his concern was with the drawing-out of implicit intentions, not with the documenting of explicit utterances. For that reason, what Husserl did not say mattered as much as what he actually did say. Following Heidegger, Merleau-Ponty argued that every thinker's work included 'an unthought-of element which is wholly his own and yet opens out on something else'.[121] And phenomenology, for Merleau-Ponty, opened out onto the world.

As understood and practised by Merleau-Ponty, phenomenology consisted almost entirely of the first of the two steps in the 'non-Cartesian way' Husserl outlined in *Experience and Judgement*: the 'retrogression from the pregiven world . . . to the original life-world'.[122] It was thus primarily 'a matter of describing, not of explaining or analysing'.[123] Far from feeling that phenomenology should work to transform philosophy into a 'rigorous science', Merleau-Ponty felt that Husserl's initial directives involved 'a rejection of science'. Science was but a 'second order expression' of a 'basic experience of the world' which phenomenology had the unique responsibility of reawakening with a 'return to that world which precedes knowledge, of which knowledge always *speaks*, and in relation to which every scientific schematization is an abstract and derivative sign-language'.[124] This world – that 'life-world' which we come to know through practical endeavours before we reflect on it with more theoretical interests – was, for Merleau-Ponty, the 'homeland of our thought', the 'horizon of all horizons, the style of all possible styles', and 'the only pre-existent Logos' on which philosophy could draw.[125]

Phenomenology thus moved in the shadow of science, attempting to give voice to what had been denied expression in its more precise, but also more restrictive, formulations.[126] At a colloquium held shortly after the publication of the *Phenomenology of Perception*, Emile Bréhier commented that Merleau-Ponty's goal might be 'better expressed in literature and painting than in philosophy'.[127] In a somewhat backhanded way, Bréhier indicated the company which Merleau-Ponty himself came to feel that philosophy must keep if it was to remain faithful to Husserl's insights. In the introduction to *Signs*, he wrote:

> Philosophy does not hold the world supine at its feet. It is not a 'higher point of view' from which one embraces all local perspectives. It seeks contact with brute being, and in any case informs itself in the company of those who have never lost that contact. It is just that whereas literature, art, and the practice of life . . . can (except at their extreme limits) have and create the illusion of dwelling in the habitual and the already constituted, philosophy – which paints without colors and in black and white

like copperplate engravings – does not allow us to ignore the strangeness of the world, which men confront as well as or better than it does, but as if in half-silence.[128]

In this concern to make manifest the strangeness of the world – or, as he put it in *Phenomenology of Perception*, 'the mystery of the world and of reason' – phenomenology was 'a movement before becoming a doctrine'. With Hegel, Kierkegaard, Marx, Nietzsche, and Freud as its forerunners, and Balzac, Proust, Valéry, and Cézanne as its fellow travellers, phenomenology 'merges into the general effort of modern thought'.[129]

But what of Husserl survived the merger? And what, in Husserl, resisted Merleau-Ponty's nudgings? Let us look briefly at the fate of a few of Husserl's central concepts.

The phenomenological reduction

At first glance, it would appear that the various techniques by which Husserl sought to bracket the general thesis of the natural attitude and open the transcendental sphere for analysis would have little relevance for a conception of phenomenology as resolutely worldly as that of Merleau-Ponty. Merleau-Ponty's position, however, was as straightforward as it was peculiar. Far from leading to a transcendental consciousness, the phenomenological reduction – as an attempted disengagement from the world which could never be carried through to completion – restored our 'wonder' at the 'strange and paradoxical' hold which the world has on us.[130] With this interpretation of the goal of the phenomenological reduction, all the distinctions Husserl had so laboriously drawn between the natural and transcendental attitudes crumbled. Merleau-Ponty argued that psychological reflection, when consistently carried out, 'outruns itself', and that starting from the question of the relationship between mental phenomena and the objective world, it is ultimately forced to account for the way in which this world is given. At that point, 'the phenomenal field becomes a transcendental field'.[131] Likewise, he claimed that the attack launched by *Gestalt* psychologists on the 'constancy hypothesis' – the belief that stimuli elicit responses which vary only with respect to variations in those stimuli – 'assumes the value of a genuine "phenomenological reduction"'.[132]

The ultimate implications of these arguments were drawn out in his 1959 essay 'The Philosopher and His Shadow' – one of the places where he pushed Husserl the hardest. Within the natural attitude, he argued, one can find a 'preparation for phenomenology':

> It is the natural attitude which, by reiterating its own procedures, topples into phenomenology. It is the natural attitude which goes beyond itself in phenomenology – and so it does not go beyond itself. Reciprocally, the transcendental attitude is still and in spite of everything 'natural'.[133]

Out of the intertwining of psychological and transcendental standpoints which he found in Husserl's *Crisis*, he wove a chiasmus where the transcendental attitude was as natural as the natural was transcendental.

The intuition of essences

Husserl's distinction between sciences of fact and sciences of essence suffered much the same fate. Merleau-Ponty argued that Husserl could maintain such a strict demarcation only so long as he held 'a dogmatic conception of *Wesenschau* [intuition of essence]'.[134] In the first book of the *Ideas*, Husserl was at pains to stress that knowledge of essence was, like knowledge of fact, a matter of *seeing*: '*Essential insight is still intuition*, just as the eidetic object is still an object.'[135] What set insight into essences apart from insight into facts was that reference could be made to essential objects without advancing the claim that such objects actually exist (for example, we can recite the essential features of a unicorn without claiming that there really are unicorns).[136] Through a variation of the attributes of an object – real or imagined – one comes to 'see' what is essential to it (for example, bearded and beardless unicorns are possible, but not hornless ones).

What Merleau-Ponty saw as 'dogmatic' in this was Husserl's insistence that 'the meaning of eidetic science excludes in principle every assimilation of the theoretical results of empirical sciences' while nevertheless maintaining that 'no fully developed science of fact could subsist unmixed with eidetic knowledge'.[137] Merleau-Ponty argued that this strict hierarchy of eidetic over empirical sciences was eventually called into question by Husserl himself in his exchange of letters with the French anthropologist Lucien Lévy-Bruhl.[138] Having studied Lévy-Bruhl's analysis of primitive mentality, Husserl was willing to grant that the findings of empirical sciences could have a decisive impact on eidetic analyses within the human sciences. Husserl now saw that philosophy must 'accept all the acquisitions of science' and only then try to work towards an understanding of the world which transcends, but does not ignore, empirical contingency.[139]

Thus phenomenology, in Merleau-Ponty's reading, completely transforms the relationship between the *de facto* and the *a priori*.[140]

> From the moment that experience . . . is recognized as the beginning of knowledge, there is no longer any way of distinguishing . . . what the world must necessarily be and what it actually is. The unity of the sense, which was regarded as an *a priori* truth, is no longer anything but the formal expression of a fundamental contingency: the fact that we are in the world – the diversity of sense, which was regarded as given *a posteriori*, including the concrete form that it assumes in a human subject, appears as necessary to this world, to the only world which we can think of consequentially; it therefore becomes an *a priori* truth.[141]

The notion of essence is borrowed from the world of perception.[142] Eidetic analysis is an *a posteriori* clarification of concrete, factual experience.[143] Hence it too is properly understood as a technique of existential rather than transcendental phenomenology. It is a way of enabling reflection to grasp the pre-reflective life of an incarnate consciousness; it is the means by which 'our effective involvement in the world' is brought to conceptualisation.[144]

Intentionality

While Husserl's notion of intentionality would eventually cause Merleau-Ponty considerable difficulties, as presented in the

Phenomenology of Perception it was neither a central category in Husserl's phenomenology – 'too often cited as the main discovery of phenomenology . . . it is understandable only through the reduction' – nor a particularly original one – Kant had already recognised that 'all consciousness is consciousness of something'.[145] Husserl's real insight, Merleau-Ponty argued, lay 'in the discovery, beneath the intentionality of representations, of a deeper intentionality, which others have called existence'.[146]

In the 'classic conception' of intentionality – embraced by both neo-Kantians and by the Husserl of the *Ideas* – consciousness is defined as 'absolute non-being' and the experience of the world is treated 'as a pure act of constituting consciousness'.[147] In this understanding of intentionality, consciousness builds up a meaningful world through a series of judgements, definitions, and other conscious acts which impose significance on the raw stuff of sense data (Husserl's '*hylé*').[148] Against this notion, Merleau-Ponty argued that Husserl came to elaborate a conception of 'operative [*fungierende*] intentionality' which – prior to all acts of positing, intending, judging, reflecting, or signifying – reveals a world which, far from being a blank state awaiting the bestowal of significance, already had a distinctive physiognomy.[149]

Husserl's mature approach, then, should not be confused with that of Descartes or Kant. Their retreat to transcendental subjectivity 'ceases to remain part of our experience and offers, in place of an account, a reconstruction'.[150] Husserl turned away from 'a noetic analysis which bases the world on the synthesizing activity of the subject' and instead embraced a ' "noematic reflection" which remains within the object and, instead of begetting it, brings to light it fundamental unity'.[151] Intentionality, like the phenomenological reduction and eidetic analysis, was pressed into the service of an existential phenomenology which argued that the relationship of subject and world 'is not a thing which can be further clarified by analysis: philosophy can only place it once more before our eyes and present it for our ratification'.[152]

The transcendental ego

Merleau-Ponty's presentation of phenomenology in the *Phenomenology of Perception* delayed the break with Husserl until the last possible moment. He insisted on the centrality of the phenomenological reductions, he argued for the continued utility of eidetic analyses, and he sought to purge intentionality of its idealist overtones. But he was forced to reject the one thing in Husserl's work which gave sense to all of these other notions: the transcendental ego. For Merleau-Ponty, the fatal error of the 'intellectualist' philosophies of Brunschvicg, Alain, and Lagneau was their attempt to found all mental activity in the epistemological subject, their attendant inability to recognise that subjectivity is always situated in and engaged with a world, and their ultimate failure to see that finitude, temporality, and carnality were not blemishes detracting from absolute subjectivity, but were, rather, the only terms on which truth was possible. Although he tried to recruit Husserl to his side here as well, he could not hide the fact that Husserl's attempted reform of the Cartesian *cogito* was plagued by a fatal intellectualism as well.

The 'true *cogito*', he argued in *Phenomenology of Perception*, neither defined 'the subject's existence in terms of the thought he has of existing' nor sought to convert 'the indubitability of the world into the indubitability of thought about the world'.[153] Instead, it 'must reveal me in a situation', as 'being-in-the-world', as 'through and through compounded of relationships with the world'.[154] Properly understood, it thus exemplified what Merleau-Ponty saw as the basic experience of reflection: it revealed a level of experience which was present before reflection and which served as the ground on which reflection was possible, but which was nevertheless governed by a set of rules different from those 'clear and distinct ideas' which, since Descartes, had been the ultimate criterion for knowledge. 'There is absolute certainty of the world in general,' Merleau-Ponty wrote, 'but not of any one thing in particular.'[155]

The *cogito* is misrepresented if it is presented as leading to a 'psychological immanence' which reduces all phenomena to 'private states of consciousness', or even if – following Husserl – it terminates in a 'transcendental immanence' which sees all phenomena as the result of the operations of a constitutive consciousness. Rather, Merleau-Ponty argued, it testifies to 'the deep-seated momentum of transcendence which is my very being'.[156] The 'ultimate consciousness is not an eternal subject perceiving itself in absolute transparency'; it is, rather, 'a comprehensive project, or a view of time and the world which . . . needs to unfold itself into multiplicity'.[157] It is not 'a transcendental Ego freely positing before itself a multiplicity in itself'; it is, rather, 'an I which dominates diversity only with the help of time'.[158] The transcendental ego 'posits a world'; the incarnate subject must first of all 'have a world or be in the world' and thus has around it 'a system of meanings whose reciprocities, relationships and involvements do not require to be made explicit in order to be exploited'.[159]

The *cogito*, in short, testifies to the ability of an incarnate subject to pull itself away from involvement in the world and reflect on that world:

> there are acts in which I collect myself together in order to surpass myself. The *cogito* is the recognition of this fundamental fact. In the proposition: 'I think, I am', the two assertions are to be equated with each other, otherwise there would be no *cogito*. Nevertheless we must be clear about the meaning of the equivalence: it is not the 'I am' which is pre-eminently contained in the 'I think', not my existence which is brought down to the consciousness I have of it, but conversely the 'I think', which is re-integrated into the transcending process of the 'I am', and consciousness into existence.[160]

Cartesian analysis falsified the experience of the *cogito*, in Merleau-Ponty's view, not – as Husserl would have it – because of a confusion of transcendental and psychological subjectivity, but rather because it failed to see that the body was the vehicle through which we have a world and the means by which we sustain communications with it.[161] Descartes gave only a secondary expression of this more fundamental experience and elaborated, within discourse and on the level of reflection, an analysis which made sense only because of its implied reference to a 'tacit *cogito*' which had 'upon itself and upon the world only a precarious hold'.[162] This 'presence to oneself, being no less than existence, is anterior to any philosophy'.[163] It is a subject whose unity, like the unity of the world, is 'invoked rather than experienced'; it is the 'background' against which all acts of positing, reflecting, thinking, and perceiving stand out.[164]

Phenomenology had the unenviable task of catching this elusive presence. Merleau-Ponty's reinterpretations of the phenomenological reduction, of eidetic analysis, and of intentionality were all attempts to retool phenomenology so that it could do justice to this subtle intertwining of subject and world:

> The world is not an object such that I have in my possession the law of its making; it is the natural setting of, and field for, all my thought and all my explicit perceptions. Truth does not 'inhabit' only the 'inner man', or more accurately, there is no inner man, man is in the world, and only in the world does he know himself. When I return to myself from an excursion into the realm of dogmatic common sense or of science, I find, not a source of intrinsic truth, but a subject destined to be in the world.[165]

Descartes and Augustine, Husserl's mentors, had led him nowhere. Against the phantom of the 'inner man', Merleau-Ponty appealed, in one of his finest essays, to Montaigne.[166] Montaigne knew that

> We are equally incapable of dwelling in ourselves and in things, and are thrown back from them to ourselves and from ourselves to them.[167]

Tossed into this cross-fire, Montaigne saw that 'To be conscious is, among other things, to be somewhere else.'[168] Husserl had joined Descartes in the attempt 'once for all' to cast off received opinions and start anew, 'building from the foundations up'.[169] Montaigne taught Merleau-Ponty a different lesson. The study of man was destined to be 'an inquiry without discovery, a hunt without a kill'.[170]

Phenomenology and the human sciences

On the basis of this peculiar reading of Husserl, Merleau-Ponty went on to relate phenomenology and the human sciences in a way which diverged markedly from Husserl. Husserl's concern was to 'purify' phenomenology, to set it apart from 'worldly' sciences which might compromise its radicalism. Merleau-Ponty sought instead to intertwine phenomenology and the human sciences.

That Merleau-Ponty's position was different from Husserl's is, however, by no means immediately obvious. In his course at the

Sorbonne on 'The Human Sciences and Phenomenology' (1950–1; 1951–2) as well as in the closely related essay 'The Philosopher and Sociology' (1951) Merleau-Ponty made one of those excursions into 'intentional history' which tend to blur the line between what a thinker actually wrote and what a reader would like to find.[171] Discussing Husserl's treatment of the relationship between phenomenology and the empirical sciences in the 1951 article, Merleau-Ponty observed:

> We know that he began by affirming – and always maintained – a rigorous distinction between them. It seems to us, however, that his idea of a psycho-phenomenological parallelism – speaking more generally: his thesis of a parallel between positive knowledge and philosophy, in which each affirmation of the one corresponds to an affirmation of the other – leads in fact to a reciprocal envelopment.[172]

To see what of this 'reciprocal envelopment' was Husserl's doing and what Merleau-Ponty's, we must begin by once again insisting on the differences between them.

From 'rigorous distinction' to 'reciprocal envelopment'

Merleau-Ponty saw this trajectory from 'rigorous distinction' to 'reciprocal envelopment' traced in Husserl's discussion of the relationship of phenomenology to psychology, to linguistics, and to history. In each case, an early attempt to subordinate empirical inquiries to an eidetic science was replaced by a 'movement back and forth from facts to ideas and from ideas to facts'.[173] The early Husserl argued that empirical psychology must defer to an eidetic psychology for the clarification of its basic concepts; he maintained that the understanding of any individual language was impossible without a comprehension of the 'essence of language in general'; and he held that since history was 'unable to judge an idea', historians must rely on 'an *a priori* science which would determine the real meaning' of the concepts which they use 'blindly and without careful examination'.[174] The later Husserl, in contrast, saw that there could be no 'basic discord' between phenomenology and psychology since they study 'the same subject, man'; he abandoned his project of constructing an ideal language by turning to the study of the experience of the 'speaking subject'; and he recognised that 'the eidetic of history cannot dispense with factual investigation'.[175] In spite of his early attempts to separate the 'empirical' from the 'essential' and the 'natural' from the 'transcendental', he came to see that they in fact encroached upon and interpenetrated one another. Or, at least, this is how *Merleau-Ponty* claimed that Husserl came to see it.

Husserl in fact came closest to the ultimate position Merleau-Ponty attributed to him in the discussion of the relationship between psychological and phenomenological standpoints which concludes the *Crisis*. As we have seen, he argued there that 'a concretely executed psychology could lead to a transcendental philosophy', while conversely, 'the transcendental accomplishment in and through which I "have" the world' could be found once more 'in a psychological internal analysis'.[176] Phenomenology and psychology were not, however, equal members of this chiasmus. The psychology which leads to transcendental philosophy is no longer a science like other 'positive sciences':

A psychology which would investigate universally the human beings living in the world as real facts in the world, similarly to other positive sciences . . . does not exist. There is only transcendental psychology, which is identical with transcendental philosophy.[177]

Hence, the envelopment of psychology by phenomenology is not reciprocated. Empirical psychology contributes nothing to phenomenology. Indeed, it can exist only once it has been recast along the lines of a phenomenological psychology.

In his discussion of the relationship between phenomenology and the human sciences, Merleau-Ponty consistently downplayed the pre-eminence Husserl accorded eidetic inquiries over empirical disciplines and, at the same time, argued that the reforms which Husserl felt phenomenology could introduce into the human sciences were already in the process of being carried out by these sciences themselves. As a consequence of this reading of Husserl, Merleau-Ponty directed the bulk of his criticism of attempts to set phenomenological inquiries off from positive sciences, not at Husserl himself, but rather at those of Husserl's 'followers' who, oblivious to the allegedly altered position of the later Husserl, continued to enforce Husserl's initial distinctions. Thus Heidegger, by distinguishing his 'analytic of *Dasein*' from those 'ontical' inquiries such as anthropology, ethnology, psychology, and biology – inquiries which presuppose 'ontological' accounts of *'Dasein'* without actually carrying them out[178] – remained, in Merleau-Ponty's opinion, 'fixed' in a 'pure and simple opposition between philosophy and the sciences of man' which, for Husserl, 'was only a point of departure'.[179] Sartre's studies of the imagination and the emotions likewise 'illustrate very well Husserl's conception as it was presented in the middle period of his career'.[180] But they also demonstrate the shortcomings attendant on a view which argues that 'phenomenological, or eidetic, psychology ought to come *first* and ought to rule over all fundamental questions'.[181] By presenting phenomenology as if it were an exercise in conceptual clarification, totally removed from empirical questions – as Sartre did, for example, when he proposed that 'I can try to grasp the essence of the "proletariat" through the word "proletariat" '[182] – one runs the risk of 'seeing an essence when, in fact, it is not an essence at all but merely a concept rooted in language'.[183] The only way to avoid this danger would be to abandon the attempt to set eidetic psychology apart from empirical inquiries and to admit a 'very close relation between induction . . . and *Wesenschau* and consequently a final homogeneity among the different psychologies, whether they be inductive or phenomenological'.[184]

Merleau-Ponty was willing to allow for this homogeneity because he sensed a growing recognition within the human sciences of the inadequacy of the inherited frameworks of 'naturalism', 'empiricism', and 'positivism'. The human sciences, like phenomenology, were unveiling 'a dimension of being and a type of knowledge which man forgets in his natural attitude'.[185] The development of *Gestalt* psychology, he argued on a number of occasions, illustrated the way in which empiricist prejudices could, to a limited degree, be undermined through rigorous empirical research.[186] Likewise, Saussure's revolution in linguistics rested on the replacement of a positivist approach – the treatment of language 'as a thing' – by a study of language which took up 'the perspective of the speaking subject'.[187] But the most important of Merleau-Ponty's examples for our immediate purposes is his discussion of developments in sociology, ethnology, and anthropology since Durkheim. For it is here, in his confrontation with the work of Claude Lévi-Strauss, that he encountered a rejection of positivism which could only with the greatest of difficulty be understood as a movement toward phenomenology.

Durkheim, Mauss, Lévi-Strauss: a rapprochement with phenomenology?

Emile Durkheim's *Elementary Forms of Religious Life* demonstrated, to Merleau-Ponty, the utter bankruptcy of the famous command of the *Rules of Sociological Method* to 'consider social facts as things'. The attempt to explain religion as a consequence of social cohesion, he argued, either 'begs the whole question' or 'hides the problem'.[188] That religious practices always take place within a community is as certain as 'that literature, art, science, and language are social facts in the sense of facts of communication'.[189] But to go on and argue that the fact of social cohesion somehow *explains* the existence of religious practices only results in our finding 'the same obscurity or the same problem hiding under another name'.[190]

Merleau-Ponty saw two basic problems in Durkheim's account. First, Durkheim merely asserted that Australian totemism – the case he studied – was in fact an 'elementary form' of religious life; he never gave a rigorous demonstration that Australian totemism indeed exemplified all that was essential to religious experience.[191] To do this, a preliminary eidetic analysis, similar to the conceptual clarification which phenomenological psychology was to bring to empirical psychology, would be needed.[192] Second, Durkheim's conception of society itself was confused and misleading:

> Recourse to social ties cannot be considered an explanation of religion or of the sacred unless one makes an immutable substance of the social, an all-round cause, a vague force defined only by its power of coercion; that is, if one makes oneself blind to the ever-original operation of a society in the process of establishing the system of collective meanings through which its members communicate.[193]

Durkheim's attribution of the characteristics of 'externality' and 'constraint' to 'social facts' resulted in a relationship between the '*conscience collective*' and the individual which, 'like that between two things, remained external'.[194] Against this way of looking at society, Merleau-Ponty argued

> the social is not *collective consciousness* but intersubjectivity, a living relationship and tension among individuals. Sociology should not seek an explanation of the religious in the social . . . but must consider them two aspects of the real and fantastic human bond as it has been worked out by the civilization under consideration and try to objectify the solution which that civilization invents, in its religion as in its economy or in its politics to the problem of man's relation with nature and with other men.[195]

To do this was to realise that while 'objective indices' could serve as a guide for the sociologist, sociological knowledge required that 'we recover the human attitude which makes up the spirit of a society'.[196]

Had subsequent sociologists overcome Durkheim's failings? Was sociology, like linguistics and psychology, contributing to the 'reciprocal envelopment' of phenomenology and the human sciences? Merleau-Ponty felt it was and found in the work of Marcel Mauss a contribution which in effect paralleled that of *Gestalt* psychology. He understood Mauss's concept of the 'total social fact' as a tacit break with Durkheim's tendency to see social facts as connected only by the external linkage of cause and effect. For Merleau-Ponty, Mauss's most important insight was that society was 'a totality where phenomena give mutual expression to each other and reveal the same theme'; social facts thus constitute 'an efficacious system of symbols . . . inserted into the depths of the individual'.[197] 'We are concerned with "wholes", with systems in their entirety', Mauss wrote in his classic *Essai sur le don*:

> It is only by considering them as wholes that we have been able to see their essence, their operation, and their living aspect, and to catch the fleeting moment when society and its members take emotional stock of themselves and their situation as regards others . . . We see social facts themselves, in the concrete, as they are. In society there are not merely ideas and rules, but also men and groups and their behaviours.[198]

Mauss's concern to see society as an expressive totality broke with the atomistic positivism which still plagued Durkheim, just as his commitment to capture the way in which social facts were experienced by the members of a society was a rejection of öbjectivism and a recognition of the importance of subjective interpretation. With these reforms, Merleau-Ponty suggested, Mauss had moved sociology closer to phenomenology.

Merleau-Ponty came to feel, however, that Mauss's elaboration of his position had fallen short of these original insights. In an important 1959 essay, 'From Mauss to Claude Lévi-Strauss', he advanced a series of criticisms which repeated those Lévi-Strauss himself had mounted a decade earlier.[199] Mauss had been unable to provide a theory of exchange or magic, the argument ran, because he fell back on explanations used by members of the societies he studied. To explain exchange, he turned to a Maori account of '*hau*'; to explain magic, he examined the Melanesian concept of '*mana*'.[200] Such notions, Merleau-Ponty wrote, 'do not so much provide a theory about the facts as reproduce the society's own theory'.[201] Or, as Lévi-Strauss put it:

> The '*hau*' is not the ultimate reason for exchange; it is the conscious form under which men of a particular society, where the problems have a particular significance, have apprehended an unconscious necessity whose reason is elsewhere.[202]

The reason for exchange, Merleau-Ponty argued, must be sought in the 'demands of an invisible totality' of which the giver and the recipient of gifts were but a part. Exchange was not 'an effect of society'; it was 'society itself in action'.[203] Terms like *mana* and *hau* could be likened to the 'zero phoneme' or the 'floating signifier' in linguistics. Lévi-Strauss – whose reformulation Merleau-Ponty was following to the letter – explained their function this way:

> In that system of symbols which constitutes every cosmology, there will ordinarily be a *symbolic value zero*, that is to say a sign marking the necessity of a symbolic content supplementary to that with which the signified is already loaded, but able to be any value on the condition that it still forms part of the available reserve and is not already, as the phonologists say, a term of the group.[204]

Terms like *hau* and *mana* thus 'draw attention to the fact that in certain circumstances . . . a relation of inadequacy exists between the signified and the signifier'.[205] Because of the surplus of signifiers that members of a society have at their disposal, it is possible for them to deploy signifiers of an indeterminate and shifting meaning which, thanks to their very indeterminacy, are able to oppose potential absences of signification without imparting any positive meaning. Such terms cannot *explain* a society's practices; they instead play a crucial role in the continuing enactment of these practices.

'Lived experience' and the unconscious: the problem of sociological meaning

This agreement between Merleau-Ponty and Lévi-Strauss, like the more general rapprochement between phenomenology and ethnology which Merleau-Ponty sought to illustrate, is at best a tenuous one. Merleau-Ponty agreed with much of Lévi-Strauss's critique of Mauss. Lévi-Strauss, in turn, accepted at least some of Merleau-Ponty's formulations of the relationship between ethnology and philosophy.[206] But, on the rather basic level of what Mauss's work suggested about what it meant for a sociological explanation to be at all meaningful, they diverged sharply.

Mauss, as Merleau-Ponty read him, required that the sociologist's explanations both grasp society as a coherent totality and show how this totality is experienced by the members of the society. 'Structure,' Merleau-Ponty insisted, 'like Janus, has two faces.' On the one side it organises 'its constituent parts according to an internal principle'.[207] Such an organising principle may be extremely complex, might be capable of being formalised mathematically, and perhaps could even be comprehended within a 'universal code of structures' whose transformation rules would 'allow us to deduce them from one another'.[208] But however far anthropology might advance in this direction, its 'most proper task' consists in tracing 'the connecting links of a thought network which lead us back from itself to the other face of structure and to its own incarnation':

The surprising logical operations attested to by the formal structure of societies must certainly be effected in some way by the populations which live these kinship systems. Thus there ought to be a sort of lived equivalent of that structure.[209]

Anthropology's unique position within the human sciences lay in its insistence that its models must at some level 'have an immediately human significance'.[210]

This insistence that the theorist's structures find a 'lived equivalent' in the experience of social actors brought sociology into agreement with phenomenology. 'Philosophy,' Merleau-Ponty argued, 'is indeed, and always, a break with objectivism and a return from *constructa* to lived experience, from the world to ourselves.'[211]

> It is essential never to cut sociological inquiry off from our experience of social subjects . . . For the sociologist's equations begin to represent something social only at that moment when the correlations they express are connected to one another and enveloped in a certain unique *view* of the social and of nature which is characteristic of the society under consideration . . . If objectivism or scientism were ever to succeed in depriving sociology of all recourse to significations, it would save it from 'philosophy' only by shutting it off from knowledge of its object. Then we might do mathematics in the social, but we would not have the mathematics *of* the society being considered. The sociologist engages in philosophy to the extent that he is charged not only to record the facts but to comprehend them. At that moment, he is himself already a philosopher.[212]

In turning from abstract constructs to the experience of the members of the society under scrutiny, the sociologist traces the same path which, for Merleau-Ponty, defined phenomenology: the retrogression from the 'second order expressions' of science to the 'basic experience of the world' which is the ultimate ground of every abstraction.

Lévi-Strauss, in contrast, demanded not a return to 'lived experience' but rather a search 'beneath the rationalized interpretations of the native' for those 'unconscious categories' which Mauss had argued were 'the determinants of magic, religion, and language'.[213] Where Merleau-Ponty argued, against Durkheim, that society be conceived not as a *'conscience collective'* but rather as 'intersubjectivity', Lévi-Strauss maintained that what Durkheim had sought to grasp as the *'conscience collective'* could be more adequately comprehended by developing Mauss's comments on the function of the 'unconscious'.[214] While Mauss, in Merleau-Ponty's reading, was groping – however tentatively – towards Husserl, Lévi-Strauss saw him as bringing to consummation that 'end of the *cogito*' which Rousseau – in Lévi-Strauss's rather idiosyncratic reading – had announced.[215]

Structuralism, as Lévi-Strauss conceived it, could engineer an escape from the prison of the *cogito* only if it developed Mauss's insights and thus played the role of Rousseau against Husserl's Descartes. Like Rousseau, it would turn away from the conscious subject – 'that unbearably spoilt child who has occupied the philosophical scene for too long now'[216] – and seek instead to comprehend the anonymous 'he' who ' "thinks" through me' and thus 'causes me to doubt whether it is I who am thinking'.[217] It sought, again like Rousseau, to refuse all immediate and forced identities in order to find a solidarity *'beyond* man with all that is alive' and thus form 'an identification also *before* the function or the character, with a being not yet shaped but given'.[218] The sciences of man must thus dispense with man and instead 'seek the society of nature to meditate there on the nature of society'.[219]

This approach to Mauss disregarded that 'face' of structure which Merleau-Ponty saw as leading back to 'lived experience'. In abandoning the requirement that structure find a 'lived equivalent' in the experiences of members of the society, Lévi-Strauss saw himself as following the path taken by structural linguistics. Language is the most social of all 'social facts'. Yet, much linguistic behaviour 'lies on the level of unconscious thought'. Speakers are unaware of the syntactic and morphological laws of their language and even the linguist's knowledge of these laws 'always remains dissociated from his experience as a speaking agent'.[220] Language thus presents a paradigm of an 'unreflecting totalization', beyond or beneath both consciousness and will. It shows us a 'human reason which has its reasons and of which man knows nothing'.[221]

The analogy to language – an analogy which Lévi-Strauss pursued most persistently after the completion of *Elementary Structures of Kinship* (1949), a work whose reliance on certain formulae taken from *Gestalt* psychology left it far more open to the sort of reading Merleau-Ponty was attempting than the works which followed[222] – provided Lévi-Strauss with the tools he needed to give primacy to the unconscious in the achievement of intersubjective understanding:

> As the organ of a specific function, the unconscious merely imposes structural laws upon the inarticulated elements which originate elsewhere – impulses, emotions, representations, and memories. We might say, therefore, that the preconscious is the individual lexicon where each of us accumulates the vocabulary of his personal history, but that this vocabulary becomes significant, for us and for others, only to the extent that the unconscious structures it according to its laws and thus transforms it into language.[223]

Taking up Paul Ricoeur's critical comments and affirming them as his own intentions, Lévi-Strauss described this unconscious as 'a combinative, categorizing, unconscious', 'a categorizing system unconnected with a thinking subject', a 'Kantianism without a transcendental subject'.[224]

From the flux of 'Erlebnisse' to the field of Being

In drawing out the implications of Mauss's work, Lévi-Strauss and Merleau-Ponty were thus led to radically different conceptions of the goal of sociological explanation. According to Lévi-Strauss, the theorist must uncover, beneath the concepts employed by the members of a society, the combinatory operations of the unconscious. According to Merleau-Ponty, no explanation is meaningful unless it recovers the 'lived equivalent' of the relations it formalises and thus returns 'from *constructa* to lived experience'.

Merleau-Ponty's apparent agreement with Lévi-Strauss's critique of Mauss thus conceals a fundamental disagreement over the nature of sociological explanation. At the basis of this dispute lay a still more fundamental disagreement over the relationship between philosophy and the human sciences. Lévi-Strauss rejected phenomenology because it 'postulated a kind of continuity between experience and reality' which his study of geology, psychoanalysis and Marxism had taught him to suspect. Existentialism struck him as an even more dubious enterprise. A 'sort of shop-girl metaphysics', it allowed people 'to play fast-and-loose with the mission incumbent on philosophy until science becomes strong enough to replace it: that is, to understand being in relationship to itself and not in relation to myself'.[225] The human sciences, accordingly, had as their peculiar mission not the recovery of the human meaning of social interactions but rather the 'dissolving' of the category of 'man' and the 'reintegration of culture in nature'.[226]

Merleau-Ponty's initial conception of the task of philosophy could not have been more opposed to Lévi-Strauss's views. In his 1945 essay 'The Metaphysical in Man' he wrote:

> Metaphysics begins from the moment when, ceasing to live in the evidence of the object – whether it is the sensory object or the object of science – we apperceive the radical subjectivity of all our experience as inseparable from its truth value. It means two things to say that our experience is our own: both that it is not the measure of all imaginable being in itself and that it is nonetheless co-extensive with all being of which we can form a notion. This double sense of the *cogito* is the basic fact of metaphysics: I am sure that there is being – on the condition that I do not seek another sort of being than being-for-me.[227]

Where Lévi-Strauss sought to understand being in relation to itself, Merleau-Ponty conceived metaphysics as consisting of an inquiry which concerned itself only with 'being-for-me'. Could Lévi-Strauss have asked for a more telling illustration of the continued hold Descartes exercised over even the most unorthodox of phenomenologists?

'The Metaphysical in Man', however, was not Merleau-Ponty's final word on the subject. Even as he was arguing in 'From Mauss to Claude Lévi-Strauss' that the ethnologist must find a 'lived equivalent' to the structures he formalises, Merleau-Ponty was questioning, in one of the working notes to *The Visible and the Invisible*, whether the notion of 'lived experience' had anything at all to do with the proper tasks of the philosopher:

> Philosophy has nothing to do with the privilege of the *Erlebnisse*, with the psychology of lived experience . . . The interiority the philosopher seeks is . . . intersubjectivity, the *Urgemein Stiftung* [primordially common foundation] which is well beyond 'lived experience'.[228]

The note does not completely reject his earlier argument – he had insisted in 'The Philosopher and Sociology' that the return to lived experience did not lead back to a 'private life' but, rather, returned to 'an intersubjectivity that gradually connects us ever closer to the whole of history'.[229] But it does raise doubts as to whether this journey back to the *Urgemein Stiftung* on which communication with others ultimately rests could be made with the means Husserl had provided.

This doubt, however, had been voiced much earlier – but not by Merleau-Ponty. At the close of the 1946 colloquy on *Phenomenology of Perception*, Jean Beaufret (who two weeks earlier had addressed the series of questions to Martin Heidegger which occasioned his critique of Sartrean existentialism, the 'Letter on Humanism') commented:

> The only reproach I would make to the author is not that he has gone 'too far', but rather that he has not been sufficiently radical. The phenomenological descriptions which he uses in fact maintain the vocabulary of idealism. In this they are in accord with Husserlian descriptions. But the whole problem is precisely to know whether phenomenology, fully developed, does not require the abandonment of subjectivity and the vocabulary of subjective idealism as, beginning with Husserl, Heidegger has done.[230]

The transcript of the session records no response from Merleau-Ponty, but a decade and a half later one of the working notes to *The Visible and the Invisible* gave as decisive an assent as Beaufret could have wished for:

> It is the Cartesian idealization applied to the mind as to the things (Husserl) that has persuaded us that we were a flux of individual *Erlebnisse*, whereas we are a field of Being.[231]

By his last writings he had journeyed far indeed from a defence of the *cogito* as the 'basic fact of metaphysics'.

Merleau-Ponty had tried to read Husserl in a way which played down the idealist tendencies which Beaufret had criticised. He had also tried to conceive of a relationship between phenomenology and the human sciences which would maintain a balance between the claims of phenomenology and the results of empirical inquiries. On both counts there were limits as to how far Husserl could be pushed. Descartes's ghost was not easily exorcised. Nowhere was this clearer than with the problem of the existence of others. We must turn to that question in order to understand why Merleau-Ponty at the close of his life spoke not of a 'flux of *Erlebnisse*' but rather of a 'field of Being'.

3
Others

Merleau-Ponty and his other

The 'problem of the other' pervades Merleau-Ponty's writings. He concluded *The Structure of Behaviour* with a brief discussion of how we make sense of the action of others.[1] The analysis of the perceived world in the *Phenomenology of Perception* culminated with an account of 'Others and the Human World'.[2] He devoted a course at the Sorbonne to 'The Child's Relations with Others' and spent part of his course on 'Consciousness and the Acquisition of Language' reviewing the discussion of the other in Husserl and Scheler.[3] The penultimate chapter of *The Prose of the World* dealt with 'Dialogue and the Perception of the Other'.[4] The problematic status of 'Being-for-others' played a major role in the critique of Sartre in *Adventures of the Dialectic*.[5] The problem of the other likewise occupied a prominent place in his last courses at the Collège de France.[6] And finally, one of the more fecund working notes for *The Visible and the Invisible* argued that a successful resolution of dilemmas surrounding the problem of others 'requires a complete reconstruction of philosophy'.[7]

A few points of reference remain constant. Husserl's account – most notably in the second volume of the *Ideas* and in the fifth of the *Cartesian Meditations* – was the basic paradigm for Merleau-Ponty's own analyses.[8] Hegel's dialectic of 'Lordship and Bondage' was usually lurking in the background and, when read through Marx, it imparted a political dimension to the discussion of intersubjectivity that is lacking in analyses of 'other minds' by Anglo-American philosophers.[9] Descartes was often invoked as well, primarily as an example of pitfalls to be avoided.[10] But the greatest spur to Merleau-Ponty's reflections on the other was Jean-Paul Sartre's account in *Being and Nothingness*.[11]

Another Sartre?

It is only fitting that Sartre's discussion of 'Being-for-others' should play this role. He was, after all, the 'other' who most decisively influenced Merleau-Ponty's development. There are few works by Merleau-Ponty in which Sartre is not cited, alluded to, or argued with. His hold over Merleau-Ponty was matched only by Husserl. But where Husserl could only inspire, Sartre could also annoy.

It is easy, on first reading, to find in Merleau-Ponty only another Sartre, a junior partner – three years younger – in the existentialist enterprise.[12] But from the start Merleau-Ponty had reservations about his friend's philosophy. Shortly after the publication of *Being and Nothingness* he observed that 'the book remains too exclusively antithetic'. The dichotomies of self and other and of 'for-itself' and 'in-itself' more often than not 'seem to be alternatives' rather than poles in 'communication' with one another. As a consequence, its dialectic was 'truncated'.[13]

He responded to these perceived shortcomings with a sort of syntactic jujitsu which, by rewriting some of Sartre's more notorious statements, turned them to his own cause. Thus, 'We are condemned to freedom' became 'We are condemned to meaning'; 'Hell is others' became 'History is others'.[14] He could also be less Aesopian. The *Phenomenology of Perception* concluded with a critique of a notion of freedom that looked suspiciously like Sartre's.[15]

The rationale behind the muting of his criticisms was that he seemed to feel, at least at first, that there was still another Sartre to be heard. There were implications yet to be articulated, analyses yet to be completed. While *Being and Nothingness* was in many respects problematic, 'all manner of clarification and completion' could be expected.[16] Its account of freedom would doubtless appear in a different light once Sartre elaborated the expected 'theory of passivity'.[17] It lacked a social theory, but it had made a start by posing 'the problem of reciprocal relations between consciousness and the social world'.[18] And, whatever failings the book might have, it nevertheless did confront 'the central problem of philosophy':

After Descartes, it was impossible to deny that existence as consciousness is radically different from existence as thing and that the relationship between the two is that of emptiness to plenitude. After the nineteenth century and all it taught us about the historicity of spirit, it was impossible to deny that consciousness always exists in a situation. It is up to us to understand both things at once.[19]

The 'us' in the last sentence meant, among others, Sartre and Merleau-Ponty. Collaborating with Sartre in the publication of *Les Temps Modernes*, Merleau-Ponty seems to have hoped that the differences between the *Phenomenology of Perception* and *Being and Nothingness* would pass away as he and Sartre elaborated in tandem their accounts of language, politics, and history.

Sartre as other

The differences did not disappear. The works which followed only made them more obvious. *What is Literature?* moved Merleau-Ponty to wonder, in *The Prose of the World*, if 'professional users of language' like Sartre had not overlooked an aspect of linguistic expression which could only be uncovered by examining the silent medium of painting.[20] *The Communists and Peace* moved him to charge, in *Adventures of the Dialectic*, that the antitheses of *Being and Nothingness* had only been repeated, not overcome, when Sartre turned from personal history to literature and politics.[21] Finally, in *The Visible and the Invisible* he mounted a critique of Sartre's pre-reflective *cogito* which was so thoroughgoing that it was also a critique of the author of the *Phenomenology of Perception*.[22]

He was not entirely fair to Sartre, a point Simone de Beauvoir stressed in her bitter rejoinder to *Adventures of the Dialectic*.[23] Throughout the 1950s he accentuated those differences with Sartre which, in the first years after the Liberation, he had downplayed. 'I borrow myself from others,' he wrote toward the end of his life, 'I make them from my own thoughts. This is no failure to perceive others; it is the perception of others.'[24] In 1945, to understand the implications of his own work, he tried to invent another Sartre. He finally understood them only by creating a Sartre who was totally other. And one of the central themes which sustained these inventions and reinventions was the 'problem of the other'.

Wrestling with monsters: Descartes, Hegel and Husserl

What is the problem with others?

The 'problem of the other' is not one of the more inspiring objects of philosophical scrutiny. To have come to the point where it is necessary to prove that others exist should be warning enough that something has gone awry. To fail to come up with a convincing proof is even more embarrassing.

'That others than you can think,' Paul Valéry wrote in one of the pithier statements of the problem, 'is an hypothesis and an acquired notion; it is not obvious.'[25] Certainty that others have thoughts, feelings, or other 'mental states' is alleged to be elusive since thoughts and feelings, unlike tables or human bodies, cannot be seen. One might argue in response that just as one knows that certain of one's own mental states are associated with certain of one's own physical states (for example, this feeling of pain and that finger, hit by a hammer) so, too, similar bodily states in others must be accompanied by the appropriate mental states (for example, that man, who just hit his finger with a hammer, must feel pain). But the problems with this solution – the so-called 'argument from analogy' – are legion. It rests on an inference, not otherwise verifiable, from one case (one's own experience of one's own body) which may not be typical and may not be even coherent (do we really have a way of denoting mental and physical states which does not already presume the existence of others?; wouldn't this require a private language?).[26] At best the argument yields, as Sartre noted, only a 'probable knowledge' that the other is more than a body.[27] At worst it tells us nothing and, as Merleau-Ponty insisted, 'presupposes what it is called on to explain'.[28]

As traditionally conceived, the problem of the other necessitates a sorting-out of the relations between four terms: my mental states, my physical states, the other's mental states, and the other's physical states.[29] To pose the problem is thus, inevitably, to presume that 'mind' and 'body' can be given distinct and unequivocal definitions. Conversely, to resolve the problem may well require a dismantling of the philosophical tradition which assumes that mind and body can be clearly distinguished. And to do this, Merleau-Ponty realised, was to confront those monsters which Descartes had set loose on succeeding generations of philosophers.

The well-dressed automaton: the Cartesian legacy

The problem of the other originates with Descartes's solution to Montaigne's 'What do I know?' What I know, Descartes argued, and know with absolute certainty, is that I am a *'res cogitans'*, a 'thinking thing'. What I am less sure of, at least at the start of the *Meditations*, is the existence of the *'res extensa'*, things beyond me, extended in the world. This latter class of objects includes those 'beings passing by on the street below'. From my window I can see nothing, Descartes writes, 'beyond hats and cloaks which might cover automatic machines'. I take these objects to be other human beings only through an act of judgement, 'a faculty proper not to my eyes but to my mind'. What is certain here is *my thinking that* I see others in the street, not their actual existence.[30]

Likewise, the evidence provided by what Descartes calls the 'inner senses' is less than compelling. How can we be sure that our experience of our own body does not deceive us as well? Amputees, for example, continue to feel pain in limbs which have been removed.[31] Descartes was able to resist the slide towards solipsism which his radical doubt inaugurated only because he thought he found at least one idea that must have an existence beyond the confines of his *cogito*: God.[32] And, having assured himself that God does not deceive, he could win back his body, the other, and the world. But what if we remove God from the picture? Are we not left with a situation in which the existence of others is at best a creature of our faculty of judgement?

Such a state of affairs is not a happy one. As Merleau-Ponty once observed, it is 'repugnant to the other . . . to be only the consciousness I have of him'[33] – which Leon Brunschvicg learned when André Cresson asked him what sort of consciousness he had of the consciousness of André Cresson:

BRUNSCHVICG: The idea that I have of his consciousness is a component in the system of my judgements about existence.
CRESSON: I cannot accept that I might be reduced to a judgement in Mr. Brunschvicg's consciousness, and I doubt whether those present, for their part, would be prepared to accept this either. Moreover, to be consistent, Mr. Brunschvicg ought to declare his as the only consciousness, and that the sole aim of knowledge is to

draw up a harmonious table of its representations for the purposes of his solitary ego.[34]

As Vincent Descombes (who ferreted out this priceless exchange in the first place) has suggested, Brunschvicg's response should be annoying to entities other than André Cresson:

> If Brunschvicg's work-table or his pen – objects whose status in his doctrine is equally that of phenomena integral to the sum of his judgements concerning existence – could talk, they would no doubt protest with the same vigour as André Cresson against their reduction to such a purely intentional status.[35]

What is at stake, then, is not simply the existence of 'other minds'. It is ultimately a question of whether the *cogito* admits of 'otherness' of any kind. If the *cogito* meets everywhere only its own *cogitationes* then has it not become, as Lévi-Strauss suspected, a prison? In search of a way out, Sartre and Merleau-Ponty turned to Hegel and Husserl.

Pugnacious solipsists: Kojève's Hegel

What they found in Hegel was the dialectic of 'Lordship and Bondage'.[36] That this brief section of the *Phenomenology of Spirit* came to be viewed by an entire generation of French intellectuals as the key to all the secrets of Hegel's philosophy was in no small way the achievement of Alexandre Kojève, a Russian refugee who lectured on the book at the École des Hautes-Études between 1933 and 1939.[37] His reading of Hegel had the effect of translating the sort of farcical exchanges which transpired between Brunschvicg and Cresson into the stuff of which epics are made.[38] The struggle for 'recognition' – Hegel's term for the concession that Cresson was trying to wring out of Brunschvicg that he indeed had an existence beyond Brunschvicg's consciousness of him – was for Kojève the driving force of Hegel's entire philosophy of history. Hegel, he taught, saw man as a 'desiring being' who, aiming at the 'nihilation of being', is motivated by a desire which transcends simple physical satisfaction. This desire, the desire for recognition as an 'independent consciousness', leads inevitably to what Kojève terms a 'battle of pure prestige'. Made of rougher stuff than the run-of-the-mill Cartesian, Kojève's solipsists risk their lives to show that they value the affirmation of their autonomy as minds more highly than their survival as bodies.[39]

This struggle has two possible outcomes: either one contestant kills the other (thus destroying the only possible source from which recognition could come), or one of the combatants, feeling the terror of death, surrenders to the other, recognising him as an independent being and consenting to serve as his slave. But even here, Kojève stresses, the desired recognition by the other is not forthcoming; the master cannot be affirmed as an independent consciousness by an individual who has been reduced to a mere instrument of another's whims. At the close of the episode we find a master who is still seeking recognition and a slave who has sublimated his fear of death into a labour which transforms the world. For Kojève, the entire *Phenomenology* is the working out of the consequences of the episode, since only with the creation of a world in which recognition is possible can the dialectic at last come to rest. All human history is thus 'the history of the labouring slave'.[40]

The degree of Kojève's influence on Sartre is unclear,[41] but there is no denying the importance of Hegel's discussion of Lordship and Bondage for Sartre's account of the other. He found Hegel's analysis to be 'filled to overflowing' with a 'richness and profoundity' that few other thinkers approached. In Hegel the Cartesian priorities had been reversed: the other was the ground on which self-consciousness emerged, 'the road of interiority passes through the other', and 'solipsism seems to be put out of the picture once and for all'.[42] But Sartre had reservations. Hegel, he argued, saw the other as an epistemological rather than an ontological problem while Sartre, for his part, maintained that any attempt to link self and other 'externally' on the level of knowledge was doomed to failure.[43] We do not merely *know* the other; we also *exist* for others. He argued as well that Hegel was guilty of a double optimism. He was guilty, first, of an 'epistemological optimism' which presupposed that there was a 'common measure' between the 'other-as-object' and 'Me-as-subject' which enabled me to see myself as an object for the other and to understand that the other was a subject for himself.[44] Second, he was guilty of an 'ontological optimism':

placing himself from the start of the account 'at the vantage point of truth' and forgetting 'his own consciousness', he refused to take the standpoint of any particular consciousness and thus already presupposed that intersubjectivity which his account was supposed to prove.[45] 'But if Hegel has forgotten himself,' Sartre concluded, 'we cannot forget Hegel. This means that we are referred back to the *cogito*.'[46]

Merleau-Ponty, unlike Sartre, attended Kojève's lectures and was greatly influenced by them. They were a crucial impetus in the genesis of Merleau-Ponty's atheism and a decisive influence on his post-war political writings.[47] But as an account of the experience of others, the dialectic of Lordship and Bondage was invoked by Merleau-Ponty only as a preliminary gesture, and quickly taken back. Consider, for example, a pivotal passage in the *Phenomenology of Perception*:

> With the *cogito* begins that struggle between consciousnesses, each one of which, as Hegel says, seeks the death of the other. For the struggle ever to begin, and for each consciousness to be capable of suspecting the alien presences which it negates, all must necessarily have some common ground and be mindful of their peaceful co-existence in the world of childhood.[48]

The disparity with Sartre's critique of Hegel is striking: for Sartre, Hegel had erred in presuming a 'common measure' which was in fact nonexistent; for Merleau-Ponty, Hegel's error lay in his ignoring of a 'common ground' which was the prerequisite for conflict itself.

The spectre in the dark corner: Husserl and the problem of solipsism

The thinker who, in Merleau-Ponty's eyes, made the greatest contribution to the elucidation of this 'common ground' was Edmund Husserl. Husserl carried out his inquiries with the full recognition that phenomenology seemed to promise, at first glance, only a 'pure solipsism'.[49] He was by no means ignorant of the troubling implications of the 'monstrous' notion that the ultimate basis on which the world rests is the *cogito*'s 'I am':

For children in philosophy, this may be a dark corner haunted by the spectres of solipsism and, perhaps, of psychologism, of relativism. The true philosopher, instead of running away, will prefer to fill the dark corner with light.[50]

His attempt to illuminate the problem of the other had taken but a scant two pages in the Sorbonne lectures. It came to occupy a little under half of the hundred-and-forty-page *Cartesian Meditations*.[51]

The terms on which he posed the problem were uncompromising. He began by invoking a 'second epoché' which, by disregarding everything which made reference to the existence of others, attempted a 'reduction to my transcendental sphere of peculiar ownness'.[52] This reduction, as Paul Ricoeur has noted, had the effect of 'transforming the objection of solipsism into an argument'.[53] It forced Husserl to find within 'my own concrete being' an 'immanent transcendency' which could account for my experience of the other and of the objective world.[54]

The goal of this reduction was to reveal a stratum of experience that was so peculiarly my own that it could serve as the benchmark for all subsequent distinctions between 'mine' .and 'other'.[55] Examining our concept of an objective world, open to anyone's experience, Husserl removed all reference to others, all imputations of objectivity, and thus arrived at the abstraction of a 'mere nature', uniquely my own. Within this sphere, my body has a unique status. Unlike those objective bodies (*Körper*) which I must manipulate externally, it is a living body (*Leib*) which I can animate immediately.[56]

Thus far, the reduction seems only to have thrown us into the arms of solipsism. But 'something remarkable strikes us'. Here, at what Suzanne Bachelard has called 'the farthest limit to which the phenomenological reduction can be carried', we find that 'my whole world of experiencing life' including my 'actual and possible experience *of* what is other' continues, oblivious to the 'screening off' of all that is other.[57] The 'reduced' ego still functions as 'a member of the world' with others outside it. Otherness continues to be constituted intentionally within it.[58]

The challenge Husserl faces is thus that of explaining how the experience of the other *as* other can be given within this uniquely personal field. The hinge on which his account turns is the peculiar way in which the body of the other is perceived. In my perception of physical objects, the perception of the front of an object is regularly accompanied by an 'appresentation' of the back. To see the front of a house is to see an object whose other side is given to me as something I could see were I to walk around it. Likewise, to perceive the body of the other is also to be presented with an object which has 'another side' – it is a *Leib* for the other as well as a *Körper* for me. But this 'other side' can never be seen by me; no modification of my location will allow me to experience the other's body as the other lives it.[59] Husserl argues that the motivation for this 'appresentation' of the other's body as another animate body is founded on my own experience of my own body. Through an ' "analogizing" apprehension', resting on 'a similarity connecting within my primordial sphere that body [*Körper*] over there with my body [*Körper*]', the other's body is seen as an animate body.[60]

This animate body 'continues to prove itself' to be a body similar to mine through 'its changing but incessantly harmonious "behaviour" '.[61] A concordance of expression, gestures, and behaviours verifies 'what is not originally accessible' and allows me to confirm the other's body as 'an analogue of something included in my peculiar ownness'.[62] Further, even though I cannot occupy the position the other occupies with respect to his own body, I can take up – in reality or in my imagination – the positions which the other takes up in the face of the world. Thus, just as my 'here' can appear as 'there' for the other, so too the 'there' that I see can also be the other's 'here'.[63] In this way the other comes to be known as a fellow member of that 'community of monads' who inhabit a shared world.

Little in this account impressed Sartre. His allegiances lay more with the 'non-egological' theory of consciousness elaborated in the *Logical Investigations* than with the 'transcendental egology' of the *Cartesian Investigations*. The latter approach 'loaded down' consciousness and deprived it of that essential spontaneity which was the distinctive attribute of a consciousness defined solely as intentionality.[64] The spectre of solipsism, he argued in his 1937 essay 'The Transcendence of the Ego', was a creature born of Husserl's abandonment of his earlier standpoint. As 'an object which appears only to reflection', the Ego was by definition 'radically cut off from the world'.[65] But, once one realises that the Ego is a product of reflective consciousness, it and all of the states it is alleged to have cease to be 'my exclusive property':

Consequently, if Paul and Peter both speak of Peter's love . . . it is no longer true that the one speaks blindly and by analogy of that which the other apprehends in full. They speak of the same thing. Doubtless they apprehend it by different procedures, but these procedures may be equally intuitional. And Peter's emotion is no more *certain* for Peter than for Paul. For both of them, it belongs to the category of objects which can be called into question.[66]

Thus 'solipsism becomes unthinkable' from the moment that the Ego ceases to have a privileged status.[67]

In *Being and Nothingness* Sartre modified his stance slightly. While no more enthusiastic about the transcendental ego, he now conceded that getting rid of it 'does not help one bit to solve the question of the existence of others'.[68] The problem he now saw in Husserl's account was that it did not succeed in doing what it would have to do to free transcendental phenomenology from the onus of solipsism – namely, show that the other is equally a transcendental ego – and instead tried to prove the one thing which no reasonable person had ever doubted: that empirical others exist.[69] In other words, Husserl does not refute the charge that *transcendental* phenomenology terminates in solipsism; the *Cartesian Meditations* shows us only how the other is constituted on the *mundane* level.[70] Even on the mundane level, Sartre felt that Husserl's account left a good deal to be desired. Like Kant and Hegel before him, Husserl saw the problem of the other as an epistemological rather than ontological question: knowledge of the other is the 'indispensable condition for the constitution of the world'.[71]

Husserl replies to the solipsist that the Other's existence is as sure as that of the world, and Husserl includes in the world my psycho-physical existence. But the solipsist says the same thing: it is as sure, he will say, but no more sure.[72]

Thus Husserl does not answer the solipsist's objections; he only repeats them.

While Merleau-Ponty was a good deal more appreciative of the *Cartesian Meditations* than Sartre, he too had reservations. The book crystallised for him a fundamental ambivalence in Husserl's thought. On the one hand, Husserl attempted 'to gain access to others by starting with the *cogito*, with the "sphere of ownness" '.

On the other hand, he denied that there even was a 'problem of the other' and abandoned the standpoint of the *cogito* in order to begin his analysis 'with a consciousness which is neither self nor other'.[73] Merleau-Ponty's Husserl – the 'existentialist' Husserl – of course preferred the latter approach. Hence, where Sartre opposed the Husserl of the *Cartesian Meditations* with arguments drawn from the *Logical Investigations*, Merleau-Ponty read the *Cartesian Meditations* from the perspective of the *Crisis*.

For this reason, the criticisms which Sartre mounted against Husserl fell most heavily on what mattered least to Merleau-Ponty: the transcendental egology. Much of what Sartre wrote could either be granted or ignored. *The Structure of Behaviour* closed with an endorsement of Sartre's position in 'The Transcendence of the Ego'.[74] In the *Phenomenology of Perception* he drove the argument home with an appeal to the *Crisis*, arguing that the self which perceives and the self which is perceived are 'not *cogitationes* shut up in their own immanence, but beings which are outrun by their world, and which consequently may be outrun by each other'.[75] Maintaining that Husserl's best instincts moved him to incarnate transcendental subjectivity into the world as intersubjectivity, Merleau-Ponty had few quarrels with Sartre's rejection of the transcendental ego.

Sartre's criticisms of the adequacy of Husserl's analysis of the problem of the other on the *mundane* level were, in contrast, of relevance to Merleau-Ponty's argument. But they could easily be shown to have missed the point. Husserl did not, as Sartre charged, pose the relationship between self and other as a matter of knowledge. Rather, Merleau-Ponty stressed, Husserl had been at pains to insist that the 'assimilative apprehension' of the other was not an 'inference from analogy'. Apperception 'is not inference, not a thinking act'.[76] We are no more confronted here with an *argument* from analogy than we are in the case of a child who, finally having understood what scissors are, 'from now on sees scissors at first glance *as* scissors' without 'explicit reproducing, comparing, and inferring'.[77] Every apperception, Husserl argued, 'points back to a "primal instituting" [*Urstiftung*] in which an object with a similar sense became constituted for the first time'.[78] In the encounter with others, my lived body serves as a 'primarily institutive original [*urstiftende Original*]' which is 'always livingly present'. Ego and alter ego are thus 'always and necessarily given *in an original "pairing"* ' through which they are always associated but never completely identified.[79] The other is thus always present, as the partner of my body, but nevertheless always 'other'.

In this account of the other, Merleau-Ponty found the most fecund of Husserl's analyses and the most powerful of the concepts which he would eventually marshall against Sartre. But, as we shall see, what he took from Husserl cut in two ways. In criticising *Being and Nothingness*, he came to criticise the *Phenomenology of Perception* as well.

Regarding the regard of the other: *Phenomenology of Perception* vs *Being and Nothingness*

Merleau-Ponty criticised Sartre's account of the other on at least three occasions. His discussion of 'Others and the Human World' in the *Phenomenology of Perception* was in large part a restrained but penetrating critique of the analysis of 'Being-for-Others' in *Being and Nothingness*.[80] In *Adventures of the Dialectic* his polemic against Sartre's essay *The Communists and Peace* examined the failings of Sartre's account of Being-for-Others so as to clarify the foundation on which Sartre's questionable politics rested.[81] Finally, in the second chapter of *The Visible and the Invisible* he sought once again to illuminate the failings of Sartre's ontology by focusing on his treatment of the other.[82]

Each time he returned to *Being and Nothingness* the stakes were raised. The critique in the *Phenomenology of Perception* was sympathetic to Sartre's general project, but anxious to see it purged of those overly antithetic tendencies which Merleau-Ponty felt plagued Sartre's presentations of his philosophy. In *Adventures of the Dialectic*, spurred by irreconcilable political differences with Sartre, Merleau-Ponty made explicit what had been held back throughout the *Phenomenology of Perception*: the extent to which he and Sartre disagreed on most of the fundamental issues at stake in the analysis of the other. Finally, in the more temperate but no less uncompromising critique of *The Visible and the Invisible*, Merleau-Ponty came to see that Sartre's inability to do justice to our experience of others had important ramifications for the argument of the *Phenomenology of Perception* as well.

Looks that kill: the other in 'Being and Nothingness'

Let us sketch, then, the main points of the analysis to which Merleau-Ponty returned again and again.[83] The account in *Being and Nothingness* began by describing the transformation my experience of the world undergoes with the appearance of another person. The other is not simply another part of my world; it is rather an alternative locus around which the world may be organised. With the entry of another person into my visual field

> suddenly an object has appeared which has stolen the world from me. Everything is in place, everything still exists for me; but everything is traversed by an invisible flight and fixed in the direction of a new object.[84]

The other is 'a kind of drain hole' in the middle of the world; into it flow all of the objects of my world.[85]

Unsettling as this experience may be, my seeing the other is only the prelude to an even more convulsive experience: 'Being-seen-by-another'. To be seen by an actual, physically present other person – the *locus classicus* is Sartre's famous description of the voyeur surprised at a keyhole by another person[86] – is to begin to fathom a dimension of our experience which can occur even in the absence of an actual person: the experience of falling under the '*regard d'autrui*':

> What *most often* manifests a look [*regard*] is the convergence of two ocular globes in my direction. But the look will be given just as well on occasion when there is a rustling of branches, or the sound of a footstep followed by silence, or the slight opening of a shutter, or a light movement of a curtain. During an attack men who are crawling through the brush apprehend as a *look to be avoided*, not two eyes, but a white farm-house which is outlined against the sky at the top of a little hill.[87]

The omnipresence of the '*regard d'autrui*' testifies to the fact that I am open to the other in the very depths of my being. 'Being-for-others' is a permanent possibility. 'At each instant,' Sartre intones ominously, 'the other *is looking at me* [*me regarde*].'[88]

The unveiling of the new ontological dimension of 'Being-for-

Others' has wide-ranging implications for Sartre's philosophy. The other binds the 'for-itself' to the 'facticity' of its past and its situation. It spatialises and temporalises the 'for-itself', strips it of its transcendence, and thus brings about that connection between the 'for-itself' and the 'in-itself' which had been one of the major concerns of Sartre's inquiry.[89] All of this persists, however, only so long as the *'regard d'autrui'* is not returned. When it is, it is the other who is transformed into an in-itself, stripped of its transcendence, fixed in a situation, spatialised and temporalised.[90] We are presented with a duel of gazes, a contest with no final victor. The ever-shifting alternatives, *consciousness as object/other as subject* and *consciousness as subject/other as object*, are the two poles between which Sartre's extended and frequently dazzling discussion of such 'concrete relations with other' as 'love, language, and masochism' (on the one side) and 'indifference, desire, hate, and sadism' (on the other) vacillates.[91]

What sustains conflict? The other in 'Phenomenology of Perception'

However much Sartre criticised Hegel, the analysis of 'Being-for-Others' was cut from the same cloth as the dialectic of Lordship and Bondage. In Sartre, relations with the other are achieved by means of an 'internal negation', by a mutual denial and nihilation. They are fundamentally conflictual.

As we have seen, Merleau-Ponty argued that Hegel's account of the 'conflict of consciousness' was dependent on the more fundamental experience of a 'common ground'.[92] The *'regard d'autrui'* was unbearable 'only because it takes the place of a possible communication'. As a *refusal* of communication, it 'is still a form of communication'.[93] Consequently, the most important task facing his account of the other was that of comprehending the primordial community which sustained both conflict and co-existence.

Like Husserl he sought a solution in the way the body of the other was perceived. As 'the vehicle for a form of behaviour', it is both 'the very first of all cultural objects' and 'the one by which all the rest exist'.[94] Rejecting the argument from analogy, he maintained that something akin to Husserl's 'analogizing apperception' was achieved by the lived body itself:

The observed correlations between my physical behaviour and that of others, my intentions and my pantomime, may well provide me with a clue in the methodical attempt to know others . . . but they do not teach me the existence of others. Between my consciousness and my body as I experience it, between this phenomenal body of mine and that of another as I see it from the outside, there exists an internal relation which causes the other to appear as the completion of the system.[95]

What is crucial here, as for Husserl, is that the body of the other is given to me as animate – as a *Leib.* – and not simply as a physical object – a *Körper*. The naturalistic picture of the body 'as a chemical structure of an agglomeration of tissues' is constructed 'by a process of impoverishment, from a primordial phenomenon of the body-for-us, the body of human experience or perceived body'.[96] The 'for-itself' is likewise a creature of an impoverishment which can be undone only if consciousness is conceived 'no longer as a constituting consciousness . . . but as a perceptual consciousness . . . as being-in-the-world or existence'.[97] In Merleau-Ponty's account, self and other meet as incarnate beings, not as sovereign *regards*.

The animate body spontaneously achieves what no analogy working from physical body to mental states could possibly accomplish. My body and the body of the other are 'two sides of one and the same phenomenon'; an anonymous existence 'inhabits both bodies simultaneously'.[98] A simple experiment illustrates the point. If an adult takes the finger of a fifteen-month-old baby and playfully pretends to bite it, the child will open its mouth. There can be no analogy constructed here since the child has 'scarcely looked at its face in a glass' and its teeth are unlike those of the adult. Instead of speaking of an argument from analogy, we must understand that the child's mouth and teeth 'are immediately for it capable of the same intentions' as those of the adult. The intention of 'biting' has 'immediately, for it, an intersubjective significance'.[99]

To account for such behaviour, Merleau-Ponty made recourse, in his course on 'The Child's Relations with Others', to Husserl's discussion of 'pairing' or – as Merleau-Ponty translated the term – 'coupling' [*accouplement*]:

In perceiving the other, my body and his are coupled, resulting in a sort of action which pairs them [*action à deux*]. This conduct which I am able only to see, I live somehow from a distance. I make it mine; I recover it or comprehend it. Reciprocally I know that the gestures I make myself can be the objects of another's intention. It is this transfer of my intentions to the other's body and of his intentions to my own, my alienation of the other and his alienation of me, that makes possible the perception of others.[100]

The 'problem of others' is thus not resolved on the level of constitutive consciousness. The certainty that others exist is, rather, the consequence of a 'passive synthesis' which precedes and sustains the activities of the conscious subject.

Merleau-Ponty's exploration of how this synthesis was achieved led him most immediately in two directions: into an intensive study of developmental psychology and into an increased concern with the role of dialogue in the perception of the other. Both themes had been touched upon in the *Phenomenology of Perception*, but their implications were more fully elaborated only after the publication of the book. And these implications began to suggest the extent to which the problem of the other strains the entire apparatus of Husserlian phenomenology.

The child, the other, and the mirror

The attention Merleau-Ponty devoted to the cognitive development of the child in his courses at the Sorbonne may well have been simply an artifact of his peculiar teaching responsibilities: he held a chair in Child Psychology and Pedagogy.[101] But regardless of his reason for offering these courses, their content proved to be of considerable relevance to the problems he had struggled with in the *Phenomenology of Perception*. Husserl had chosen a most peculiar example to illustrate the phenomenon of 'assimilative apperception': a child's learning, and then applying, the notion 'scissors'. Would not a more relevant question be how the child learns to employ the notion 'other person'? Could not the research of psychologists such as Wallon, Guillaume, and Piaget illuminate the 'primal instituting' that pairs my body with that of the other?

In their writings Merleau-Ponty found discussions of the emergence of the concept of the other which confirmed and completed Husserl's account. The child, at about six months of age, leaves behind an initial phase of 'pre-communication', in which 'there is not one individual over against the other but rather an anonymous collectivity', and begins a process – never fully completed – of segregation and distinction between self and other.[102] The acquisition of knowledge of the other *as other* is coupled with the realisation by the child that its own body is *distinct* and *bounded*. My body and the others's body are, as Husserl had described it, 'paired'; they are both given in the same stroke. Children do not begin from the *cogito* and then learn that others exist. Rather, they begin from a diffuse standpoint, which admits of no distinction between self and other, and come to know themselves only in so far as they make progress in knowing others.

The child's fascination with its own image in a mirror – a phenomenon that had been noted by Köhler, Guillaume, and Wallon among others[103] – is paradigmatic of this dual achievement. By giving the child, for the first time, the opportunity to see its own body as a discrete and bounded entity, it also enables the child to distinguish between itself and others.[104] But to understand the affective dimension of the child's experience of the mirror image, Merleau-Ponty turned from the classic discussion in Wallon's *Les Origines du caractere chez l'enfant* to consider a more recent contribution by one of his fellow auditors in Kojève's lectures on the *Phenomenology*: Jacques Lacan's 1949 paper 'The Mirror Stage as Formative of the Function of the I'.[105]

Following Lacan, Merleau-Ponty argued that the most important lesson which the child learns in the process of recognising the image in the mirror as its own is that 'there can be a viewpoint taken on him'. The mirror teaches the child 'that he is *visible*, for himself and for others'.[106] This recognition that one is – as Merleau-Ponty put it in *The Visible and the Invisible* – a 'visible seer' is the precondition for the development of the 'imaginary me' or 'ideal ego'. But with the acquisition of this consciousness of oneself as a distinct and separate individual comes 'a sort of alienation':

I am no longer what I felt myself, immediately to be; I am that image of myself that is offered by the mirror. To use Dr. Lacan's terms, I am 'captured, caught up' by my spatial image. Thereupon I leave the reality of the lived *me* in order to refer myself constantly to the ideal, fictitious, or imaginary *me*, of which the specular image is the first outline. In this sense I am torn from myself, and the image in the mirror prepares me for another still more serious alienation . . . the alienation by others. For others have only an exterior image of me, which is analogous to the one seen in the mirror. Consequently others will tear me away from my immediate inwardness much more surely than will the mirror.[107]

The image in the mirror 'turns the child away from what he effectively is' and orients him instead 'towards what he sees and imagines himself to be'.[108]

There was one aspect of Lacan's argument, however, which Merleau-Ponty passed over. Lacan's essay closed by drawing out the implications of the mirror stage for 'any philosophy directly issuing from the *cogito*', especially the 'contemporary philosophy of being and nothingness'.[109] Sartrean existentialism, Lacan argued, was refuted by the implications psychoanalysis drew from the mirror stage. The ego must be seen as 'the function of *méconnaissance* [misrecognition]'; it is an imaginary object, which tears the subject away from what it is and chains it to what Lacan, drawing on Kojève, later characterised as 'the desire of the other'.[110] To take the *cogito* as the starting-point for philosophy would thus condemn philosophy to a foundation which vanished under scrutiny.

While Lacan's critique was directed at Sartre, his argument had troubling implications for Merleau-Ponty's position as well. The *Phenomenology of Perception* argued that the lived body is our primordial means of contact with the world. But, given Lacan's analysis of the mirror stage, what sort of relation can we posit between the 'lived me' and the 'imaginary me'? It was on this score that Lacan, in an article written shortly after Merleau-Ponty's death, expressed severe reservations about the degree to which Merleau-Ponty had appreciated the full implications of the mirror stage.[111] Recourse to a 'tacit' or 'pre-reflective' *cogito* did not, in Lacan's opinion, overcome the superficiality which plagued all 'philosophies of consciousness'. No matter how indeterminate the *cogito* is made, Lacan argued, it continued to imply 'all the powers of reflection by which subject and consciousness are confounded'.[112] Merleau-Ponty still clung to the pre-Freudian tendency to equate 'consciousness' (be it 'reflective' or 'pre-reflective') with 'subjectivity' and thus to ignore the important role played by unconscious processes in the creation of the subject.[113]

In the *Phenomenology of Perception*, drawing more on Binswanger's *Daseinanalysis* than on Freud, Merleau-Ponty had argued that psychoanalysis uncovered an 'incarnate significance' which was the original phenomenon of which 'body and mind, sign and significance are abstract moments'.[114] Likewise in a 1951 lecture he had suggested that what Freud had tried to introduce '*between* the organism and ourselves' under the rubric of 'unconscious' was, in fact, what 'other thinkers have more appropriately named *ambiguous perception*'.[115] In these formulations, critics sympathetic to Lacan have found a blurring of the boundary between the 'conscious/preconscious system' and the unconscious.[116] Such formulations seem to suggest that the psychoanalyst's passage back from the conscious to the unconscious is the same thing as the phenomenologist's passage from the objective to the pre-objective. But this is precisely an analogy which Lacan rejected.

For Lacan – as for Lévi-Strauss – phenomenology was unable to appreciate the radical heterogeneity which the concept of the unconscious introduces into the account of subjectivity. Husserl, like Descartes, had assumed that the reflecting ego could make a complete inventory of its own contents. But the split between the ego and the unconscious – a rift whose origin Lacan traced to the imaginary identifications of the mirror stage – plays havoc with the Cartesian project. Lacan's reformulation of the *cogito* was a good deal more extensive than Husserl's: 'I am not wherever I am the plaything of my thought; I think of what I am where I do not think to think.'[117]

If the unconscious – that place where, in Lacan's formulation, I think of what I am without realising that I am thinking at all – is conceived as the locus of the 'discourse of the other',[118] it is difficult to accept Merleau-Ponty's description of it as the 'other side' of consciousness. It is rather, as J. B. Pontalis suggested, what Freud once called 'an other scene'.[119] The contents of this 'other scene' cannot be explored through self-reflection, since to stay on the level of philosophical reflection is to remain on the level where, as Lacan would have it, 'I am the plaything of my thought'. To reach this 'other scene' one must enter into the complex dialectic of the analytic process in which the task of interpretation, in Lacan's words, 'consists precisely in distinguishing the person lying on the analyst's couch from the person who is speaking'.[120] And that was precisely the step which Merleau-Ponty, at this point, was unable to take.

Dialogue, de-centering, and institution

He did, however, complement his analysis of the child's relations with others with a second concern, broached in *Phenomenology of Perception* but pursued more extensively in his courses at the Sorbonne and in his unpublished study *The Prose of the World*: the way in which relations with others are mediated through language. For Sartre, dialogue was a continuation of conflict by other means. The discussion of language in *Being and Nothingness* was but a parenthesis in the analysis of 'seduction' within the first cycle of 'concrete relations with others' ('Love, Language, and Masoch-ism').[121] Merleau-Ponty, by contrast, had argued in *Phenomenology of Perception* that while the other, 'by inserting me in his field, stripped me of part of my being', this loss could be recovered 'by establishing relations with him, by bringing about his clear recognition of me'.[122] Language was uniquely capable of accomplishing this task:

> In the experience of dialogue, there is constituted between the other and myself a common ground; my thought and his are interwoven into a single fabric, my words and those of my interlocutor are called forth by the state of the discussion, and they are inserted into a shared operation of which neither of us is the creator. We have here a dual being, where the other is for me no longer a mere bit of behaviour in my transcendental field, nor I in his; we are collaborators for each other in consummate reciprocity.[123]

To learn to speak, he stressed in his course 'Consciousness and the Acquisition of Language' (1949–50), is not simply to master a new intellectual faculty; it is also to acquire the capacity of living with others.[124]

Language could play this role, Merleau-Ponty went on to argue in *The Prose of the World*, because the relationship between 'speaking' or 'expressive' subjects 'is no longer that alternation which makes a rivalry of the relations between minds':

> I am not active only when I am speaking; rather, I precede my thought in the listener. I am not passive while I am listening; rather, I speak according to . . . what the other is saying. Speaking is not just my own initiative, listening is not submitting to the initiative of the other, because as speaking subjects we are *continuing*, we are resuming a common effort more ancient than we, upon which we are grafted to one another and which is the manifestation, the growth, of truth.[125]

Dialogue provided a paradigm of interaction which differed radically from Sartre's analysis of the '*regard d'autrui*'. It did not culminate in the unstable dyads of 'consciousness as object/other as subject' and 'consciousness as subject/other as object'. Rather, self and other were reciprocally de-centered and hence able to 'encroach upon one another'. Both drew upon expressive acts which 'derive from the same institution'.[126]

Thus, against Sartre's primordial conflict of self and other, Merleau-Ponty invoked Husserl's conception of a 'pairing' of self and other which rested on a 'primal instituting' that assured their co-existence in a shared world. But, as has already been suggested, to stress this aspect of Husserl's work was to embark on a reading of phenomenology which was at odds with certain of Husserl's more Cartesian arguments. And to develop this aspect of Husserl's thought by recourse to a philosophy of language was implicitly to call into question the extent to which phenomenology, as a 'philosophy of consciousness', could come to terms with the problem of the other.

Merleau-Ponty confronted these issues head-on in his course on 'Institution in Personal and Public History' (1954–5) at the Collège de France. Asking whether the notion of 'institution' might not resolve 'certain difficulties in the philosophy of consciousness' – not least among them its tendency to treat the other as 'the negation of itself' – he came to the conclusion that to accept the notion of 'institution' was necessarily to abandon the notion of 'constitution':

> If the subject were taken not as a constituting but an instituting subject, it might be understood that the subject does not exist

instantaneously and that the other person does not exist simply as the negative of myself . . . an instituting subject could coexist with another because the one instituted is not the immediate reflection of the activity of the former and can be regained by himself or by others without involving anything like a total recreation. Thus the instituted subject exists between others and myself, between me and myself, like a hinge, the consequence and guarantee of our belonging to a common world.[127]

Husserl's notion of institution thus provided Merleau-Ponty with a means of curbing those tendencies in Husserl's discussion of 'constitution' which led to Sartre's picture of self and other as eternal antagonists, each forever negating the other. But there is something peculiar in his argument: the subject which he is analysing here is presented both as an 'instituting subject' and as an 'instituted subject'. To speak of the subject as 'institut*ing*' is to see consciousness as actively creating meaning through a series of intentional acts. To speak of the subject as 'institut*ed*' is to open the door to a rather different view of the subject and to see the subject not as an agent creating meaning but as a creature whose meaning must be sought outside its own actions.

Does the subject institute or is it instituted? Merleau-Ponty would appear to want to have it both ways – a stance which is by no means unreasonable but which is, at least at this point, scarcely supported by anything else in his philosophy. *The Prose of the World*, in its role as prolegomena to Merleau-Ponty's philosophy of expression, was to have taken up this curious status of the subject in greater detail. But that work remained unfinished. When Merleau-Ponty next examined the problem of the other it was in a markedly different context: a critique of Sartre's politics.

The political dimension: *Adventures of the Dialectic* **and** *The Communists and Peace*

Breaking points

Merleau-Ponty's long and bitter critique of Sartre in *Adventures of the Dialectic* was provoked by a series of articles which Sartre wrote in response to the bizarre sequence of events which followed the arrival in Paris, on 28 May 1952, of General Matthew B. Ridgway. Ridgway, who was to assume command of NATO forces from Dwight David Eisenhower, had been the target of attacks in the communist press because of the alleged American use of bacteriological weapons in Korea. He was greeted in Paris by a demonstration which was swiftly and forcefully dispersed by the police. In the aftermath, Jacques Duclos, a leading figure in the French Communist Party and a member of parliament, was arrested – allegedly with a loaded pistol, a truncheon, a wireless transmitter, and two carrier pigeons in his car. Only after he had been imprisoned on charges of conspiracy did it become widely known that the pistol and truncheon belonged to his driver/bodyguard, that the wireless transmitter was, in fact, an ordinary radio, and that the pigeons were neither carrier pigeons nor even alive; they were destined not for a meeting with the KGB in Moscow but rather for a rendezvous with some *petits pois* in a casserole.[128]

For Sartre, these events – which opened a campaign to outlaw the French Communist Party – were the 'one straw' which pushed him past the 'breaking point'. 'In the language of the Church,' he later wrote, 'this was my conversion.'[129] Swearing 'an undying hatred of the bourgeoisie' and taking up the defence of the French Communist Party, he wrote day and night and produced the first of a series of articles which appeared in *Les Temps Modernes* between July 1952 and April 1954 under the title 'The Communists and Peace'.[130]

For Merleau-Ponty, these articles were the final straw. In an attack which consumed over half of *Adventures of the Dialectic* he gave public expression to the private disagreements which, since the outbreak of the Korean War, had increasingly estranged him from Sartre. And this attack on Sartre's *politics* culminated in a re-examination and rejection of Sartre's *philosophy*.

The problem of communism

The immediate cause of the quarrel was a mutual redefining of political allegiances. As Sartre wrote in 1961:

Each of us was conditioned, but in opposite directions. Our

slowly accumulated disgust made the one discover, in an instant, the horror of Stalinism, and the other, that of his own class.[131]

Prior to his 'conversion', Sartre had been a good deal less concerned with politics and a good deal further from Marxism than Merleau-Ponty. In the division of labour that grew up at *Les Temps Modernes* Merleau-Ponty assumed the responsibilities of editor-in-chief and political editor. He refused, however, to allow his name to appear along with Sartre's on the masthead of the journal, apparently fearing – Sartre later conjectured – that Sartre might move the journal to the right. He wanted to be able to dissociate himself without a public breach with Sartre.[132]

In the years immediately following the Second World War, *Les Temps Modernes* maintained a position of neutrality toward both the United States and the Soviet Union, with Merleau-Ponty concerned to defend the principles of communism against liberal critics while at the same time ready to criticise the Soviet Union and the French Communist Party for betraying their Marxist heritage.[133] He held to this stance as late as January 1950 when, in an editorial on recent revelations of the extent of the concentration camp system in the Soviet Union, he both argued that 'there is no socialism when one out of every twenty citizens is in a camp' and yet nevertheless maintained that 'whatever the nature of the present Soviet society may be, the USSR is on the whole situated, in the balance of powers, on the side of those who are struggling against the forms of exploitation known to us'.[134]

The outbreak of the Korean War forced his hand. His 'wait and see' attitude towards Marxism now seemed 'a dubious dream'. The independence on which such an attitude rested placed him 'outside communism'.[135] In 1952, ostensibly in protest over the deletion of a critical preface he had attached to an article by Pierre Naville on 'The Contradictions of Capitalism', Merleau-Ponty resigned from *Les Temps Modernes* and terminated his friendship with Sartre.[136]

The party as other: from 'Being and Nothingness' to 'The Communists and Peace'

Political issues such as these would appear to be far removed from the philosophical problem of our relations with others. But for both

Merleau-Ponty and Sartre, the connection could not have been more intimate. Once the arguing started, Sartre later recalled, their differences could not be confined to politics:

> Suddenly his tongue loosened. And so did mine. We launched into a long and futile explanation which bounced from one subject to another and from one discussion to another. Is there a spontaneity of the masses? Can groups find their cohesion from within? Ambiguous questions which at times took us back to politics ... and at other times back to sociology, to existence itself, which means, to philosophy, to our 'style of life', to our 'anchorage' and to ourselves.[137]

The two 'ambiguous questions' which Sartre mentioned were, in fact, the point of departure for Merleau-Ponty's critique in *Adventures of the Dialectic*. And in the book, as in their discussions, the critique of *The Communists and Peace* irresistibly led Merleau-Ponty back to *Being and Nothingness*.

The reasons for Merleau-Ponty's focusing on Sartre's treatment of class are not far to seek. *The Communists and Peace* was concerned not so much with the anti-Ridgway demonstration as with the failure of French workers to support the June 4 strikes called by the French Communist Party to protest against the May 28 arrests. Segments of the liberal press hailed this inaction as evidence of the proletariat's having begun to act independently of its representatives in the party.[138] Sartre, denying that the proletariat was capable of such action against the party, developed an argument which was greatly indebted to his account of the other in *Being and Nothingness*. His analysis of the failed June 4 strike – which, at this point, Merleau-Ponty would have rejected on political grounds alone – was thus linked to parts of *Being and Nothingness* which had long been suspect to Merleau-Ponty on philosophical grounds.

In *Being and Nothingness* Sartre had dealt with class consciousness as an example of the two modalities in which feelings of community with others can be experienced: as an us-object [*nous-objet*] and a we-subject [*nous-sujet*]. The former occurs when the dyad of self and other is confronted by a third party. One possible outcome is that the 'third' will regard both the 'I' and the 'other' as a single entity, fusing both into a similar situation and imputing to both a common project. Sartre noted that certain contexts are more conducive than others to this taking place, the situation of communal work being among the most favourable. It is not work *per se* that integrates individuals into a collectivity, Sartre argued, but rather work carried out for another under the watchful eye of an other.[139] Solidarity with other members of a class is thus introduced from the outside, by the 'Other', and the goal of class struggle can only be the abolition of this status of being an 'us-object', a goal which requires the eradication of the other.[140]

The main lines of this account were carried over into *The Communists and Peace*, where Sartre argued that, as a consequence of transformations in the French economy, a blurring of class distinctions had taken place which frustrates the constitution of a proletarian 'us-object'. Workers rarely find themselves watched by capitalist 'thirds'; the complex hierarchy of workers and managers defuses class conflicts.[141] The party must step into the role abandoned by the capitalist 'third'. Described by Sartre as 'pure action', unencumbered by facticity, and without divisions, it provides the *'regard d'autrui'* which binds the proletariat together.[142]

The account in *Being and Nothingness* thus leads inexorably to the conclusions of *The Communists and Peace*: the proletariat did not assert its independence on June 4 since, by definition, only 'individuals' and never the 'proletariat' criticise or fail to follow party directives:

'Then, *who* refused to strike?' Well, *individuals*, and a great number of them at that; if you like, the great majority of workers. 'And isn't that what's called the proletariat?' No, it is not . . . The worker restricts himself to refusing to participate *personally*; he doesn't pass judgement. And far from wishing, like Kant and the drunks of the Fourth Republic, 'to raise the principle of his own act to a universal law', he strives to keep it private.[143]

For the *proletariat* to criticise the party it would have to become a 'we-subject' – an active, collective subject. And that is no simple feat.

The concept of 'we-subject' is among the more obscure aspects of Sartre's early social thought and one of the more important concerns of his later *Critique of Dialectical Reason*.[144] The analysis in *Being and Nothingness* focuses on the way the production and use of manufactured objects shapes an anonymous, collective subject. These objects, having been produced by non-individualised 'they-subjects', reveal their users as 'an undifferentiated transcendence'.[145] Thus active solidarity with others is won, paradoxically, only at the price of a surrender to the power of objects.[146]

A similar argument emerges in the final instalment of *The Communists and Peace*.[147] While continuing to insist that the masses are 'the object of history' and 'never act by themselves', Sartre granted that the militant's transformation of the 'masses-object' into a 'proletarian-subject' requires some 'prior unity' within the proletariat. This unity, he argued, arises through a process of mimesis in which I imitate, not the 'Other', but rather 'myself become my own object'. Imitator and imitated are both 'interchangeable and separated' and the proletarian's capacity for imitation resides in his being 'anyone at all'.[148]

> Each sees the other come to him as anyone at all, that is, as himself. To the extent that massification engenders both isolation and interchangeability, it gives rise to imitation as a mechanical relationship between molecules; and imitation is neither a *tendency* nor a psychic characteristic: it is the necessary result of certain social situations.[149]

While this prior unity may serve as fodder for the militant, taken by itself it remains 'a false unity of isolations, masking a perpetual dispersion'.[150] The party still constitutes the proletariat.

Appalled by this argument, Merleau-Ponty began a critique of Sartre's essays which returned to the ultimate basis on which they rested: the account of the other in *Being and Nothingness*. But was he simply recasting what was essentially a political squabble into a difference of philosophies? How serious was his attack on Sartre's *philosophy*? Might it not be merely a tactic designed to make more serious a disagreement which was, after all, primarily political?[151] To answer these questions we must look briefly at Merleau-Ponty's analysis of class and party in the period *before* his break with Sartre.

Class and party in 'Phenomenology of Perception' and 'Humanism and Terror'

Merleau-Ponty had countered Hegel's description of the 'struggle of consciousnesses' by recalling their 'peaceful coexistence in the world of childhood'. But he never assumed that history was an affair of children. In *Humanism and Terror* he wrote that it was

> essentially a struggle – the struggle of the master and slave, the struggle between classes – and this is a necessity of the human condition; because of the fundamental paradox that man is an indivisible consciousness no one is able to affirm himself except by reducing the other to objects.[152]

His mentors in politics were Machiavelli, Marx, and Weber. 'Political action is of its nature impure,' he wrote in *Humanism and Terror*, 'since it is the action of one person upon another.'[153] Violence cannot be expelled from politics; to that extent he agreed with Weber's 'Politics as a Vocation'.[154] All one could do was apply Machiavelli's test to see if violence – something that was inherently evil – could nevertheless be 'used well'. Was its use 'economical'? Did it lessen or increase with use?[155] Or, to speak like Marx, did violence eventually lead to the ending of the domination of masters over slaves? Did it serve, as Kojève put it, the cause of mutual recognition?[156] Phenomenological analyses may show that conflict is impossible without a more basic commonality, but this does not mean that history knows no incidents of domination and struggle. The primacy intersubjectivity enjoyed over conflict in Merleau-Ponty's phenomenology is not – and *need not* be – carried over into his philosophy of history.[157]

Merleau-Ponty did not, however, interpret all forms of social interaction in terms of a conflict between self and other. A theory of class consciousness had been sketched in the *Phenomenology of Perception* which diverged sharply from Sartre's account. Merleau-Ponty saw class consciousness as 'a mode of dealing with the world and society' which grounds both specific political practices and reflective judgements about class identity.[158] Class consciousness thus exists before the advent of the other as a 'shared lot' or 'general style of existence'.[159] This is of the utmost importance for Merleau-Ponty's account of the party since it allows him to see the party as the nexus where the prethematic experience of class consciousness is articulated through an encounter with leaders whose function is in essence 'pedagogical'.[160] The party is thus not a *regard* which creates the proletariat; it is instead an interlocutor in the dialogue through which the proletariat comes to self-consciousness.

The major themes of Merleau-Ponty's subsequent dispute with Sartre were present well before their explicit political disagreements of the early 1950s. The conflict, however, remained latent. When facing concrete political problems, both Sartre and Merleau-Ponty could very well reach similar conclusions, analysing the situation in terms borrowed from Hegel's dialectic of Lordship and Bondage. Such agreements, however, were of the most fragile sort, resting as they did on a more fundamental disagreement over the primacy of conflict at the level of social ontology. When they came at last to disagree on political issues, and were forced to make explicit the bases on which their commitments rested, Merleau-Ponty found himself driven to confront once again all of the shortcomings of Sartre's treatment of the problem of others.

The 'intermonde' lost: 'Being and Nothingness' revisited

Merleau-Ponty could not, then, treat *The Communists and Peace* simply as a wrong-headed analysis of contemporary events. By its very 'reference to the present' it was already theoretical, treating the event as 'ineffaceable, as a decisive test of our intentions and an instantaneous choice of the whole future of all that we are'.[161] It implied, in short, Sartre's entire philosophy of consciousness, facticity, and time.[162] It was an attempt 'to annex history to his philosophy of freedom and the other'.[163]

The Communists and Peace, Merleau-Ponty argued, was less a development of Sartre's social theory than a repetition of an unchanging set of ontological motifs. Relationships between classes, relationships within classes, and ultimately history itself had all been treated as if they were nothing more than slightly more complex variants of the contests Sartre had analysed in *Being and Nothingness*; never mediated through things, these relationships were always 'immediately readable in the accusation of a *regard*'.[164] Throughout *The Communists and Peace* 'we remain within the philosophy of the subject'.[165]

> The social can enter his philosophy of the *cogito* only by way of the *alter ego*: if I am a thinking being, only another I can contest the thought I have of myself. Inversely, the other can have the status of a self only by taking it away from me, and I can recover it only by reacting to the magic of the *regard* with the countermagic of pure action. 'Sociality' as a given fact is a scandal for the 'I think'.[166]

Sartre's ontology did not ground a social theory; it had become a substitute for one.

At its most basic level, Merleau-Ponty argued, Sartre's project is marked by a paradox. He regularly invokes a 'middle ground . . . between consciousness and things' but then revolts against it.[167] While Merleau-Ponty once argued that the revolt was only apparent – and waited for Sartre to remedy the overly antithetical character of his ontology – in *Adventures of the Dialectic* he concluded that it was Sartre's commitment to explore the 'middle ground' between his antinomies which was only apparent:

> Contrary to appearances, being-for-itself is all that Sartre has ever accepted, with its inevitable correlate: pure being-in-itself . . . There is no hinge, no joint or mediation, between myself and the other.[168]

Lacking this mediation, Sartre could not, like Marx, conceive of history as a 'mixed milieu, neither things nor persons' in which intentions are 'absorbed and transformed'; in Sartre there can be no 'coming-to-be of meaning in institutions'.[169] Since 'men and things are face to face' nothing is ever *continued*; it is only willed anew.[170]

> The question is to know whether, as Sartre says, there are only *men* and *things* or whether there is also the interworld, which we call history, symbolism, truth-to-be-made. If one sticks to the dichotomy . . . each man, in literature as well as in politics, must assume all that happens instant by instant to all others . . . If, on the contrary, one agrees that no action assumes as its own all that

happens, that it does not reach the event itself, that all actions, even war, are always symbolic actions . . . if one thus renounces 'pure action', which is a myth (and a myth of the spectator consciousness), perhaps it is then that one has the best chance of changing the world.[171]

Sartre now joined Brunschvicg, behaviourism, and the other partisans of the 'philosophy of the spectator consciousness'.[172] He too failed to appreciate the density of history and society as an interworld of symbols.

Visibility, carnality, reversibility: *The Visible and the Invisible*

The panorama and the chiasm

In *Adventures of the Dialectic* Merleau-Ponty's critique of Sartre's ontology had been subordinated to the exigencies of his polemic against Sartre's politics. That quarrel now behind him, Sartre's ontology was given a more direct – and slightly more charitable – accounting in the second chapter of *The Visible and the Invisible*.[173] Here, Merleau-Ponty granted that Sartre's 'philosophy of the negative' was a considerable improvement over the idealism of the 'philosophy of reflection' – a term in Merleau-Ponty's lexicon which was elastic enough to encompass a philosophy like Brunschvicg's as well as the Kantian tendencies within Husserl's phenomenology. While reflective philosophy had been unable to show how a constitutive consciousness could 'pose another that would be its equal' – witness Brunschvicg's difficulties with Cresson – Sartre had managed to turn this 'stumbling block' into 'the principle of a solution'.[174] The very struggle between self and other showed that consciousness was not shut up in its own world. Each individual world opens onto 'a background world that exceeds all its perspectives'. It is but a 'partial being', connected to 'the whole of Being'.[175]

Sartre's solution, nevertheless, left Merleau-Ponty with a sense of 'uneasiness'. *Being and Nothingness*, he wrote,

described our factual situation with more penetration than had ever before been done – and yet one retains the impression that this situation is one that is being surveyed from above, and indeed it is: the more one describes experience as a compound of being and nothingness, the more their absolute distinction is confirmed; the more the thought adheres to experience, the more it keeps it at a distance. Such is the sorcery of the thought of the negative.[176]

Under Sartre's spell the elements which comprise 'perceptual faith' – the term Merleau-Ponty used to denote our unshakeable conviction that the world and others indeed exist[177] – undergo a strange mutation. The 'one who sees' becomes a 'seer who forgets that he has a body', an abstract, disembodied consciousness, a 'for-itself'.[178] The thing seen is transformed into the 'in-itself', an absolute plenitude, a 'positivity' bereft of 'density, depth, the plurality of planes, the background worlds'.[179] And the relationship of the seer to other seers is presented only in an 'ambivalent' or 'labile' form.[180]

All this, Merleau-Ponty argued, was the consequence of Sartre's vantage point. Being and nothingness opposed one another in a clear and unequivocal fashion only for an observer who looked at the world from a high enough altitude.[181] From such a position it was possible to overlook the 'inherence of being in nothingness and of nothingness in being'; from such a perspective the world appeared monochromatic, one-dimensional, and unambiguous.[182] A philosophy perched here enshrined as 'dialectic' not our immediate contact with being, but rather the experience of vision as 'a panorama'.[183] Given this vantage point it was impossible to ameliorate the antithetic character of Sartre's philosophy which had for so long bothered Merleau-Ponty. Antitheses could never be overcome; they only 'more quickly succeed one another before thought'.[184]

The blindness inherent in Sartre's panoramic vision was particularly evident in his treatment of the other. 'Vision ceases to be solipsistic only up close,' Merleau-Ponty wrote,

when the other turns back upon me the luminous rays in which I had caught him, renders precise that corporeal adhesion of which I had a presentiment in the agile movements of his eyes, enlarges beyond measure that blind spot I divined at the center of my sovereign vision, and, invading my field through all its frontiers, attracts me into the prison I had prepared for him and, as long as he is there, makes me incapable of solitude.[185]

For a description of the relation between self and other that was more faithful to what transpired 'up close', Merleau-Ponty drew on Paul Valéry's account of the 'exchange' of *regards*:

> Once gazes interlock, there are no longer *quite* two persons and it's hard for either to remain alone. This exchange . . . effects . . . a transposition, a metathesis, a chiasm of two 'destinies', two points of view. You take my appearance, my image, and I take yours. You are not I, since you see me and I don't see myself. What is missing for me is this 'I' whom you can see. And what *you* miss is the 'you' I see.[186]

Just as Sartre's panoramic vision had overlooked the interweaving of being and nothingness, so too it had been blind to the chiasm in which self and other were tangled. Sartre viewed the *regard* as a 'look that kills'; in Valéry, the crossing of *regards* initiates a process of 'simultaneous, reciprocal limitation' which yields a 'decentering', not an 'annihilation'. Sartre knew only 'a me–other rivalry'; in Valéry we have a 'co-functioning' of self and other.[187]

Valéry did something more, however, than simply confirm Merleau-Ponty's misgivings about Sartre's description of the '*regard d'autrui*'. His use of the term 'chiasm' – a word which denoted X-shaped configurations of the sort frequently encountered in anatomy (for example the interweaving of optic nerves) and by extension referred to all those interweavings, reciprocal interpenetrations, and crossings that Merleau-Ponty had sought to evoke through his use of rhetorical chiasmata – suggested an alternative to Sartre's panoramic vision.

At the close of *Adventures of the Dialectic*, Merleau-Ponty had been groping towards an understanding of dialectical thought which would free itself from the standpoint of a 'spectator consciousness':

> There is dialectic only in that type of being in which a junction of subjects occurs, being which is not only a spectacle that each subject presents to itself for its own benefit but which is rather their common residence, the place of their exchange and of their reciprocal interpenetration.[188]

To remain faithful to this conception of the dialectic, he went on to argue in *The Visible and the Invisible*, was to recognise that the dialectic was above all else 'the refusal of panoramic thinking'.[189] But, then, how was it to be conceived? Drawing on Valéry, he suggested in one of the working notes to *The Visible and the Invisible* that the dialectic must be grasped as a 'chiasm', a 'reversal'.[190] The intertwining of self and other which Valéry had described can be generalised to all of our ties with the world:[191] 'every relation with being is simultaneously a taking and a being taken; the hold is held'.[192] This was how Hegel's expression *'an sich oder für uns'* [in-itself or for-us] was to be understood: every attempt at grasping things as they are 'in themselves' culminates in a 'retiring into oneself', just as every attempt at grasping things as they are 'for us' throws us back into the world of things in themselves.[193] The proper task of philosophy is not to try to untangle this intertwining of self and world; 'every analysis which *disentangles* renders unintelligible'.[194] Rather, philosophy must be content with 'interrogating' this tangle, situating itself 'neither in the for Itself nor in the in Itself' but, rather, 'at the joints, where the multiple *entries* of the world cross'.[195]

Tangible touchers and visible seers: transforming the problem of the other

One of Merleau-Ponty's favourite tangles, the one which occurs when one hand touches the other hand while this other hand is touching something else, is particularly helpful in attempting to fathom the implications of the notion of the chiasm for his philosophy. As early as *Phenomenology of Perception* – before his first recourse to Valéry's 'chiasm of *regards*' – Merleau-Ponty had discussed this example.[196] He returned to it once again in the last two years of his life – *after* having made the chiasm the central metaphor in his 'new ontology'.[197] By contrasting the two discussions, we can begin to perceive the differences between *The Visible and the Invisible* and the *Phenomenology of Perception* and begin to understand the implications these differences had for his approach to the problem of the other.

The discussion in *Phenomenology of Perception* was yet another of his tacit dissents from *Being and Nothingness*. Sartre had argued that 'to touch and be touched' were 'radically distinct' phenomena that 'exist on two incommunicable levels'.[198] Merleau-Ponty granted that 'the two hands are never simultaneously in the relationship of touched and touching to each other', but he refused to concede that this meant that the touched hand is simply an object in the world like any other thing:

> In passing from one rôle to the other, I can identify the hand touched as the same one which will in a moment be touching . . . In this bundle of bones and muscles which my right hand presents to my left, I can anticipate for an instant the integument or incarnation of that other right hand, alive and mobile, which I thrust towards things in order to explore them. The body catches itself from the outside engaged in a cognitive process; it tries to touch itself while being touched, and initiates 'a kind of reflection' which is sufficient to distinguish it from objects.[199]

This equivocation between touching and being touched is one of the 'structural characteristics of the body itself'; the body is both subject and object, capable of both 'seeing' and 'suffering'.[200]

The disagreement with Sartre over the status of the touched hand reflects their more basic divergence regarding the nature of the 'pre-reflective *cogito*' – that 'non-positional' self-consciousness which, for both, grounded all reflective acts. Sartre's distinction between the body which touches and the body which is touched is, as M. C. Dillon has argued, merely one instance of 'the ontological distinction he draws between consciousness and its objects'.[201] Consciousness is always of a different order than its objects; my experience of my body is no exception. I am no more intimately related to it than I am to any of the other objects I confront. Indeed, I come to know it first through the agency of the other.[202] Throughout the *Phenomenology of Perception*, Merleau-Ponty had argued for a different understanding of the pre-reflective *cogito*. It must be understood as an incarnate consciousness, as a body-subject. Hence, there can be no question of the body being simply an object among other objects in the world.[203]

Without downplaying the extent of Merleau-Ponty's dissent from *Being and Nothingness*, it is necessary to stress what he shared with Sartre here: both saw the concept of the pre-reflective *cogito* as a necessary and adequate response to the idealism in which they had been trained. In Sartre, the argument that the pre-reflective *cogito* is always *other* than its objects neatly summarised his earlier attack on Brunschvicg's 'digestive philosophy'. In Merleau-Ponty, the argument that the reflective *cogito* was supported and sustained by a tacit, incarnate *cogito* marked the culmination of his effort to show – contra Brunschvicg – that perception could not be reduced to judgement. But, in *The Visible and the Invisible*, the very coherence of the notion of a pre-reflective *cogito* is called into question. A working note from January 1959 makes it clear that it is not simply *Sartre's* notion which is being rejected:

> What I call the tacit *cogito* is impossible. To have the idea of 'thinking' (in the sense of 'thought of seeing and of feeling'), to make the 'reduction', to return to immanence and to consciousness of . . . it is necessary to have words. It is by the combination of words (with their charge of sedimented significations, which are in principle capable of entering into other relations than the relations that have served to form them) that I *form* the transcendental attitude, that I *constitute* the constitutive consciousness. The words do not refer to positive significations . . . Mythology of a self-consciousness to which the word 'consciousness' would refer – – There are only *differences* between significations.[204]

The tacit *cogito*, like the distinction between self and other, is an artifact of language, a creature of the sedimented meanings and the diacritical oppositions which make up the language the philosopher employs.[205] Merleau-Ponty continued to insist that there is 'a world of silence' to which the philosopher must somehow give voice; the perceived world was 'an order where there are non-linguistic significations'.[206] But the tacit *cogito* had imported into this silent world of vision the already-formulated language of the philosophy of consciousness, and in doing so had misrepresented the relationship between vision and speech.

Merleau-Ponty's later examinations of the touched hand thus proceed without recourse to the tacit *cogito*. All of the terms associated with the philosophy of the *cogito* are now suspect. In a long working note from May 1960 he stressed a point which had been noted only in passing in his earlier discussion: the touching hand is 'never exactly the touched'; it always eludes us. We cannot say that the touching and the touched 'coincide in the body' as he had implied in 1945. Instead, he wrote somewhat cryptically, 'Something other than the body is needed for the junction to be made; it takes place in the *untouchable*.'[207] We gain nothing by foisting another name onto this untouchable and saying that the touching and the touched 'coincide "in the mind" or at the level of "consciousness" '. These words only transform 'a true negative' into 'a positive that is elsewhere (a transcendent)'.[208] The place where the toucher and the touched meet is not simply *de facto* untouchable; it is untouchable *de jure*. It, like the 'invisible of vision' or the 'unconsciousness of consciousness', is the 'other side or the reverse (or the other dimensionality) of sensible Being'.[209]

In stressing that the touching hand always escapes the hand that tries to touch it, Merleau-Ponty is not suggesting that the two 'sides' of the body, the sensible and the sentient, are divided by an abyss of the sort that Sartre posits between the in-itself and the for-itself. Rather than an 'abyss', we must speak here of an *'écart'* – a 'spread' or 'divergence'.[210] The non-coincidence of the touching and the touched is not a 'failure' which must either be set right by further analysis or installed as absolute.[211] It is, rather, the sort of joining of obverse and reverse which is typical of the chiasm.[212] The analysis of the touched hand must take as its starting-point the fundamental lesson the chiasm teaches: 'there is not identity, nor non-identity . . . there is inside and outside turning around one another'.[213]

The relation of self and other needed to be rethought along similar lines. 'There is not the For Itself and the For the Other', he wrote in a working note from November 1960, 'They are each the other side of the other.'[214] Self and other are not to be taken as 'positive subjectivities', each unknowable by the other. Their relationship is rather that of 'two entries into the same Being', two 'moments of the same syntax'. They are 'not two contradictories, but rather each the reverse of the other'.[215] I never have the other's experiences; if I did there would be no reason to talk of self and other. But this non-coincidence must be understood in the same way that we understand the non-coincidence of the touching and the touched. It points not to a failure or a problem but is, rather, that particular *écart* around which a chiasm has been tied. Although my hands are never able to coincide with one another, they neverthe-less are able – because of 'a very peculiar relation from one to the other across corporeal space' – to join together as one 'sole organ of experience' and explore the world. In the same way, the monocular views of my individual eyes are tied together into 'one sole cyclopean vision'.[216]

'Why would this generality, which constitutes the unity of my body,' Merleau-Ponty asked, 'not open it to other bodies?'

> The handshake too is reversible; I can feel myself touched as well and at the same time as touching . . . Why would not the synergy exist among different organisms, if it is possible within each? Their landscapes interweave, their actions and their passions fit together exactly: this is possible as soon as we no longer make belongingness to one same 'consciousness' the primordial definition of sensibility, and as soon as we rather understand it as the return of the visible upon itself, a carnal adherence of the sentient to the sensed and the sensed to the sentient.[217]

The problem of the other is not so much 'solved' as 'transformed'.[218] Others present a problem only to a philosophy which operates with a set of categories which separate mind and body, consciousness and world, subject and object. It was precisely this vocabulary which Merleau-Ponty abandoned in *The Visible and the Invisible*. The other is not a problem because 'it is not I who sees, not he who sees'; instead an 'anonymous visibility inhabits both of us, a vision in general, in virtue of that primordial property that belongs to the flesh'.[219]

Flesh on flesh, or the story of the eye

Merleau-Ponty's long struggle with Sartre's account of 'being for others' thus culminated with the recognition that the problem of the other defied analysis 'into being and nothingness, into existence as consciousness and existence as a thing'; its resolution required nothing less than 'a complete reconstruction of philosophy'.[220] Sartre had ventured a somewhat more suggestive approach to the problem than the 'philosophy of reflection', but in the end he too remained tied to the vantage point of the 'spectator consciousness'.[221] Just as Descartes, seated in his room, gazed out the window at the suspicious forms on the street below, so too Sartre's consciousness peered out 'through the holes of the eyes' from the depths of its 'invisible retreat' at the panorama that lay open before it.[222] For both, consciousness was a voyeur, eager to see everything, but careful to remain unseen.

In coming to terms with Sartre, Merleau-Ponty was forced to question the view of the relationship of mind and body, of consciousness and world, which had dominated philosophy since at least Descartes. As outlined, *The Visible and the Invisible* – like Husserl's *Crisis* – would attempt to trace the crisis of contemporary philosophy back to its origins in the Cartesian project.[223] Only by doing this could the presuppositions and commitments which had brought about the present state of affairs be finally revealed. While Merleau-Ponty did not live to complete this part of the manuscript, his last published essay, 'The Eye and the Mind', included a painstaking dissection of Descartes's *Dioptric*. By looking at it, we can begin to appreciate the magnitude of the reconstruction he felt was needed to save philosophy.

In the *Dioptric*, Descartes sought to apply the principles outlined in his *Discourse on Method* to the phenomena of light and reflection, the functioning of the eye and the nature of vision, and the ways in which vision might be improved through devices such as the telescope.[224] It was, of course, the discussion of vision – which he had analysed as early as *The Structure of Behaviour*[225] – that most concerned Merleau-Ponty. Descartes's essay, he wrote, was 'the breviary of a thought that wants no longer to abide in the visible'.[226] It consistently talked about vision as if it were something else. For example, at the start of the essay, vision is treated as one incidence of the more general case of touch. Light, it is argued, should be understood as a case of 'action by contact'; the blind are said to 'see with their hands' and the blind man's sticks are claimed to duplicate exactly, in his hands, the effect produced by the impact of light rays on the back of the eye.[227] With this shift from seeing to touching, Merleau-Ponty argued, Descartes managed 'at one swoop' to eliminate 'action at a distance' and relieve us 'of that ubiquity which is the whole problem of vision':

> In the world there is the thing itself, and outside this thing itself there is that other thing which is only reflected light rays and which happens to have an ordered correspondence with the real thing; there are two individuals, then, bound together externally by causality.[228]

In much the same way, looking at paintings is equated with the reading of texts. Copper engravings, Descartes wrote, 'excite our thought' in the same way as 'signs and words, which have no manner of resemblance to the things they signify'.[229] Vision thus becomes a

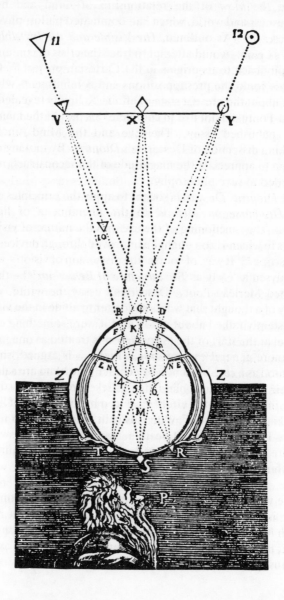

process of interpretation, a process of reflection and judgement, an activity proper to the mind, not the eye.[230]

But how can a mind *see* anything? How can a *res cogitans* be effected by a *res extensa*? The *Dioptric* provided an elaborate diagram of the path traced by light rays leaving an object and travelling into the chamber of the inner eye.[231] But, as Merleau-Ponty asked in a working note from September 1959, 'Who will see the image painted in the eyes or in the brain?'[232] At the bottom of the diagram – but never mentioned by Descartes in his discussions – is a man who, as Paul Valéry wrote, seems to be 'busy looking at the image that forms on the retina'.[233] Descartes's cleaving of mind from body obliged him to place, inside the objectified eye, a man who is able to reflect on what is there to be seen.[234] But does this little man have, in the chamber behind his eyes, yet another man? And who might be hiding in the even smaller room behind this other man's eyes? We can stop this infinite regress, Merleau-Ponty argued, only by recognising that 'the primordial vision that one must indeed come to cannot be the *thought of seeing*'.[235] It is the eye which sees, after all, not the soul. The eye – that most peculiar *res extensa* – performs 'the prodigious work of opening the soul to what is not soul'.[236]

Vision thus eludes the models suggested by the spectator consciousness. What Merleau-Ponty was attempting, in Marc Richir's apt image, was a 'defenestration of the *cogito*'.[237] The philosopher in his room, the little man behind the eye, the 'for-itself' which 'flees' from the 'in itself': all these images rest on the same understanding of vision. They assign the philosopher the role of a '*kosmotheoros*' – the seer who surveys the entire universe – and thus lose sight of the fact that, like everyone else, the philosopher looks at the world from its midst.[238] 'He who sees is of it and in it': the seer is not hidden away in a room, he is down in the street, a visible part of the world he sees.[239]

We have to reject the age-old assumptions that put the world and the seer in the body, or, conversely, the world and the body in the seer as in a box. Where are we to put the limit between the body and the world, since the world is flesh? Where in the body are we to put the seer, since evidently there is in the body only 'shadows stuffed with organs', that is, more of the visible? The world is not 'in' my body, and my body is ultimately not 'in' the visible world:

as flesh applied to flesh, the world neither surrounds it nor is surrounded by it. A participation in and kinship with the visible, the vision neither definitively envelops it nor is enveloped by it.[240]

Vision should be understood as the 'turning back' of one part of the visible upon the rest. It is an affair of what Merleau-Ponty termed 'the flesh', a name he chose to designate that for which 'there is no name in traditional philosophy'.[241] Neither 'matter', nor 'some "psychic" material', nor 'a fact or sum of facts "material" or "spiritual" ', nor 'a representation for a mind', nor 'the union or compound of two substances', the flesh – in one of the few positive definitions Merleau-Ponty ever gave – 'is the sensible in the two-fold sense of what one senses and what senses'.[242] It is an attempt to designate, without untangling, the chiasm which is our primordial relation with the world. 'The seer is caught up in what he sees, it is still himself he sees: there is a fundamental narcissism of all vision.'[243]

After Descartes

In his 1945 discussion of the reception of *Being and Nothingness*, Merleau-Ponty had hailed the book as an attempt to think through 'the central problem of philosophy': the reconciliation of the lessons of Descartes with those of nineteenth-century historicism. 'After Descartes,' he wrote, 'it was impossible to deny that existence as consciousness is radically different from existence as thing and that the relationship between the two is that of emptiness to plen-titude.'[244] But this was precisely what *The Visible and the Invisible* questioned.

By the end of his life Merleau-Ponty had come to view half of what he had once charged philosophy with understanding in a totally different light. After Descartes, 'existence as consciousness' and 'existence as thing' must no longer be juxtaposed to one another as nothingness and plentitude. Rather, they must be understood as 'obverse' and 'reverse', as abstracts from the same 'flesh'. As Marjorie Grene has argued:

Sartre is the last of the Cartesians. He shows us, brilliantly and maddeningly, the impasse to which in our time the modern mind has come. Merleau-Ponty, groping, obsessed with one paradox – the paradox of visual perception – over rhetorical, yet speaks to us as one of the first truly post-Cartesians.[245]

Being and Nothingness still inhabited a Cartesian universe. *The Visible and the Invisible* was an attempt to understand how philosophy, after the demise of the Cartesian ontology, could go on.

But what of the second of the two lessons to which contemporary philosophy was supposed to respond? In 1945 Merleau-Ponty had also argued, 'After the nineteenth century and all it has taught us about the historicity of spirit, it was impossible to deny that consciousness always exists in a situation.'[246] The importance of *Being and Nothingness* lay not simply in its faithfulness to Descartes; rather, its greatness lay in its attempt to fuse the Cartesian project with the great themes of nineteenth-century historicism. How do matters stand with the 'historicity of spirit' in the face of Merleau-Ponty's critique of Cartesian ontology? To understand the relationship between his critique of Descartes and his growing estrangement from the vision of history which found its fullest expression in that Hegelianised Marxism which he professed in the years immediately after the Second World War, we must leave behind the problem of the other and consider Merleau-Ponty's account of expression and history. And to do this is to turn from his long argument with Sartre to his peculiar dialogue with Ferdinand de Saussure.

4

Speech, Expression, and the Sense of History

From perception to history, via expression

Few concerns play as central a role in the evolution of Merleau-Ponty's thought as the problem of expression. His inquiries took him beyond linguistics and aesthetics to grapple with questions that were basic to his studies of politics, society, and history. He hoped that by turning to the models suggested by linguistics and aesthetics he could acquire the categories needed to understand the social world and thus bring to completion the project he had begun with *The Structure of Behaviour* and the *Phenomenology of Perception*. But his attempt to elaborate a theory of expression ultimately led him to question the standpoint he had adopted in his first two books and thus to submit his entire project to radical criticism.

Beyond perception

At the 1946 colloquium on the *Phenomenology of Perception*, Merleau-Ponty stressed that the book represented 'only a preliminary study, since it hardly speaks of culture or history'. It had shown a way of 'getting closer to present and living reality', but an extension of its approach to 'the relation of man to man in language, in knowledge, in society and religion' was still to be attempted.[1] The *Phenomenology of Perception* had shown that perception was 'an original modality of consciousness', reducible neither to association nor judgement, and that the perceptual world was neither 'a sum of objects' nor a set of analytic propositions.[2] The fruit of this restoration of the world of perception, however, was a 'bad ambiguity' – 'a mixture of finitude and universality, of interiority and exteriority'.

But there is a 'good ambiguity' in the phenomenon of expression, a spontaneity which accomplishes what appeared to be impossible when we observed only the separate elements, a spontaneity which gathers together the plurality of monads, the past and the present, nature and culture into a single whole. To establish this wonder would be metaphysics itself and would at the same time give us the principle of an ethics.[3]

The examination of this 'good ambiguity' was to be the task of *The Origin of Truth* and its prologue, *The Prose of the World*.

The Origin of Truth was to give 'a precise description of the passage of perceptual faith into explicit truth as we encounter it on the level of language, concept, and the cultural world'.[4] It would thus show how the 'bad ambiguity' of the perceptual world was overcome in the 'good ambiguity' of expression. This more ambitious work was to be preceded by a shorter study devoted to the problem of literary expression: *The Prose of the World*. It would examine how language is able to 'sublimate rather than suppress our incarnation' in the communication with others.[5] Its account of literature would, he hoped, provide the key to 'the more general order of symbolic relations and institutions'.[6]

The course Merleau-Ponty set for himself in the years immediately following the completion of the *Phenomenology of Perception* is thus clear enough: he hoped to work from perception to expression and onward from expression to history and truth. The study of expression would show how the world of perception is transposed into a world of signs which have meaning for others. It would thus set the stage for an inquiry into the ways in which these meanings were instituted and transformed in history. What is not so clear is why he found himself unable to bring any of this to completion.

Resources

In these inquiries – as elsewhere – he found a starting-point in the work of Husserl and Sartre. What mattered in Husserl was not the attempt in the *Logical Investigations* to construct a universal grammar but rather his late essay 'The Origin of Geometry as an Intentional-Historical Problem'.[7] Here Husserl was not constructing an eidetic of language; rather he was attempting to understand the path which led from an immediate, 'lived' contact with space to an idealised, geometrical space. He was concerned not so much with providing a rational reconstruction of grammatical forms as with showing how reason itself emerges in history.[8]

Sartre played his usual role of *agent provocateur*: *The Prose of the World* was initially conceived as 'a sort of *What is Literature?* with a longer section on the sign and prose'.[9] Sartre's essay had opened with a discussion of prose and the sign which posed a number of arguments (at one point appealing to the *Phenomenology of Perception* for support) which Merleau-Ponty eventually came to reject. Sartre began by denying that music or painting could be discussed using the same concepts employed in the study of language: 'Notes, colors, and forms are not signs. They refer to nothing exterior to themselves.'[10] He went on to distinguish the way poetry and prose regard language:

> The poet has withdrawn from the language-instrument in a single movement. Once and for all he has chosen a poetic attitude which considers words as things and not as signs. For the ambiguity of the sign implies that one can penetrate it at will like a pane of glass and pursue the thing signified, or turn his gaze toward its *reality* and consider it as an object. The man who talks is beyond words and near the object, whereas the poet is on the side of them.[11]

For the writer of prose, then, language was a tool, transparent like a window pane, which leads us directly into the world of things.[12]

Husserl and Sartre were not, however, Merleau-Ponty's only sources of inspiration. In his studies of expression, as in his account of perception, non-philosophers were as important as philosophers. He drew on studies of aphasia by Gelb and Goldstein – analyses which already had claimed a prominent place in the *Phenomenology of Perception* – and was acquainted as well with Roman Jakobson's work on aphasia and children's language.[13] Discussions of language acquisition in the writings of Henri Wallon, Paul Guillaume, and Jean Piaget also played an important role in his courses and writings in the late 1940s as did certain arguments of the linguist Gustave Guillaume.[14] But the theorist who would most decisively influence Merleau-Ponty's approach to the problem of expression was Ferdinand de Saussure.

Reading (and misreading) Saussure

Merleau-Ponty's relation to Saussure is marked by a paradox. He was, as Roland Barthes once noted, the first French philosopher to take an interest in Saussure's linguistics.[15] But his reading of Saussure was so idiosyncratic that it makes his notoriously loose readings of Husserl look like models of hermeneutic chastity. He openly admitted that he was 'pushing Husserl further than he wanted to go', but there is scant evidence that he saw anything unorthodox in his interpretation of Saussure.[16]

Merleau-Ponty's Saussure

Merleau-Ponty began a serious reading of Saussure only after the publication of the *Phenomenology of Perception*.[17] Saussure's name first appears in courses given at Lyon, the École Normale, and the Sorbonne between 1947 and 1950.[18] His work is discussed briefly in a 1947 article and examined much more extensively in the unfinished manuscript of *The Prose of the World*.[19] The discussion of history in the inaugural lecture at the Collège de France culminated in the claim that Saussure's work showed how the dilemmas which plagued Hegel and Marx could be overcome.[20] And, in his first courses at the Collège de France, Saussure's writings occupied a position of almost undisputed pre-eminence.[21]

On all these occasions, Merleau-Ponty presented Saussure's achievement in much the same way. Saussure had rejected attempts at approaching language as if it were a natural object and had maintained that it was fruitless to seek causal linkages between present facts of speech and historically antecedent states. He instead took up 'the perspective of the speaking subject who lives in his language' and founded, alongside the already established 'diachronic linguistics of language [*langue*]', a new 'synchronic linguistics of speech [*parole*]'. From the standpoint of *parole* Saussure was able to reveal an order, a system, and a totality where earlier only chaos and accident had ruled.[22]

Merleau-Ponty saw in Saussure's return to the speaking subject a way of transcending the rigid dichotomies philosophy had estab-lished between the existing and the possible, the constituted and the constituting, facts and conditions of possibility, and – ultimately –

between science and philosophy itself.[23] Saussure's approach freed
history from historicism and made a new conception of reason
possible.[24] He thus achieved something far loftier than his stated
aim of showing the linguist 'what he is doing'.[25] He revealed 'a
rationality in the contingent, a lived logic, a self-constitution' which
cast needed light on 'the union of contingency and meaning in
history'.[26] Indeed, Saussure 'could have sketched a new philosophy
of history'[27] – *could have*, but didn't; so the job was left to
Merleau-Ponty.

The Saussure of the 'Course'

It is difficult to reconcile these claims with the actual content of
Saussure's *Course in General Linguistics*.[28] The primacy Merleau-
Ponty accorded to the 'speaking subject' and the 'linguistics of
speech' flies in the face of Saussure's insistence that the sole
appropriate object of linguistics was *langue* – human speech
(*langage*) considered as a social institution whose conventions
constrain and govern individual acts of speaking (*parole*).[29] At the
very start of the *Course*, Saussure stressed the need to 'put both feet
on the ground of language [*langue*] and use language as the norm for
all other manifestations of speech [*langage*]'.[30] The 'linguistics of
speech' was, in Saussure's opinion, the concern of a set of disciplines
– anatomy, speech physiology, and phonology – whose connection
to linguistics was at best tenuous.[31]

It is even more difficult to understand why Merleau-Ponty
thought Saussure had juxtaposed 'a synchronic linguistics of speech'
to 'a diachronic linguistics of language'. A diagram printed in the
Course which summarises Saussure's view of the 'rational form' of
linguistics makes it abundantly evident that the distinction between
parole and *langue* is by no means isomorphic with the distinction
between synchrony and diachrony.[32]

$$\text{Langage} \begin{cases} \text{Langue} \begin{cases} \text{Synchrony} \\ \text{Diachrony} \end{cases} \\ \text{Parole} \end{cases}$$

Langue can be studied either synchronically or diachronically – it can be regarded either as a set of co-existing terms which constitute a functioning system or as a consequence of a series of transformations, brought on by fortuitous accidents, which have forced the system to establish a new equilibrium.[33] *Parole* is thus emphatically not the object of synchronic linguistics. Indeed, Saussure went so far as to argue: 'Taken as a whole, *parole* cannot be studied.'[34] In it one finds only momentary, individual articulations of a system whose coherence can be understood only by turning from the act of speech to consider the conventions of *langue*.[35]

Finally, beyond these terminological misunderstandings, Merleau-Ponty's portrait of Saussure as a potential philosopher of history seems strangely out of step with how Saussure himself regarded the relationship between linguistics and history. Seeking to establish the principles on which linguistics could rest, Saussure argued that the science of language should follow the practice of the 'economic sciences':

> Here, in contrast to other sciences, political economy and economic history constitute two clearly separated disciplines within a single science . . . Proceeding as they have, economists are . . . obeying an inner necessity. A similar necessity obliges us to divide linguistics into two parts, each with its own principle. Here as in political economy we are confronted with the notion of *value*; both sciences are concerned with *a system of equating things* of different orders – labour and wages in one and a signified and signifier in the other.[36]

Political economy sought to understand the relation between labour and wages without recourse to history (and that, in Marx's eyes, was its monumental blindness). Saussure urged linguistics to approach the relation of signifier to signified in the same way. The thinker that Merleau-Ponty felt could well have written a new philosophy of history had, in fact, conceived his entire project in isolation from history.

There is thus little in the *Course* to support Merleau-Ponty's reading of Saussure. To be sure, there are passages which, if pulled from context and read against the main thrust of the lectures, would support parts of his interpretation.[37] But this would be a rather perverse way of reading Saussure, and an attempt which explains Merleau-Ponty's interpretation of Saussure in this fashion leaves unanswered the most interesting question: what led Merleau-Ponty to read Saussure so queerly?³⁸

The faces of the sign

At the heart of Merleau-Ponty's reading of Saussure lies an idiosyncratic interpretation of Saussure's definition of the linguistic sign. At the start of the resumé of his 1953–4 course on 'The Problem of Speech', Merleau-Ponty argued that in 'adopting speech as his theme', Saussure launched a wholesale revision of the received categories of linguistics:

> He challenged the rigid distinction between sign and signification which seemed evident when one considered instituted language [*langue*] alone, but breaks down in speech [*parole*] where sound and meaning are not simply associated. The famous definition of the sign as 'diacritical, oppositive, and negative' means that language is present in the speaking subject as a system of differentiations [*écarts*] between signs and between significations and that speech operates, in one gesture, the differentiation in these two orders.³⁹

Like most of Merleau-Ponty's claims about Saussure, there are considerable difficulties in reconciling this with the *Course*. But unlike other misreadings, this one has a strange coherence about it.

In his famous definition of the nature of the linguistic sign, Saussure was not, as Merleau-Ponty implied, *challenging* the distinction between 'sign' and 'signification'. Rather, he was *introducing* a distinction, within the sign itself, between what he called the 'signifier' (or 'sound image') and the 'signified' (or 'concept').⁴⁰ To find anything approximating what Merleau-Ponty is alluding to we must turn to Saussure's discussion of the nature of linguistic value. There, *langue* is described as a 'series of contiguous subdivisions marked off on both the indefinite plane of jumbled ideas and equally vague plane of sounds'.⁴¹ Merleau-Ponty thus modified Saussure's position in two ways: first, he saw the operation of differentiation as being carried out on the plane of *parole*, not *langue*; second, he saw the process of differentiation as involving, not 'concepts' and 'sound images', but rather a 'perceptual chain' and a 'verbal chain'.[42] With the first move, the focus is shifted from an already existing *system* of differentiations to an *act* which fuses together sound and meaning through a process of mutual opposition. With the second move, the focus is shifted from the plane of ideas to the plane of perception.[43] While Merleau-Ponty's double displacement is inconsistent with Saussure's argument, it is congruent with a certain understanding of the nature of the linguistic sign.

Roland Barthes has suggested a typology of the ways signs have been studied which is helpful in clarifying the presuppositions which guide Merleau-Ponty's reading of Saussure. 'Every sign,' he writes, 'includes or implies three relations':

> To start with, an interior relation which unites its signifier to its signified; then two exterior relations: a virtual one that unites the sign to a specific reservoir of other signs it may be drawn from in order to be inserted in discourse; and an actual one that unites the sign to other signs in the discourse preceding or succeeding it.[44]

Each relation suggests a different way of approaching the sign. The first, which Barthes terms the 'symbolic' relation, would have us focus on individual, isolated signs and investigate the analogical relation between the signifier and the signified. The signifier here is viewed as 'less a (codified) form of communication than an (affective) instrument of participation'.[45] The signifier is seen as an attempt to capture the inexhaustible meaning of the signified through an always insufficient act of mimesis. For example, the cross 'symbolises' Christianity, but Christianity is always more than the cross.[46] To investigate the inner relation of signifier and signified is thus to ask whether the signifier resembles the signified adequately, whether it captures it, whether it sufficiently embodies or expresses it.

These are precisely the questions Saussure told us *not* to ask. His 'first principle' of linguistics, the dictum that 'the linguistic sign is arbitrary' means – if nothing else – that there is no resemblance, no analogy, no natural bond between signifier and signified. The sole reason for preferring the sound ' ^{1} kat' to any other possible series of sounds (for example, ' $\int$ a') as a way of signifying small, carnivorous mammals who shed hair on furniture is that it is an established convention among speakers of English to use the sound-image

' kat' to signify the concept 'cat'.[47] Beyond noting that it is indeed the convention to use a certain sound image to designate a certain concept, there is simply nothing more to be said about the internal relationship between signifier and signified.

The doctrine of the 'arbitrary nature of the sign' thus shifts attention to the two exterior relations Barthes noted: the virtual or 'paradigmatic' relation of the sign to other signs which might have stood in its place, and the actual or 'syntagmatic' relation of the sign to neighbouring signs within the discourse itself.[48] If the 'symbolic consciousness' saw the act of signification as a relation in 'depth' with the signifier pointing to the foundation on which all acts of signification draw, the 'paradigmatic consciousness' sees the sign in 'perspective':

> It sees the signifier linked, as if in profile, to several virtual signifiers which it is at once close to and distant from . . . The dynamics attached to this vision is that of a summons: the sign is chosen from a finite organized reservoir, and this summons is the sovereign act of signification.[49]

For the paradigmatic consciousness, the act of signification cannot be understood as a simple gesture pointing unequivocally to a particular content. It is, rather, an act which takes its meaning as much from what it rejects – the series of other possible signifiers – as from what it takes up. Meaning here is diacritical, not indexical.

While the paradigmatic consciousness is still concerned with the connecting of signifiers to signifieds, the 'syntagmatic conscious-ness' takes up a stance which is even further removed from the standpoint of the 'symbolic consciousness'. Its concern is with the relation of signs to one another on the level of discourse itself. Focusing on the play of signifiers, it 'most readily renounces the signified' and is thus 'more a structural consciousness than a semantic one'.[50]

Let us now try to determine which of these conceptions is most commensurate with Merleau-Ponty's reading of Saussure. It is clear, first of all, that his reading resists a thoroughgoing syntagma-tic conception. Maurice Lagueux has suggested that his misreadings of Saussure can at least partially be understood as a consequence of his overriding interest in questions of meaning.[51] His *was* a semantic, not a structural consciousness, while the syntagmatic consciousness is, as Barthes has stressed, 'a strictly fabricative or even *functional* imagination', concerned with the ways in which chains of signifiers fit together and not with the signifieds they designate.[52]

To what extent does Merleau-Ponty's reading of Saussure appear to be grounded in a paradigmatic approach to the sign? Here his interest in questions of meaning presents fewer problems and, indeed, Barthes himself uses Merleau-Ponty's philosophy of expression as an example of the paradigmatic consciousness.[53] Such an approach to the sign may have been the position towards which Merleau-Ponty's philosophy of expression advanced, but his account of expression nevertheless carried in its wake crucial elements of a conception of expression which had been elaborated *before* his appropriation of Saussure. This account not only placed the speaking subject at the centre of the discussion of the process of signification, it also conceived of the process in terms which are closest to the one relationship between signifier and signified which Saussure expressly excluded: the symbolic relation.

Speech as gesture, history as perception

If we wish to understand Merleau-Ponty's peculiar reading of Saussure, we would do well to examine the account of expression and history he articulated prior to his study of Saussure's work. The *Phenomenology of Perception* included a chapter on 'The Body as Expression and Speech' whose premises regarding the nature of speech differed significantly from the arguments Merleau-Ponty advanced in *The Prose of the World.* In the years immediately after the publication of *Phenomenology of Perception* – and most notably in his 1947 study *Humanism and Terror* – Merleau-Ponty outlined an approach to history which drew on the theory of expression sketched in the *Phenomenology of Perception.* By looking at these first efforts at a theory of expression and history, we can understand the questions which Merleau-Ponty brought to his reading of Saussure and thus comprehend a bit more clearly the reasons behind his idiosyncratic account of Saussure's work.

The word which points

The problem of language entered the *Phenomenology of Perception* on much the same terms as the analyses of spatiality and motility or the discussion of sexuality: all of these phenomena testify to the body's 'intentionality and sense-giving powers'.[54] Just as Merleau-Ponty argued that the body projects itself into the perceptual world 'by an "intentional arc" ' . . . which brings about the unity of the senses, of intelligence, of sensibility and motility' and just as he maintained that the body enters the erotic world thanks to 'an intentionality which follows the general flow of existence and yields to its movements', so too the act of speech brought home to him 'the enigmatic nature of our body'.[55]

> It is not a collection of particles, each one remaining in itself, nor yet a network of processes defined once and for all – it is not where it is, nor what it is – since we see it secreting in itself a 'significance' which comes to it from nowhere, projecting that significance upon its material surrounding, and communicating it to other embodied subjects.[56]

We understand thoughts and intentions only because our body is capable of appropriating and expressing these thoughts and intentions: 'It is the body which points out, and which speaks.'[57]

Speech is thus 'a genuine gesture' and is meaningful in the same way as any non-linguistic gesture.[58] The meaning of words should no more be sought in their sounds than the meaning of a gesture should be sought in the physical act itself.[59] I do not improve my understanding of what someone is pointing at by examining his index finger more intently; I must, rather, follow his gesture and see what it is that he is pointing towards. And what he is pointing towards is neither a 'concept' nor a 'mental image'; it is the world itself.[60]

> My friend Paul and I point out to each other certain details of the landscape; and Paul's finger, which is pointing out the church tower, is not a finger-for-me that I *think of* as oriented towards a church-tower-for-me, it is Paul's finger which itself shows me the tower that Paul sees, just as, conversely, when I make a movement towards some point in the landscape that I can see, I

do not imagine that I am producing in Paul, in virtue of some pre-established harmony, inner visions merely analogous to mine: I believe, on the contrary, that my gestures invade Paul's world and guide his gaze.[61]

It is much the same with language: 'It presents or rather it *is* the subject's taking up a position in the world of meanings.'[62] The phonetic 'gesture' brings about 'a certain structural co-ordination of experience, a certain modulation of existence' between speaker and listener.[63] Like the finger pointing to the church tower, *'le mot a un sens'*: the word has a meaning, a direction.[64]

Both connotations of the French *sens* – 'meaning' and 'direction' – are crucial; throughout the *Phenomenology of Perception*, meaning is understood *as* orientation:

In all uses of the word *sens*, we find the same fundamental notion of a being oriented or polarized in the direction of what he is not, and thus we are always brought back to a conception of the subject as *ek-stase*, and to a relationship of active transcendence between the subject and the world.[65]

This conception of meaning as orientation allowed Merleau-Ponty to reject the 'empiricist' treatment of the word as simply a mark left by a stimulus without embracing the 'intellectualist' alternative of viewing the word as a category which structures experience.[66] *Sens* is to be understood less 'in terms of the indescribable quality of its "mental concepts" than in terms of a certain manner of presenting its object'.[67] While idealism had understood signification as an act which imposes meaning – in Husserl's terminology, signification is a *Sinn-gebung* – Merleau-Ponty argued that *Gestalt* psychology suggested a more profound conception of meaning. The *significa-tion* 'circle' may well be recognised by 'an understanding which engenders it as the abode of points equidistant from a centre'. But the *Gestalt* of the circle is grasped only by a subject 'familiar with his world' who is able to seize the circle 'as a modulation of that world, as a circular physiognomy'.[68]

We have no way of knowing what a picture or a thing is other than by looking at them, and their significance is revealed only if we look at them from a certain point of view, from a certain distance and in a certain direction, in short only if we place, at the service of the spectacle, our collusion with the world.[69]

This, then, is the sort of meaning that gestures deliver to us. We do not understand them on the level of conscious, reflective acts of interpretation. They are, rather, grasped by a sort of 'blind recognition' by which 'I lend myself to the spectacle' and learn through my body what it is that the other's body is urging me towards.[70]

The speech which breaks the silence

However persuasive this may be as an account of gestures,[71] is the act of speech really best understood as a gesture? Do words turn us toward the world or do they only bring us to other words, to concepts, to a 'mental setting which is not given to everyone'? How convincing is it to treat the words as a gesture when we know – because different languages use different sounds to refer to the same objects – that the link between sound and meaning is arbitrary? These objections, which might well have been voiced by a reader attentive to the implications of Saussure's approach to the linguistic sign, were in fact raised by Merleau-Ponty himself against his own presentation of the word as a gesture.[72] But the speed with which he brushed them aside shows how far from Saussure his initial conception of expression was.

In response, Merleau-Ponty invoked the 'celebrated distinction' between '*langages*' – 'constituted systems of vocabulary and syntax' – and '*parole*' – acts of speech in which 'unformulated meaning [*sens*] not only finds the means of being conveyed outwardly, but moreover acquires existence for itself, and is genuinely created as meaning [*sens*]'.[73] This distinction (which is close to, but not identical with, Saussure's distinction between *langue* and *parole*) is immediately restated, transposed onto the level of *parole*, as a distinction between the 'word in speaking' (*parole parlante*) and the 'spoken word' (*parole parlée*).[74] It is only in the former that we find a 'significative intention' through which existence comes to be 'polarized into a certain "*sens*" '.[75]

Merleau-Ponty's account of speech is thus concerned with a quite specific class of speech acts, epitomised for him by the child's first entering into the world of language or a writer's expressing something for the first time – speech acts which 'transform a certain kind of silence into speech'.[76] While rather rare – and, one would assume, rather different from what goes on in ordinary discourse – these acts are absolutely central to Merleau-Ponty's account.

Constituted speech, as it operates in daily life, assumes that the decisive step of expression has been taken. Our view of man will remain superficial so long as we fail to go back to that origin, so long as we fail to find, beneath the chatter of words, the primordial silence, and as long as we do not describe the action which breaks this silence.[77]

It is this word which breaks the silence, and *only* this sort of word, which is truly a gesture.

This distinction – which owes more to Heidegger's distinction between *Rede* and *Gerede* than to anything in Saussure[78] – limits the class of speech acts which Merleau-Ponty likens to gestures, but it does not respond to the main thrust of the objections raised against his account of speech. He still must show how, in the face of the multiplicity of languages, even this sort of 'originary expression' can be viewed as resembling the gestures which we use to point out objects in the world. Merleau-Ponty's response here is twofold: he argues, first, that non-linguistic gestures are by no means 'natural' – they too vary from culture to culture – and, second, that the linguistic gesture is 'not entirely arbitrary'.[79] It is this second part of the response that commits him to a position diametrically opposed to Saussure.

Signs will appear to be arbitrary, Merleau-Ponty argues, only so long as we consider spoken speech and examine only the 'final conceptual meaning' of words.

But it would no longer appear so if we took into account the emotional content of the word . . . It would then be found that the words, vowels, and phonemes are so many ways of 'singing' the world, and that their function is to represent things not, as naive onomatopoeic theory had it, by reason of an objective resemblance, but because they extract, and literally express, their emotional essence. If it were possible, in any vocabulary, to disregard what is attributable to the mechanical laws of phonetics, to the influence of other languages, the rationalization of grammarians, and assimilatory processes, we should probably discover in the original form of each language a somewhat restricted system of expression, but such as would make it not entirely arbitrary.[80]

The arbitrary relation between signifier and signified is thus only apparent. Once the linguistic sign has been restored to its original, emotive function, it will become apparent that the signifier does indeed bear a certain resemblance to what it signifies. When we perform Merleau-Ponty's proposed linguistic *epoché* and make our return to 'originary speech', we find that what appeared to have been a sign was in fact a symbol.

The *Phenomenology of Perception* thus contained an account of expression which differs markedly from Saussure's understanding of the nature of the linguistic sign. What, then, was the motivation for Merleau-Ponty's attempt, in *The Prose of the World*, to elaborate a theory of expression which was more clearly an attempt to appropriate Saussure's approach? An answer can be found by examining the three works described by Merleau-Ponty in a prospectus drawn up at the time of his candidacy to the Collège de France as having 'touched upon' certain themes which were still to be developed in *The Origin of Truth* and *The Prose of the World*: two essays from *Sense and Non-Sense* ('Cézanne's Doubt' and 'Metaphysics and the Novel'), and *Humanism and Terror*.[81] In the prospectus, Merleau-Ponty presents these essays as anticipations of an account whose 'philosophical foundations . . . are still to be rigorously elaborated'.[82] Yet it is possible to read these works in a different light. Far from lacking a philosophical foundation, all three are firmly grounded in the account of expression of the *Phenomenology of Perception*. But in developing the implications of this account, Merleau-Ponty was led to recognise its limitations. The three essays lack a philosophical foundation only because they provoked a renewed reflection which undermined the theory of expression sketched in the *Phenomenology of Perception*.

Cézanne, 'L'Invitée', and the Moscow Trials

Let us examine the three works Merleau-Ponty mentioned, but do so with our eyes cast back to the *Phenomenology of Perception*, not forward to *The Prose of the World*. The debts owed to the *Phenomenology of Perception* by the two essays in *Sense and Non-Sense* are readily apparent. Cézanne's work is claimed to exemplify the risks that artists invariably run.

> Because he returns to the source of silent and solitary experiences on which culture and the exchange of ideas have been built up in order to know it, the artist launches his work just as a man once launched the first word, not knowing whether it will be anything more than a shout, whether it can detach itself from the flow of individual life in which it originates and give the independent existence of an identifiable *meaning* [*sens*] either to the future of that same individual life or to the monads coexisting with it or to the open community of future monads.[83]

'Cézanne's difficulties,' Merleau-Ponty concluded, 'are those of the first word.'[84] His work testified to the ambiguity of expression: it is impossible to find 'a single gesture which is not spontaneous', since there are no innate or inherited gestures, but it is also 'impossible to have a single gesture which is absolutely new in regard to that way of being in the world which . . . is myself'.[85] Freedom is always situated. The lesson we learn from Cézanne is the one we have learned in the *Phenomenology of Perception*.

It is also the lesson we learn from Simone de Beauvoir's novel *L'Invitée*, the subject of the second essay in *Sense and Non-Sense*. Morality is not something which can simply be presumed; harmony can be 'taken for granted' only among 'Kantian consciousnesses'.[86] For the characters in *L'Invitée*, value must be created by 'actively being what we are by chance'. Neither completely created nor entirely discovered, value emerges in the process of taking up a situation 'which we have not completely chosen'.[87] Like 'Cézanne's Doubt', 'Metaphysics and the Novel' explores 'the revolt of life's immediacy against reason', and attempts, without losing sight of the experience of 'unreason' (*déraison*), to formulate 'a new idea of reason'.[88] What *sens* we are able to make in the world must emerge against a background of *non-sens*.

The same general theme may be found in *Humanism and Terror*, although the argument here is a good deal more complex and, when all is said, a good deal less convincing. On the most immediate level, the book is a critique of Arthur Koestler's novel *Darkness at Noon*. It seeks, through an examination of Nikolai Burkharin's testimony at the 1937 Moscow trials, to draw different lessons about the relationship between violence and history than those reached by Koestler and other liberal critics. Koestler, as Merleau-Ponty read him, presented the trials as a struggle between the 'yogi' and the 'commissar' – between moral conscience and political Machiavellianism. Rubashov, Koestler's fictitious amalgam of Zinoviev and Bukharin, vacillates between the two alternatives. He confesses his guilt before the tribunal because of his commitment to a philosophy of history which allows the Party to manipulate individuals like objects, but as he awaits execution in his call he loses himself in the 'oceanic feeling' of pure inwardness.[89]

For Merleau-Ponty the significance of the Moscow Trials lay elsewhere. They revealed the tragedy inherent in politics: the objective consequences of actions can be quite different from the intentions of their authors. The charges against Bukharin are false when judged against his *intentions*, but true when judged against the *consequences* of his acts. For this reason Bukharin's confession should not be understood as the collapse of the yogi before the commissar. It must instead be seen as Bukharin's attempt to show how actions, born of a certain reading of history, could display to an observer a pattern which was 'objectively' counter-revolutionary in spite of their subjective innocence.[90] Bukharin's plight thus lay bare the 'maleficence' of history:

> It solicits men, tempts them so that they believe they are moving in its direction [*sens*], and then suddenly it unmasks, and events change and prove that there was another possibility. The men whom history abandons in this way and who see themselves simply as accomplices suddenly find themselves the instigators of a crime to which history has inspired them. And *they are unable to look for excuses or to excuse themselves from even a part of the responsibility*. For at the very moment when they were following the apparent curve of history, others were deciding to back off and to commit their lives along another road to the future.[91]

There is no 'science of the future', it cannot be predicted with the certainty with which events in the natural world can be foretold.[92] The future is instead presented to us in a series of 'perspectives'; it is a 'horizon of possibilities' analogous to our perceptual horizon. Just as an object on our perceptual horizon may reveal itself, as we move closer to it, to be something quite different from what we originally took it to be, so too the future which we approach may turn out to be quite different from what we initially supposed.[93] Political actors such as Stalin, Trotsky, and Bukharin each have different perspectives within the ambiguous field of history and, on the basis of their different readings of the future, they each formulate different projects which seek to realise different ends.[94]

The drama of the Moscow Trials, then, lay in their attempt to confront 'the collaborator before he was wrong historically'.[95] Merleau-Ponty insists that Bukharin's testimony represents a confession that the future he was working towards was not a possible future. His opposition to forced collectivisation and rapid industrialisation could only have rendered the Soviet Union defenceless in the face of the threat posed by Nazi Germany:

> If he had been arrested a few years earlier or even judged a few months earlier Bukharin would probably have refused to surrender. But in the world situation as of 1938 the liquidation of the opposition can no longer be regarded as an accident. Bukharin and his colleagues were defeated; this means that they were up against a persistent police force and an implacable dictatorship. But their failure means something even more essential, namely, that what broke them was necessitated by that phase of history.[96]

The *sens* of history had eluded him, and in his confession he accepted the consequences.

As an analysis of Bukharin's testimony, *Humanism and Terror* is, quite simply, rather dreadful. While Merleau-Ponty, unlike Koestler, focuses on the peculiar character of Bukharin's 'confession' – Bukharin accepted complete and total 'political responsibility' for everything he and his co-defendants were charged with doing and then proceeded, point by point, to disprove and deny all the particular charges against him – to explain these peculiarities as resulting from a belated recognition on Bukharin's part that Stalin's policies had been historically vindicated by the need to oppose fascism, is to display a staggering ignorance of the real situation Bukharin faced. It was Bukharin, not Stalin, who made the earliest and in many ways most prescient appraisal of the threat posed by

Hitler. His opposition to forced collectivisation and rapid industrialisation rested at least in part on the argument that such tactics were likely to alienate the citizenry, thus making resistance to a German attack difficult to muster.[97] Further, there is precious little evidence to support Merleau-Ponty's assumption that the Soviet Union was in the end better able to withstand the German invasion because of Stalin's policies.[98] But the greatest failing in Merleau-Ponty's interpretation of the Moscow Trials lies with his willingness to take the charges against Bukharin and the 'Bloc of Rightists and Trotskyites' at face value. He seems utterly incapable of recognising the tactical importance of the trials in Stalin's drive to consolidate power, and appears blissfully unaware of the three main functions the charges served: they shifted the responsibility for Stalin's own crimes – for example, the assassinations of Kirov and Gorky – to others, they attributed the failures of collectivisation and industrialisation to the sabotage of others, and they provided a pretext for liquidating the first generation of Bolsheviks, a step which removed the Party as a possible check on Stalin's own future actions.[99]

But if these were the real functions of the charges, why did Bukharin confess? The blanket acceptance of 'political responsibility' appears to have been the price Bukharin had to pay to insure the survival of his second wife and three-year-old son – both of whom had been placed in detention within weeks of his own arrest. It was also the prerequisite for his being able to take the stand at all. But once on the stand, he proceeded to make a shambles of the charges against him through what his biographer has aptly described as 'a dazzling exhibition of double-talk, evasion, code words, veiled allusions, exercises in logic, and stubborn denunciation'.[100] To read this testament of the 'last Bolshevik', Merleau-Ponty would have had to school himself in a political hermeneutics which, at this point at least, was apparently beyond him.

Marx's wager: the 'sens' of history

Our concern here, however, is not with the often staggering naïveté of *Humanism and Terror* as a piece of political analysis but rather with the way it illustrates some characteristic features of Merleau-Ponty's initial attempt to move from perception to history. So we must disengage his dubious specific claims about Bukharin's testimony from his more general discussion of what it means to impute a *sens* to history. This uncoupling is made a bit easier by the fact that certain parts of his more general argument can also be found at the close of the *Phenomenology of Perception*.

There he argued that the conclusions reached in his discussion of the problem of others showed that my 'absolute individuality' is surrounded by 'a kind of halo of generality or a kind of atmosphere of "sociality" '. Our existence in the world thus bears a 'double anonymity'. My life has 'a *sens* which I do not constitute', both on the individual level – my body sustains certain projects which have not necessarily been consciously thematised – and the social level – I am born into a particular society, a particular class, and here too we find certain pre-reflective projects.[101]

> Provided that this is so, there can be situations, a *sens* of history, and a historical truth: three ways of saying the same thing. If I indeed made myself into a worker or a bourgeois by an absolute initiative, and if in general terms nothing solicits our freedom, history would display no structure, no event would be seen to take shape in it, and anything might emerge from anything else . . . History would never move in any direction, nor would it be possible to say that even over a short period of time events were conspiring to produce any definite outcome. The statesman would always be an adventurer, that is to say he would take advantage of events by conferring upon them a meaning which they *did not have*.[102]

History has a *sens*, then, in the same way as an individual life. Certain possibilities are offered. They are taken up and modified by a freedom which is neither bound to the terms of the situation it assumes nor completely free from the situations in which it is engaged. Nothing guarantees that a life or a history will have only *one sens* from beginning to end, but lives and histories are, nevertheless, 'condemned to meaning'.[103] It is impossible for them not to express something.

In *Humanism and Terror*, Merleau-Ponty argued that Marx's account of history rested on a similar vision of the nature of historical intelligibility.[104] Marx, like Hegel before him, rejected the view that history was only 'the simple encounter and discrete succession of absolutely autonomous individuals, without roots, without posterity, without any interaction'. In history we instead find 'situated beings' who are 'characterized by a certain type of relation to men and the world, by a certain activity, a certain way of treating other people and nature'.[105] There is, in other words, 'not a plurality of subjects but an intersubjectivity' and the actions of one group of individuals are bound to affect the lives of others in as much as all are participants in 'a single common situation'.[106]

To articulate a philosophy of history, Merleau-Ponty insisted, is to demonstrate that these various individual situations are indeed united in one common situation and that this common situation is 'moving toward some privileged state which gives the whole its meaning'.[107] Marxism rests on such a wager:

> In essence Marxism is the idea that history has a *sens* – in other words, that it is intelligible and has a direction – that it is moving toward the power of the proletariat, which as the essential factor of production is capable of resolving the contradictions of capitalism, of organizing a humane appropriation of nature, and, as the 'universal class', able to transcend national and social conflicts as well as the struggle between man and man. To be a Marxist . . . is to believe that history has a *Gestalt* . . . a holistic system moving toward a state of equilibrium, the classless society which cannot be achieved without individual effort and action, but which is outlined in the present crisis as its solution.[108]

In *Humanism and Terror*, Marxism is not simply *a* philosophy of history, 'it is *the* philosophy of history'. To renounce it is to 'dig the grave of reason in history'.[109] If the proletariat proves incapable of transcending the alternatives of lordship and bondage, if it cannot bring about mutual recognition betwen men, it would mean not merely that Marx's conjectures had been refuted. 'It would mean that there is no history – if history means the advent of humanity and humanity the mutual recognition of men as men.'[110]

The discussion of the *sens* of history in the *Phenomenology of Perception* has entered here into an uncomfortable *ménage à trois* with Kojève's Hegel and Lukács's Marx. The *Phenomenology of Perception* contributes the basic metaphors: historical meaning, like perceptual meaning, emerges as a figure against a background; it is brought to the foreground by gestures which elicit but do not constitute it; freedom is always situated freedom. Kojève's reading of Hegel defines the direction in which this history is moving: towards a state of mutual recognition in which the struggle of master and slave finally ends. And Lukács' reading of Marx identifies the major actor in the drama: it is the proletariat which, by becoming conscious of its own position in society, finally unveils the mystifications which have blinded men to the true meaning and direction of history. This vision of history is a most unstable mixture, destined to fall apart for both practical and theoretical reasons.

On the practical level, everything hinges on Marxism's not simply being an ideology of 'adventurers' who impose meaning willy-nilly on a passive and blank history. As a gesture which reveals rather than constitutes the *sens* of history, Marxism must rest on the 'extrapolation of a *praxis* already at work in history, of a reality that is already committed, namely, the proletariat'.[111] There must be something in the historical field to which Marxism can appeal, just as there must be something – however ambiguous – on the horizon of the perceptual field which I try to make my friend see as a church tower. And, sooner or later, I must get my friend to understand what it is I am pointing at, just as sooner or later, the future towards which Marxists are gesturing must become plausible to those they address.

But what if the future which Marxism tries to make palpable constantly slips from view? What if it is evident only to the party, and not to the masses, that history is moving, in spite of reversals, detours, and diversions, towards a classless society? In 1945, Merleau-Ponty held out the possibility that history might 'consist of a series of diversions' from the path Marx had projected, diversions which might last 'for as long as we live and perhaps even for centuries'.[112] In such a situation, 'Marxism could . . . only be stated in terms of negative propositions'. We would know that crises will not cease unless the means of production have been socialised, but we would know 'neither that a universal socialist production would achieve equilibrium nor that the course of events . . . is heading toward that outcome'.[113] What such a series of detours might mean on a practical level was driven home in *Humanism and Terror*:

> The contact broken between the spontaneous life of the masses and the exigencies of a proletarian victory planned by the leaders should be re-established after some foreseeable interruption and within a man's lifetime. Otherwise the proletarian will not see for

what he is sacrificing himself and we shall have returned to the
Hegelian philosophy of the State: a few functionaries of History
who possess knowledge for all and carry out the will of the World
Spirit with the blood of others. Local history must have a patent
connection with universal history without which the proletariat
lapses into the provincialism it should have transcended.[114]

By 1952 he was convinced that history had indeed strayed from the
Marxist path, and that to hold Marxism in suspension as a set of
negative truths while waiting for history to cohere once again into a
Marxian *Gestalt* was, in effect, to have already abandoned Marxism.
A philosophy of history which kept waiting for history to come back
to its true *sens* was not Marxism; it was a poorly disguised Kantian
rationalism.[115]

In addition to these troubling practical questions, Merleau-
Ponty's synthesis of Hegel, Marx, and an existentialised Husserl was
threatened on the theoretical level. Here everything hinges on
Merleau-Ponty's ability to show meaningful parallels between
perceptual meaning and historical meaning. While he was fairly
successful in drawing analogies between the way the perceptual
field is structured and the way the future is presented to historical
actors, it is less clear whether an analogy can be sustained between
the subject for whom the perceptual world is meaningful and the
subject who brings a *sens* to the historical world.

The subject of perception is an incarnate consciousness which
confronts a world it has not created and grasps this world in a series
of always partial syntheses. The subject of history as described in
the *Phenomenology of Perception* likewise has only a limited grasp;
history has some *sens*, but there is no claim that there is a single
history moving in one direction.[116] Yet Merleau-Ponty advances
precisely this claim in *Humanism and Terror* when he elevates
Marxism to the status of *the* philosophy of history. Such a claim
would be congruent with the vision of history one finds in either
Kojève or Lukács – for Kojève the entirety of history is the
labouring slave's effort to achieve recognition, for Lukács it is the
history of the coming to consciousness of the proletariat as the
'identical subject–object' of world history.[117] But such a conception
of history demands a subject with a far more comprehensive grasp
than the subject described in the *Phenomenology of Perception*. All
the theoretical obscurities of *Humanism and Terror* arise from the

fact that Merleau-Ponty has simply coupled the universal history he found in Kojève and Lukács to the perspectival account of historical meaning he outlined in the *Phenomenology of Perception.*[118] The passage from perception to history thus takes the form of a leap.

Enter Saussure

By 1952 these practical and theoretical problems had placed in question the conception of history elaborated in *Humanism and Terror.* In the discussion of history in his inaugural lecture at the Collège de France, Merleau-Ponty tried to come to grips with why Marxism had been led astray – and called on Saussure for help.

He was more careful than in his earlier works to distinguish Marx's vision of history from Hegel's. Marx refused to locate historical reason on any level other than 'the life of men'. History, for him, was 'the situation in which all meanings are developed' and 'praxis' was that peculiar sort of meaning which 'works itself out spontaneously in the intercrossings of those activities by which man organizes his relations with nature and other men'.[119] Marx did not see history as 'directed at the beginning by an idea of universal or total history' nor is it driven by a 'dialectic of matter'.[120] The *sens* of history is, rather, 'immanent in the interhuman event'.[121]

The very novelty of Marx's approach sealed its fate. 'Nothing in sociology or positive history was preparing the way for the intellectual reform which he called for' and neither he nor his followers fully understood what this notion of history implied.

Where, in fact, was this immanent meaning of inter-human events to be placed? It is not, or certainly it is not always, in men, that is, in their minds, but outside them. Once he had stopped placing any absolute knowledge in things, it seemed that there were only blind events. Where then was the historical process, and what mode of existence must be recognized in such historical forms as feudalism, capitalism, proletariat, which are spoken of as though they were persons, knowing and willing, hidden behind the multiplicity of events, without seeing clearly what these masks represent? After rejecting the expedient of the Hegelian Objective Spirit, how could the dilemma of existence as thing versus existence as consciousness be avoided?[122]

Seeking to place itself beyond idealism and materialism, Marxism wound up vacillating between the two, unable to decide between an account of history which places all hope with the voluntary action of a class which abolishes all classes, and an account which sees everywhere only the blind movement of anonymous forces.

It was here that Merleau-Ponty thought the 'theory of signs' could make a contribution. The relation between the subject's 'will to express' and the 'means of expression' provided by language could serve as a paradigm for understanding the relationship between 'productive forces and forms of production and, more generally, between historical forces and institutions':

> Just as language is a system of signs which have meaning only in relation to one another, and each of which has its own usage throughout the whole language, so each institution is a symbolic system that the subject takes over and incorporates as a style of functioning, as a global configuration, without having any need to conceive it at all. When equilibrium is destroyed, the reorganizations which take place comprise, like those of language, an internal logic even though it may not be clearly thought out by anyone.[123]

Language thus presents us with a system, governed by a logic which may not be fully understood by any of those who employ it, which is set in motion by the will of these same speakers to make themselves understood. In the same way, history can be viewed as a symbolic structure, governed by rules and beset by transformations which none of its agents fully comprehends, which is driven by the will of these agents 'to coexist and to recognize one another'.[124]

> It is in this way . . . that the forms and processes of history, the classes, the epochs, exist . . . they are in a social, cultural, or symbolic space which is no less real than physical space and is, moreover, supported by it. For meaning lies latent not only in language, in political and religious institutions, but in modes of kinship, in machines, in the landscape, in production, and, in general, in all the modes of human commerce.[125]

Here, then, was the answer to the question of where the 'immanent meaning of inter-human events' was to be placed. History, like language, was a system of signs. Marx's historical materialism will find its proper form as a Saussurian semiology of history.

Saussure, the sign, and the problem of history

In his inaugural lecture Merleau-Ponty suggested that Saussure's work 'perhaps implies a concept of historical meaning which gets beyond the opposition of things versus consciousness'.[126] The crucial word is 'perhaps'. Whether such a concept could in fact be got out of Saussure's work was, for Merleau-Ponty, a question whose final resolution depended on what could be achieved in *The Prose of the World*, a book which at the time of the inaugural lecture was unfinished, but not yet abandoned.

The written and unwritten 'Prose of the World'

As originally outlined, *The Prose of the World* was to fall into three parts. The book would begin, like Sartre's *What is Literature?*, with an analysis of the nature of prose and a discussion of the linguistic sign. The second part would focus on a few specific authors and show how they transformed conventions of discourse so as to produce new modes of expression. The concluding part, as Merleau-Ponty wrote in his prospectus, would 'elaborate the category of prose beyond the confines of literature to give it a sociological meaning'.[127] He hoped, in this final section, to extend the analysis developed in the discussion of literary uses of language to the domain of politics and religion.[128] Only the first of the projected three parts was actually begun and even it remained unfinished.

The posthumously published manuscript of *The Prose of the World* consists of a somewhat motley assortment of chapters. The short opening discussion is devoted to dispelling the 'spectre of a pure language' – a conception, close to Sartre's in *What is Literature?*, which sees language as a set of signs which function like 'an all purpose tool', referring us to particular meanings and, beyond these meanings, to particular objects in the world.[129] In the second chapter, Merleau-Ponty turned to Saussure and, drawing on his discussion of the 'diacritical' character of linguistic values, argued that signs are never meaningful in and of themselves but instead take on meaning only through their opposition to other signs.[130] As a way of exploring how meaning arises 'between' words, Merleau-Ponty proposed that we perform a 'reduction' upon language and turn away from what it signifies in order to explore how it goes about expressing meaning.[131] Thus begins an extended discussion of the parallels between literary expression and painting; the contrast to Sartre's brusque conclusion that no meaningful analogies could be constructed here is presumably intentional.[132] This complex and extraordinarily suggestive discussion – most of which was eventually published in a revised form as 'Indirect Language and the Voices of Silence'[133] – is followed by three chapters which are a good deal shorter and considerably less provocative. The first of these three chapters attempts to show that even the most formal mode of expression, the algorithm, still presupposes a primordial 'carnal' contact with the world.[134] The next focuses on the way speech allows us to move beyond our immediate perceptual experience of other people and create a community with the other through dialogue.[135] The last begins to draw parallels between the way a child's babbling is superseded by true phonemic oppositions and the way a child's scribbles give way to actual drawings, but comes to an abrupt end after only eight pages.[136]

The Prose of the World was thus broken off before it could fulfil the promise Merleau-Ponty had seen in Saussure's linguistics. In a brief aside in the chapter on children's drawings, Merleau-Ponty promised that the *next* chapter would deal with 'the nature of the relationship between the expressive operation and the thinker whom it presupposes and forms as well as the history which it continues and recreates'.[137] While he never wrote this chapter, he did give a course entitled 'Materials for a Theory of History' (1953–4) which examined the work of Max Weber – in particular *The Protestant Ethic and the Spirit of Capitalism* – and Georg Lukács – in particular *History and Class Consciousness*.[138] These inquiries may well have been undertaken with an eye towards the ultimate concern of *The Prose of the World*: the problem of meaning in history. They were, however, destined for a different use and became the first two chapters of his 1955 critique of Marxism, *Adventures of the Dialectic*.

Merleau-Ponty's attempt to resolve the problems he found in Marx by turning to Saussure thus leaves us with two works whose

relationship is quite puzzling. *The Prose of the World* was intended
to lay the basis of a new understanding of Marx's attempt to place
meaning in history; but it provides only a discussion of linguistic
expression and – apart from a few comments in the chapter on
'indirect language' – never explicitly comes to grips with the
problem of history. *Adventures of the Dialectic* does – but the
relevance of Saussure's work for its discussions of Weber, Lukács,
Trotsky, and Sartre remains obscure. It is little wonder, then, that
students of Merleau-Ponty's social thought have, for the most part,
confined their attention to the later book, leaving *The Prose of the
World* to those of their colleagues concerned with aesthetics and
literature.[139] But that option is not open to us. We have seen that
The Prose of the World was at least in part intended to resolve the
tensions which beset Merleau-Ponty's attempt, in *Humanism and
Terror*, to develop a philosophy of history on the basis of the
philosophy of expression sketched in the *Phenomenology of
Perception*. It is thus of the greatest importance to understand why
The Prose of the World was unable to reach its goal and to see what,
if anything, this might have to do with the critique of Marxism he
undertook in *Adventures of the Dialectic*. And to do this, we must
proceed as we did with his first attempt to move from expression to
history and see how he now conceived of the linguistic sign.

The diacritical gesture: the theory of expression in 'The Prose of the World'

We have seen that the relation of signifier to signified in the
discussion of expression in the *Phenomenology of Perception* could
best be described, in the terms provided by Barthes's typology, as
'symbolic'. The reduction performed on language terminated in a
conception of the sign as representative of a primordial, emotional
response to the world. In this alleged 'originary speech', the relation
between signifier and signified was held to be 'not entirely
arbitrary'.

Something of this hope for an approach to language which would
look beyond the conventions of institutionalised language and
make contact with an 'originary' gesture continued to haunt *The
Prose of the World*. Phonology, as Merleau-Ponty understood it,
was a way of looking at language which 'considers modulations

introduced by speech . . . as expressive in themselves'.¹⁴⁰ But this originary act of expression is no longer conceived as a one-to-one coupling of signifiers to signifieds. We are not led back to 'a golden age of language in which words . . . adhered to the objects themselves'.¹⁴¹ Phonology reveals, not a domain of unequivocal gestures, but rather a 'sublinguistic life whose whole effort is to differentiate signs and systematize them'.¹⁴² We no longer find a primordial language which 'sings' the world; we instead encounter a language which, oblivious to the world, would appear to be simply humming to itself. At first glance it would seem that 'language never has anything to do with anything but itself'; it 'never says anything'.¹⁴³ It is instead 'a series of gestures' which point to nothing in particular but are rather concerned with differentiating them-selves from one another in a way that 'presents differences clear enough for the conduct of language'.¹⁴⁴ If the conception of the sign in the *Phenomenology of Perception* appeared to be 'symbolic', in *The Prose of the World* we find an approach which would seem to be avowedly 'paradigmatic'.

Merleau-Ponty endorses a study of this 'primordial level of language' which adheres to the programme laid out by Saussure. Signs are not to be seen as 'representations of certain significations', they are, rather, 'the means of differentiation in the verbal chain'. A language is to be understood less as 'a sum of signs' than as 'a methodological means of differentiating signs from one another'. To speak a language is not to deploy a finite number of signs; it is, rather, to employ 'a principle of distinction'.¹⁴⁵ In his summary of the opening chapters of *The Prose of the World* at the start of 'Indirect Language and the Voices of Silence', Merleau-Ponty made his debts to Saussure quite clear:

> What we have learned from Saussure is that, taken singly, signs do not signify anything, and that each one of them does not so much express a meaning as mark a divergence [*écart*] of meaning between itself and other signs. Since the same may be said for all other signs, we may conclude that language is made of differences without terms; or more exactly, that the terms of language are engendered only by the differences which appear among them.¹⁴⁶

Because the sign is 'diacritical from the outset', meaning will arise 'at the edge of signs' as a product of a charade in which all the gestures, taken individually, are 'equivocal or banal'.[147] The ability of language to 'signify a thought or a thing directly' is thus but a 'secondary power' of language; it masks the more primitive operation of self-differentiation which lies at the heart of all speech.[148]

To say that direct signification is a 'secondary power' of language is, however, not to deny that language does indeed signify. While Merleau-Ponty embraced Saussure's account of the diacritical nature of linguistic values, his earlier concern with questions of reference – or, as he put it, 'the transcendence of signification' – is not abandoned. 'In the end language must signify something and not always be language about language', he stressed in a marginal note to *The Prose of the World* directed against Joseph Vendryès (whose *Le Langage* was a useful reference for Merleau-Ponty) and 'perhaps Saussure'.[149] *The Prose of the World* has not broken with the notion – so central to the argument of the *Phenomenology of Perception* – that language points towards the world. But what *has* been put in question is an account of the linguistic gesture which, like that in the *Phenomenology of Perception*, sees *individual* signs as gesturing towards discrete concepts or objects. Thus, while Merleau-Ponty's conception of the *nature* of the linguistic sign changed markedly between the *Phenomenology of Perception* and *The Prose of the World*, with a 'paradigmatic consciousness' increasingly displacing a 'symbolic consciousness', his conception of the *function* of the sign remain unchanged. Signs transcend the closed system of language and make reference to the world. But this reference is indirect, the product of the diacritical play of signs which, on first glance, seem only to be pointing at each other.

Let us make sure his argument is understood, for it is a rather unique one. Language makes reference to the world not *in spite* of the fact that 'originary' language seems only to refer to itself but *because* of this fact. Self-reference makes reference to the world possible:

It is words that words arouse and, to the degree that we 'think' more fully, words so precisely fill our minds that they leave no empty corner for pure thought or for significations that are not the work of language. The mystery is that, in the very moment where language is thus obsessed with itself, it is enabled, through a kind of excess, to open us to a signification . . . In an instant this flow of words annuls itself as noise, throwing us completely into what it means.[150]

In a marginal note inserted at this point in the manuscript, he reiterated the argument by making an analogy to perception:

> Just as the analysis of perception makes clear the transcendence of the thing in relation to the contents and *Abschattungen* [adumbrations; perspectival shadings]. The thing emerges over there, while I think I am grasping it in a given variation of the *hyle* where it is only in adumbration. Similarly, thought arises over there, while I am looking for it in a particular inflection of the verbal chain.[151]

For this reason – *pace* Sartre – meaningful analogies *can* be drawn between painters and writers. Both deploy the oppositions made possible by the systems in which they work – figures and grounds, colours and canvas, words and silence – in a way that allows a meaning to emerge which transcends the dots of paint on the canvas or the flecks of ink on the page.[152] Both must express 'indirectly'; for both, meaning arises in the intervals between signs. What distinguishes writing from painting is the fact that it is easier to forget all this in the act of speaking and, like Sartre, simply assume that speech takes us directly and unambiguously to the things we speak about.[153] Every time we speak, we of necessity forget everything Saussure has taught us about the nature of linguistic value.[154]

Here, as perhaps nowhere else, Merleau-Ponty has articulated a position which defies neat classification. Where Sartre reduced the sign to a simple and unequivocal reference to things, Merleau-Ponty drew on Saussure's account of the diacritical nature of linguistic value and insisted that words refer to things only by referring to other words. Where subsequent disciples of Saussure would abandon all concern with reference and see language instead as a closed system, having to do with nothing save itself, Merleau-Ponty continued to concern himself with the way in which this incessant self-differentiation nevertheless opens onto the world.[155] Little wonder that his reading of Saussure was so idiosyncratic. The questions he tried to make Saussure answer were questions Saussure had never asked. Saussure sought the proper 'object' on which a science of language could be grounded. He found it by turning from the individual act of speech to consider instead the social conventions of language.[156] Merleau-Ponty read Saussure to find a way of analysing the interaction between the will to express and the means of expression provided by language. He found it by confounding Saussure's neatly drawn distinctions and envisioning a 'synchronic linguistics of *parole*'.

Structure, event, advent: the sense of history in 'The Prose of the World'

The import of this 'synchronic linguistics of *parole*' for the philosophy of history can best be understood if we examine the dichotomies which Merleau-Ponty hoped it would resolve. His Sorbonne course, 'Consciousness and the Acquisition of Language', closed with the suggestion that, 'if generalized', Saussure's approach to language might provide a way beyond the impasse of treating history either as 'the sum of independent *chance* events' or as 'providential', as a 'manifestation of an internal structure'.[157] *The Prose of the World* stressed the need to leave behind those 'empty discussions' which posit history as an 'external power' and thus force on us the dilemma of choosing 'between this power and ourselves'.[158] In *Adventures of the Dialectic* he examined Max Weber's writings to see how one could avoid the unhappy choice between a history which 'judges, situates, and organizes' facts in light of the 'troubles and problems of the present' and an 'agnostic history which lines up civilizations one after the other like unique individuals who cannot be compared'.[159] And the preface to this same work spoke of the need to overcome Alain's dichotomy between a 'politics of reason' which 'totalizes history' and sees all particular problems as destined to be resolved in a future which will constitute 'a new beginning' and a 'politics of understanding' which 'does not flatter itself with having embraced all of history' and instead 'resolves problems one at a time'.[160] The task Merleau-Ponty assigned to his Saussure-inspired approach to history was thus that of mediating between event and structure, individual and history, present and past – in short, between concrete individual existence and universal historical meaning. Since this was the very task Hegel had set for himself, 'the Hegelian dialectic is what we call by another name the phenomenon of expression'.[161] But why did

Merleau-Ponty think that Saussure could be successful where Hegel had failed?

Saussure's distinction between *parole* and *langue* would seem to be only another *example* of the dichotomy Merleau-Ponty was seeking to avoid, and not a particularly promising way of getting around it. Saussure understood *parole* as an order of unique and incomparable *events* and conceived of *langue* as the atemporal *structure* never totally manifested in any one of these events.[162] To transpose such a view of language onto the plane of history would appear only to replicate the dichotomy as the distinction – quite out of keeping with Hegel but crucial, for example, in the work of a historian like Fernand Braudel – between history conceived as a sequence of events (Braudel's *histoire évenementielle*) and history viewed as a structure or group of structures (Braudel's *longue durée*).[163] But just as Merleau-Ponty undercut the dichotomy of *langue* and *parole* by mixing elements from both sides of the opposition to frame a new distinction between a 'synchronic linguistics of *parole*' and a 'diachronic linguistics of *langue*', so too he shifted the ground under the dichotomy between event and structure with a flanking manoeuvre which opened a new opposition between history as *event* and history as *advent*.[164]

The term 'advent' was taken from Paul Ricoeur, who used it to denote the emergence of a *sens* in history which transcends its time and continues to be effective in the present – for example, the 'advent' of the notion of the *cogito*. The advent of such a *sens* is typically the concern of philosophical readings of history; empirical historians tend to eschew such discussions in favour of a chronicling of events.[165] Merleau-Ponty needed to look no further than Edmund Husserl for an example of a philosopher who scanned history in search of such an advent of meaning. Ricoeur himself cited Husserl as one example of the genre and, as has already been noted, Husserl's essay 'The Origin of Geometry' played a central role in Merleau-Ponty's own reflections on the relation between expression and history.

Husserl had sought to work backwards from current 'handed-down forms' of geometry to the 'original beginnings of geometry as they necessarily must have been in their "primally establishing" [*Urstiftende*] function'.[166] Such an inquiry – which Husserl stressed must not be taken as a response to a 'philological–historical question' – proceeds on the level of generalities, not on the level of

actual empirical facts, and inquires into the meaning and implications of the 'primal establishment' of geometry, not into its actual
historical origins. It was, in Ricoeur's terms, a study of the advent of
geometrical meaning which concerned itself with the conceptual
transformations wrought by the beginnings of geometrical thought;
it was not a study of the historical events which led to the creation of
geometry. Its central task was to understand how geometrical
objects, which have no 'objective meaning' and accordingly must
first have been intra-psychically created, could have become 'ideal
objects' which possess an intersubjective meaning; it was not
concerned with determining where, or when, or with whom
geometry first began.[167]

In analysing the problem, Husserl made use of a concept which,
as we have already seen, is central to Merleau-Ponty's understanding of phenomenology: *Stiftung*. In his discussion of the relationship
between painters, past works, and the world, Merleau-Ponty
paused to reflect on the richness of the notion:

> Husserl had used the fine word *Stiftung* – foundation or establish-
> ment – to designate first of all the unlimited fecundity of each
> present which, precisely because it is singular and passes, can
> never stop having been and thus being universally; but above all
> to designate that fecundity of the products of a culture which
> continue to have value after their appearance and which open a
> field of investigations in which they perpetually come to life
> again.[168]

A history which sought to discover such acts of institution must
address the 'rise of styles, their mutations, their surprising transformations, and also simultaneously their solidarity in a single
history of painting'.[169] Such a history of the way in which a painter
'revives, reactivates, and renews the entire understanding of
painting in each new work' is the forgotten foundation on which a
history of events spins out its tale of 'dismemberment, ignorance,
externality'.[170] To turn from event to advent was thus to turn from a
domain where history manifested only chaos to a domain where a
sens could be found.

Saussure's approach to linguistics could provide guidance for
such a history of advents because the 'synchronic linguistics of
parole' which Merleau-Ponty thought he had discovered repre-

sented an approach to language whose task perfectly paralleled that
of the historian of advents:

> Alongside the linguistics of *langue*, which gives the impression, in
> the extreme, that language is a series of chaotic events, Saussure
> has inaugurated a linguistics of *parole*, which would reveal in it at
> each moment an order, a system, a totality without which
> communication and the linguistic community would be impos-
> sible.[171]

The diachronic study of *langue*, as Merleau-Ponty portrays it,
presents us with a series of transformations, displacements, and
rearrangements in the system of language which make sense only in
so far as we can frame causal accounts of the fortuitous events which
produced these results. The synchronic study of *parole*, in contrast,
forces us to look not at specific events but rather at a continuing
advent. The synchronic viewpoint, he stressed, is not 'instantaneous'; there is, rather, a constant overlapping of each temporal phase
upon the next.[172] Ignorant of the chance events which create in a
given language a set of structural constraints, the speaker animates
these structures with each act of speaking, just as each painter
renews and reactivates the entire project of painting in each of his
works.

A 'true history of painting' must thus treat each painter as
'something like an institution'. It must look 'beyond the immediate
aspects of the canvases' attributed to a painter and search instead
for 'a structure, a style, and a meaning against which the discordant
details (if there are any) that fatigue, circumstance, or self-imitation
has torn from his brush cannot prevail'.[173] In moving from the 'order
of events' to the 'order of expression', the historian of painting puts
aside attempts to explain individual works by particular circumstances and sees the work not as an 'effect' but rather as 'a response'
to the circumstances which it transforms into a signifying system.[174]
The task of political or social historians is no different. They too
must look beyond such labels as 'Parliament under the *ancien
régime*' or 'the French revolution' to see 'what they really signify in
the dynamics of human relations and what modulation of these
relations they represent'.[175]

The Prose of the World provides, however, only the vaguest of
suggestions as to how the emergence of meaning which Marx

claimed to find in history could be reformulated along the lines suggested by Saussure. The little discussion that one can find of the character of a 'history of advents' is devoted to problems in the history of painting, not to problems in the writing of political or social history. Indeed, even with respect to the history of painting we have less an illustration of how one might proceed than an assertion that all the historian needs to do is follow Saussure. The historian seeking guidance as to how the shortcomings of Marx's philosophy of history are to be remedied is thus presented with an analogue twice removed. A social history of advents will resemble a history of the advent of styles and schools in painting which, in turn, resembles Saussure's 'synchronic linguistics of *parole*' which – as we have seen – resembles nothing in the *Course in General Linguistics*. Our attempt to understand what Merleau-Ponty thought Saussure could do to remedy the lacunae of Marx's philosophy of history has led us, it would seem, to a dead end. But we need only turn to the first chapter of *Adventures of the Dialectic* to find what has been sought in vain in *The Prose of the World*. There, in the guise of an interpretation of Max Weber's *Protestant Ethic and the Spirit of Capitalism* we meet as clear an illustration of what Merleau-Ponty felt Saussure implied for the social sciences as one could ever hope to see.

Max Weber and the 'histoire avènementielle' of capitalism

The first chapter of *Adventures of the Dialectic* drew tacitly on the categories developed in *The Prose of the World* to provide a methodological foundation for Weber's study of the relation between Protestantism and the rise of capitalism. Weber, Merleau-Ponty argued, sought to grasp the 'intelligible nuclei' of history, those 'symbolic matrices' which 'for a shorter or longer time' structure the way in which men respond to nature, each other, and death. The rise and fall of these matrices is not to be explained through an appeal to 'external forces'; rather it must be understood by showing how these matrices either disintegrate internally or are reorganised when a previously secondary element comes to predominate.[176] 'Rationalization', the guiding theme in Weber's social theory, may thus be understood as a matrix composed of elements which can be found scattered throughout history, but which take on a unique value only when fused with other elements in a coherent structure:[177]

> In law, science, technology, and Western religion we see prime examples of this 'rationalizing' tendency. But only after the fact. Each of these elements acquires its historical meaning only through its encounter with others. History has often produced one of them in isolation (Roman law; the fundamental principles of calculus in India), without its being developed to the degree that it would have to be in capitalism. The encounter of these elements confirms in each one of them the outline of rationality which it bore.[178]

To speak of the 'advent' of 'rationalization' is thus to reconstruct the process by which a number of discrete elements arose to form a synchronic system which, once created, continues to structure the interactions between its component parts until such time as it degenerates or is replaced by a new structure.

Understood in this way, Weber's approach to history is fully commensurate with the argument of *The Prose of the World*. We need only note how Merleau-Ponty appealed in his discussion of Weber to two of the leading motifs of his earlier study:

> The meaning of a system in its beginning is like the pictorial meaning of a painting, which not so much directs the painter's movements but is the result of them and progresses with them. Or again, it can be compared to the meaning of a spoken language which is not transmitted in conceptual terms in the minds of those who speak, or in some ideal model of language, but which is rather the focal point of a series of verbal operations which converge almost by chance. Historical discourse comes to talk of 'rationalization' or 'capitalism' when the affinity of these productions of the historical imagination becomes clear. But history does not work according to a model; it is, in fact, the advent of meaning.[179]

Weber's account of capitalism thus traces how a synchronic system emerges, how a mode of signification which is composed of a number of initially discrete components comes to find an equilibrium which, for a greater or lesser period of time, is capable of maintaining a coherence in all its members.

All of this was offered by Merleau-Ponty as a reading of Weber which, while forced to 'interpret freely', nevertheless claimed to refrain from 'imputing to Weber more than he would have wished to say'.[180] Much of it flies in the face of interpretations which see Weber as requiring that social actions be understood in terms of the 'subjective meaning' which they have for their authors. Merleau-Ponty, in contrast, insists, 'It is not a question of coinciding with what has been lived but rather of deciphering the total meaning of what has been done.' The interpreter of a social action must restore 'not only the perspective of the agent but also the "objective" content'.[181]

But if Merleau-Ponty's reading is characteristically free, it is also remarkably attuned to Weber's actual achievement. It captures what is actually accomplished in *The Protestant Ethic* far more faithfully than those readings which remain content to summarise his methodological rules as outlined at the start of *Economy and Society*.[182] Weber's use of a text by Benjamin Franklin in which time is likened to money is not part of an effort to understand *Franklin's* intentions. Franklin's text provides Weber instead with an anticipation of a set of relations between temporality and economic activity which bridge the transformation from a Protestant to a capitalist ethos. In interpreting Franklin, Weber has discovered an 'objective meaning'; he has restored an 'anonymous intention, the dialectic of a whole'.[183] This, then, is how Weber's 'ideal type' must be understood:

> They give only, as Weber says, a provisional illustration of the point of view chosen, and the historian chooses this point of view in the same way that one remembers a word of an author, or someone's gesture: in one's first encounter with it, one becomes aware of a certain style.[184]

The ideal type is thus a first and one-sided attempt at grasping a symbolic matrix which will gradually be filled in more completely as subsequent perspectives are unfolded and explored.

This does not mean that the experience of agents is to be totally ignored. We have already seen how Merleau-Ponty stressed, in his discussion of Lévi-Strauss's work, that the theorist's structures must – at some point or another – have a 'lived equivalent'.[185] Likewise, the advent of a new meaning in history must not be totally unnoticed by those who live through its arrival. Merleau-Ponty notes that Weber found in Wesley's writings a realisation that religion, by producing 'both industry and frugality', could not help but also foster those riches whose increase always brings with it the decline of religion. Indeed, Wesley himself had concluded that 'although the form of religion remains, the spirit is swiftly vanishing away'.[186] The historian, like the linguist, grasps a symbolic system which both structures the actions of agents and, in turn, is structured by their actions. It is a system whose full complexity necessarily escapes those who make use of it. But its meaning could not have completely eluded them.

While this reading of Weber enables us to see what Merleau-Ponty seems to have thought an extension of Saussure's approach to the domain of history might have involved, it tells us nothing about how a Saussure-inspired philosophy of history could go about resolving the problems facing the account of history sketched in *Humanism and Terror*. Indeed, the vision of history which emerges from Merleau-Ponty's reconstruction of Weber is at loggerheads with the account of his earlier book. The double implication of *sens* – direction and meaning – which was so crucial in both the *Phenomenology of Perception* and *Humanism and Terror* is explicitly revoked in Merleau-Ponty's discussion of Weber. History for Weber 'does not have a direction [*sens*] like a river' but it does have 'a meaning [*sens*]' which, even though incapable of teaching us what truth is, can nevertheless show us what 'errors to avoid'.[187] The *sens* of history is not to be found in 'a pure development of the idea'; rather it must be sought 'in contact with contingency, at the moment when human initiative founds a system of life by taking up anew scattered givens'.[188] History is not the voice of reason. It is, rather, 'a distracted interlocutor, it allows the debate to become sidetracked; it forgets the data of the problem along the way'.[189] It eliminates valid achievements as well as false solutions and thus purges itself of both *sens* and *non-sens*.[190]

It is thus a most sceptical philosophy of history which Merleau-Ponty finds with his Saussurian reading of Weber. It is clearly a good deal less than he would have needed to redeem the analyses sketched in *Humanism and Terror* or to overcome the shortcomings of Marx's conception of history noted in his inaugural lecture. But then we must remember that the discussion of Weber stands not at the close of *The Prose of the World*, as the culmination of an analysis of expression, but rather at the start of *Adventures of the Dialectic*, as the point of departure for an examination of Marxism which concluded with a critique of the argument of *Humanism and Terror*. Having tried to fathom where *The Prose of the World* was supposed to have led Merleau-Ponty, we must now see where, in fact, his study of expression and history took him.

Beyond Marx and Husserl: a new ontology

The Prose of the World stopped short of its goal: an account of the subject which expression 'presupposes and shapes' and of the history which expression 'continues and re-creates'.[191] It was thus unable to serve as a bridge between the analysis of the perceptual world in the *Phenomenology of Perception* and the philosophy of history whose contours had been sketched in *Humanism and Terror*. In the face of the failure of *The Prose of the World*, the simplest course of action Merleau-Ponty could have taken would have been to reformulate a philosophy of expression along lines other than those suggested by Saussure. If, for whatever reasons, a paradigmatic conception of expression was problematic, the project could always be rethought along the lines suggested by his earlier 'symbolic' conception of the sign. But this is precisely what Merleau-Ponty did not do. The lesson he took from *The Prose of the World* was not that Saussure's conception was somehow deficient. Rather, he came to feel that there were severe problems with the two positions he was attempting to tie together with it. After 1953, he turned, not to a reformulation of his philosophy of expression, but rather to a critique of his earlier writings on perception and history. In *Adventures of the Dialectic* he re-examined Marx's philosophy of history and came to the conclusion that it was no longer possible to adopt the 'wait and see' attitude towards communism which he had articulated in *Humanism and Terror*. In *The Visible and the Invisible* he took up again the analysis of the perceptual world and questioned whether his existentialised Husserl had done justice to it.

Marxism and the inertia of history

The very first sentence of *Adventures of the Dialectic* betrays the
lacuna that *The Prose of the World* had failed to fill: 'We need a
philosophy of both history and spirit to deal with the problems we
touch upon here.'[192] *Adventures of the Dialectic* was an attempt at
'speaking philosophically of politics' without the guidance a fully
achieved account of expression and history would have provided.
He candidly described it as a set of 'samplings, probings, philosophical anecdotes, the beginnings of analyses'.[193]

It is, all said, not the most elegantly crafted of books. The last half
of it is taken up by a sprawling critique of Sartre, while the first half
consists of a trio of closely related chapters on Weber, Lukács, and
Soviet Marxism and a somewhat more tangential chapter on
Trotsky. But if the book is ungainly in form, it is impressive in its
content. It consists of nothing less than the careful construction and
ruthless dismantling of one of the strongest possible cases that can
be made for the Marxian philosophy of history.

He was aided in the process of construction by Georg Lukács's
classic 1923 book *History and Class Consciousness*. It is to Lukács –
who, in addition to being one of the most important Marxian
theorists of the twentieth century, was once a student of Max Weber
– that Merleau-Ponty turned in search of a way beyond Weber's
sceptical philosophy of history. By pursuing 'the relativization of
relativism to its limits', Lukács attempted to regain 'a sort of
totality' and thus hoped to restore to history that *telos* which Weber
had evicted.[194] Merleau-Ponty's juxtaposition of Weber and Lukács
is an impressive achievement on two levels. First, considered simply
as an account of Lukács' book, *Adventures of the Dialectic*
articulated the concerns that lay at the heart of *History and Class
Consciousness* with a seriousness, a passion, and a clarity which has
rarely been matched by subsequent interpreters.[195] Second, the
juxtaposition of Weber and Lukács made manifest, in the most
compelling possible way, the tension between the philosophy of
history which had inspired Merleau-Ponty's works prior to *The
Prose of the World* and the view of history which *The Prose of the
World* seemed to imply. Merleau-Ponty had read *History and Class
Consciousness* as early as 1946 and much in his discussion of
Marxism during the late 1940s was indebted to Lukács' work.[196]
Hence, if Weber speaks for the implications of *The Prose of the*

World, it is Lukács who expresses the position that Merleau-Ponty now found himself forced to abandon – but not without giving it a few last words.

Lukács, he argued, found 'the road to follow' through his study of Weber.[197] For Weber, ideal types were partial, one-sided representations of historical reality which of necessity are relative to our own time. Lukács, however, argued that their very relativity bound them to the history they sought to capture; the advent of 'scientific history' is itself a part of the process of rationalisation which it claims to describe.[198] Since our concepts inhere in the history they describe, history should not be thought of as an object separate from us; 'it is also our awakening as subjects'.[199]

We give a form to history according to our categories; but our categories, in contact with history, are themselves freed from partiality. The old problem of the relations between subject and object is transformed, and relativism is surpassed as soon as one puts it in historical terms, since here the object is the vestige left by other subjects, and the subject – historical understanding – held in the fabric of history, is by this very fact capable of self-criticism.[200]

Weber had not been able to recognise these implications of his work because he remained committed to 'the idea of a truth without condition and without point of view'.[201] Lukács, however, went further, and relativised Weber's relativism by conceiving of history as 'that movement in which knowledge looks back on its origins, recaptures its own genesis, equals as knowledge what it was as event, gathers itself together, and tends towards self-consciousness'.[202]

Writing a history of the development of capitalism would thus involve a providing of an account of the '*Vergesellschaftung der Gesellschaft*' – 'the becoming social of society':[203]

To say that there is a 'becoming social of society' is to say that men begin to exist for one another, that the social whole retraces its dispersion in order to totalize itself, that it goes beyond various partitions and taboos, toward transparency, that it arranges itself as a center or an interior from which it is possible to think it, that it gathers itself around an anonymous project in relation to which various attempts, errors, progress, and a history would be possible, and, finally, that brute existence is transformed into truth and tends toward meaning [*signification*].[204]

There is a 'complicity' between the consciousness of the historian and the 'structuration realized by history' which 'allows consciousness to become knowledge of the social'.[205] There is a *sens* to history, then, not because of 'an irresistible orientation toward certain ends' but rather because 'there is no event which does not bring further precision to the permanent problem of knowing what man and his society are'.[206] History is the story of the 'emergence of a subjectivity'; in it one sees the genesis of a subject which can look backward and comprehend its own advent.[207] Lukács thus pointed the way towards a 'philosophical reading of history' which finds . 'behind the prose of everyday existence, a recovery of the self by itself which is the very definition of subjectivity'.[208]

The 'ballast' or 'counterpart' of this interpretation of history lies with a 'historical fact': the proletariat.[209] A commodity which comes to understand the way it had been forced to become a commodity, an object of history which can become aware of the forces which have reduced it to the status of a thing, the proletariat brings to full consciousness that 'becoming social of society' which is the ultimate meaning of capitalism. The proletariat is the identity of subject and object which philosophy had postulated as the criterion of truth; it is the Archimedian point on which the philosophy of history must rest.[210] But the peculiar character of the proletarian consciousness must be emphasised. It is neither 'a state of mind, nor is it knowledge'. It is instead 'a praxis':

It is less than a subject and more than an object; it is a polarized existence, a possibility which appears in the proletariat's situation at the juncture of things and this life.[211]

For this reason Marxism is not simply 'a materialist transposition of Hegel'; the concept of 'praxis' forces a rethinking of the way in which meaning can appear in history:

For a philosophy of praxis, knowledge itself is not the intellectual possession of a signification, of a mental object; and the proletarians are able to carry the meaning of history, even though this meaning is not in the form of an 'I think' . . . The profound philosophical meaning of the notion of praxis is to place us in an order which is not that of knowledge but rather of communication, exchange, and association.[212]

For this reason, the theory of the party 'is not a corollary of Marxism – it is its very center'.[213] The party is the locus where 'the meaning which is understands itself'. Here the intepretation of the theorist and the experience of the proletarian are played off against one another in a process of 'indefinite verification' which gives rise to a notion of truth far different from that correspondence of idea and external *ideatum* which is the hallmark of the natural sciences. In this context truth is understood as 'non-falsity', 'the maximum guarantee against error that men may demand and get'. It is the knowledge that 'there is no *disagreement* between the theoretician and the proletarians'.[214]

These, then, were the main arguments of Lukács's 'lively and vigorous essay', a work which was immediately condemned by the Comintern as 'a revision and criticism of Marxism' and subsequently disowned by its author.[215] *History and Class Consciousness* was denounced for its 'subjective idealism' and its 'ultra-leftism', positions which had become heretical once Lenin's *Materialism and Empirico-Criticism* had been made the canonical text on all philosophical issues facing the international communist movement. Merleau-Ponty had little respect for Lenin's book – it was a work, he wrote, which annulled 'all that has been said about knowledge since Epicurus'[216] – but he did not regard the rejection of *History and Class Consciousness* as simply the triumph of mechanistic dogma over dialectical truth. He maintained, rather, that the Party's recourse to Lenin's naturalism and Lukács's subsequent retreat from his own arguments testified to 'an internal difficulty of Marxist thought'.[217] Lukács's reading of Marx recaptured a vision of the relation between philosophy and praxis that Marx had expressed in his own writings prior to 1850. But after 1850 (and, indeed, as early as the *German Ideology*) Marx had begun to speak of 'destroying philosophy rather than realizing it'.[218] 'Scientific' socialism became the new ideal 'and what is given to science is taken from philosophy'.[219] While Marx would continue to affirm his debts to Hegel, Merleau-Ponty stressed that something crucial had changed in Marx's stance towards the dialectic.

What he looks for in Hegel is no longer dialectical inspiration;

rather it is rationalism, to be used for the benefit of 'matter' and 'relations of production', which are considered as an order in themselves, an external and completely positive power. It is no longer a question of saving Hegel from abstraction, of recreating the dialectic by entrusting it to the very movement of its content, without any idealistic postulate; it is rather a question of annexing Hegel's logic to the economy.[220]

The conflict between 'western' Marxism and Marxism–Leninism was thus already prefigured in Marx himself. The 'circuit which always brings the dialectic back to naturalism' cannot be written off to the 'errors of epigones'. It has its truth; it 'testifies to an obstacle that Marxist thought tried, for better or worse, to get around'.[221]

Drawing on Karl Korsch's *Marxism and Philosophy* – a work which appeared in the same year as *History and Class Consciousness* and was condemned at the same meeting of the Comintern[222] – Merleau-Ponty argued that the 'dialectical' and 'philosophical' Marxism of the young Marx and *History and Class Consciousness* were 'suited to soaring periods, when revolution appears close at hand'. The orthodox and scientistic Marxism of Lenin's *Materialism and Empirico-Criticism* and the old Marx, in contrast, predominates during those 'stagnant periods' when the meaning alleged to be inherent in history vanishes under the press of contemporary events and 'the weight of infrastructures makes itself felt'.[223] The vision of history articulated by the young Lukács and the young Marx was out of step with such times:

> The Marxism of the young Marx as well as the 'Western' Marxism of 1923 lacked a means of expressing the inertia of the infrastructures, the resistance of economic and even natural conditions, and the swallowing-up of 'relations between persons' in 'things'. History as they described it lacked density and allowed its meaning to appear too quickly. They had to learn the slowness of mediations.[224]

Unable to do justice to this inertia, dialectics bowed before naturalism, Lukács accepted the judgement of the Comintern, and the young Marx made way for the old.[225]

The explanation Merleau-Ponty gives as to why the young Marx and the young Lukács were unable to come to terms with the density of history has a familiar ring to it:

> In order to understand the logic and shifts of history, its meaning [*sens*] and what, within it, resists meaning, they still had to conceptualize the sphere proper to history, the institution, which develops neither according to causal laws, like a second nature, but always in dependence on that which it signifies, nor according to eternal ideas, but rather by bringing more or less under its laws events which, as far as it is concerned, are fortuitous and by letting itself be changed by their suggestions . . . This order of 'things' which teaches 'relationships between persons', sensitive to all the heavy conditions which bind it to the order of nature, open to all that personal life can invent is, in modern language, the sphere of symbolism, and Marx's thought was to find its culmination here.[226]

What Merleau-Ponty found lacking in Marx in *Adventures of the Dialectic* was what he had turned to Saussure to find in his inaugural lecture: an adequate account of the 'inter-human meaning of events'. In 1952 he had emphasised the inadequacy of naturalism in the face of Marx's conception of praxis. In 1955 he argued that the surrender of Marxism to naturalism was part and parcel of the way Marx had understood the *sens* of history. Neither a mechanical nor a dialectical Marxism could understand that history is both movement and stagnation, both progress and regress, both *sens* and *non-sens*. [227]

What was ultimately at stake was the coherence of the notion of revolution. Lukács had envisioned, in the revolutionary party, a unity of subject and object, individual and history, past and future, and discipline and judgement.[228] But could such a 'sublime point' be preserved once it enters into history as a regime?

> Marx was able to have and to transmit the illusion of a negation realized in history and in its 'matter' only by making the non-capitalist future an absolute Other. But we who have witnessed a Marxist revolution well know that revolutionary society has its weight, its positivity, and that it is therefore not the absolute Other.[229]

Everything in history, Merleau-Ponty concluded, is 'at the same time movement and inertia'. Marx had denied that this was 'the very *structure* of history' by assigning the principle of movement to one class – the proletariat – and the principle of inertia to the other – the bourgeoisie.[230] But this was to ignore the density of history and to dream the political equivalent of the 'spectre of pure language': a politics unencumbered by the ambivalences which plague institutions:

> It is no accident that all known revolutions have degenerated: it is because as established regimes they can never be what they were as movements; precisely because it succeeded and ended up as an institution, the historical movement is no longer itself: it 'betrays' and 'disfigures' itself in accomplishing itself. Revolutions are true as movements and false as regimes.[231]

Had Marxism learned to conceptualise the field of history properly, it would have had to abandon the dream of a revolution which, once and for all, exorcises the ghosts of the past, lifts the weight of dead generations from the brain of the living, and brings an end to the long reign of human 'pre-history'.[232] It would have placed much more modest hopes in regimes which sought only to change history, not to remake it from top to bottom. It would have learned as well that a rather different critique of capitalism was needed, a critique which

> does not believe that capitalist institutions are the only mechanisms of exploitation, but . . . also does not judge them to be any more natural or sacred than the polished stone hatchet or the bicycle. Like our language, our tools, our customs, our clothes, they are instruments, invented for a definite purpose, which found themselves little by little burdened with an entirely different function. A complete analysis of this change in meaning has to be made, going beyond the famous analysis of surplus value, and a program of action established consequent upon it.[233]

But having learned all this, Marxism would cease to be Marxist – it would have become instead Max Weber's 'tragic liberalism'.[234]

Phenomenology and the opacity of the cogito

The critique of Marxism carried out in *Adventures of the Dialectic* was followed by a critique of phenomenology itself. Beginning with his 1954–5 course 'The Problem of Passivity', continuing through two courses on the concept of nature, and culminating in his 1959–60 course 'Husserl at the Limits of Phenomenology', Merleau-Ponty questioned the degree to which phenomenology could do justice to those phenomena which resist being treated as the products of a constitutive subjectivity. As he wrote in his 1959 essay on Husserl!

> the ultimate task of phenomenology as philosophy of conscious-ness is to understand its relationship to non-phenomenology. What resists phenomenology within us . . . cannot remain outside phenomenology and should have its place within it. The philosopher must bear his shadow, which is not simply the factual absence of future light.[235]

He had suggested as early as 1951 that the problem of language presented one of the more provocative starting-points for 'inter-rogating phenomenology and recommencing Husserl's efforts instead of simply repeating what he said'.[236] But the path these inquiries took in *The Visible and the Invisible* led beyond phenomenology altogether. With respect to Husserl as with respect to Marx, the point of departure for his increasingly heretical reflections was the failure of *The Prose of the World* to provide the promised account of 'the nature of the relationships between the power of expression and the thinker whom it presupposes and shapes, as well as the history which it continues and recreates'.[237]

Even though *The Prose of the World* lacked the promised chapter on the expressive subject, the relation between perception, lan-guage, and thought had been broached at a number of places in the book. One of the more notable was a passage, taken over into the essay 'Indirect Language and the Voices of Silence', where Merleau-Ponty reflected on the relationship between the 'advent' of painting as a collective practice and the individual 'events' which are circumscribed within this *'histoire avènementielle'*:

Advent is the promise of events. The domination of the many by the one in the history of painting, like that domination which we have encountered in the use of the perceiving body, does not consummate succession in an eternity. On the contrary it insists upon succession; it needs it at the same time that it establishes its signification. And there is not simply a question of an *analogy* between the two problems; it is the expressive operation of the body, begun by the smallest perception, which is amplified into painting and art.[238]

The subordination of individual events to an advent can be likened to the subordination of various individual movements and gestures to the more general 'motor project' or 'intentional arc' which carries the body into the world. And – as Merleau-Ponty argued with fewer reservations in 'Indirect Language and the Voices of Silence' than in *The Prose of the World*[239] – the subordination of event under advent in history is not simply *analogous* to the subordination of the many under the one in the *Phenomenology of Perception*: 'the quasi-eternity of art is of a piece with the quasi-eternity of incarnate existence'. In our use of our own body 'we have the means of understanding our cultural gesticulation insofar as it involves us in history'.[240] Any use of the body, including the act of perception, 'is already primordial expression' and, conversely, all acts of expression have as their substratum 'not a pure "I" . . . but rather an "I" endowed with a body'.[241]

The way he posed this chiasm of perception and expression was dependent in crucial ways on the discussion of the tacit *cogito* in the *Phenomenology of Perception*. There, it will be recalled, it was argued that Descartes's *cogito* – an expressive act of crucial importance for the advent of a certain style of philosophising – is incomprehensible in the absence of the tacit *cogito* which it presumes:

The *cogito* at which we arrive by reading Descartes . . . is, then, a spoken *cogito*, put into words and understood in words, and for this reason not attaining its objective, since that part of our existence which is engaged in fixing our life in conceptual forms, and thinking of it as indubitable, is escaping focus and thought. Shall we therefore conclude that language envelops us, and that we are led by it . . . ? This would be to forget half the truth . . . I should be unable even to read Descartes' book, were I not, before any speech to begin, in contact with my own life and thought, and if the spoken *cogito* did not encounter within me a tacit *cogito*. This silent *cogito* was the one Descartes sought when writing his *Meditations*.[242]

Descartes's book, like any successful act of expression, possesses a generality which allows it to be understood by others. But, Merleau-Ponty insists, this generality 'is not that of the idea, but that of a behavioural style "understood" by my body in so far as the latter is a behaviour-producing power, in this case a phoneme-producing one'.[243] This generality of the body, then, allows me to 'catch on' to the expressive acts of others, just as our original, mute contact with the world ultimately grounds all language.

This is why consciousness is never subordinated to any empirical language, why languages can be translated and learned, and finally, why language is not an attribute of external origin, in the sociologist's sense. Behind the spoken *cogito*, the one which is converted into discourse and into essential truth, there lies a tacit *cogito*, myself experienced by myself.[244]

All texts thus have a 'pretext'; the activities of the expressive subject are dependent on the originary activities of the perceptual subject.[245]

As we know from our discussion of Merleau-Ponty's treatment of the problem of others, by the end of the 1950s he had come to regard the tacit *cogito* as 'impossible'. Such a notion, he argued, only serves to perpetuate the 'mythology of a self-consciousness to which the word "consciousness" would refer'.[246] The tacit *cogito*, no less than the spoken *cogito*, was a creature of language. Descartes's naïveté in failing to see that the spoken *cogito* rested on a tacit *cogito* had only been seconded by the 'naïveté . . . of a silent *cogito* that would deem itself to be an adequation with the silent consciousness, whereas its very description of silence rests entirely on the virtues of language'.[247] He did not deny that there was a domain of 'non-linguistic significations'. He did reject the idea that one could treat this domain as if it were composed of positive entities which could be catalogued and named without radically changing their character.[248] *'One cannot make a direct ontology'*; the only path open was an 'indirect' path and the only philosophy possible was a 'negative' one.[249]

One of his reasons for questioning the coherence of the notion of the tacit *cogito* speaks directly to our interests here: the inability of the tacit *cogito* to generate a convincing account of the passage from perception to expression. A note from February 1959 entitled 'Tacit *Cogito* and Speaking Subject' went to the heart of the problem. Arguing that the chapter on the *cogito* in the *Phenomenology of Perception* 'is not connected with the chapter on speech', Merleau-Ponty stressed that the book could offer no insight into 'the problem of the passage from the perceptual meaning to the language meaning, from behaviour to thematization'. It was not enough to invoke a tacit *cogito*. Rather one had to construct 'a theory of the savage mind, which is the mind of praxis'. The task of such a theory would be to grasp *'what*, across the successive and simultaneous community of speaking subjects, *wishes, speaks*, and finally *thinks'*.[250]

It is this question which dominates the discussion of expression in *The Visible and the Invisible*. A working note from September 1959 entitled 'Perceiving Subject, Speaking Subject, Thinking Subject' sketched what it meant to understand the speaking subject as 'the subject of praxis':

> It does not hold before itself the words said and understood as objects of thought or ideates . . . It is a certain lack of . . . such or such a signifier, which does not construct the *Bild* [image] of what it lacks. There is therefore here a neo-teleology, which no more permits being supported by a *consciousness of* . . . nor by an ec-stasy, a constructive project, than does the perceptual teleology.[251]

The perceiving subject must likewise be seen as 'a tacit, silent Being-at [*Etre-a*] which returns from the thing itself blindly identified, which is only a separation [*écart*] with respect to it'; perception must be understood as 'imperception, evidence in non-possession: it is precisely because one knows too well what one is dealing with that one has no need to posit it as an object'.[252] The perceptual and the expressive subject are conceived in similar terms, but the organising metaphors are now taken from Saussure's linguistics, not from the vocabulary associated with the pre-reflective cogito. Saussure's approach to language can thus be generalised beyond its original domain. It 'confirms and rediscovers the idea of perception as divergence [*écart*] by relation to a level'.[253]

With perception and expression now conceived in a fashion that dispenses with the tacit *cogito*, the relationship between them can be approached in a different way. In *The Visible and the Invisible*, Merleau-Ponty no longer speaks of expression as the 'sublimation of perception'. Rather, it is 'a sublimation of the flesh'.[254]

> It is as though the visibility that animates the sensible world were to emigrate, not outside of every body, but into another less heavy, more transparent body, as though it were to change flesh, abandoning the flesh of the body for that of language, and thereby would be emancipated but not freed from every condition.[255]

The tacit *cogito* had been the last refuge for a view of subjectivity which still conceived of the relationship between subject and world as that of interior to exterior, and accordingly subordinated language to a private, pre-linguistic contact with the world. With the 'defenestration of the *cogito*' and with the opposition of subject and object now suspended in the chiasm of the sensing and the sensible, meaning is no longer to be seen as adhering to words 'like the butter on the bread, like a second layer of "psychic reality" spread over the sound'.[256] Meaning is, rather, 'the integral of all the differentiations of the verbal chain, it is given with the words for those who have ears to hear':[257]

> When the silent vision falls into speech, and when the speech in turn, opening up a field of the nameable and the sayable, inscribes itself in that field, in its place, according to its truth – in short, when it metamorphoses the structures of the visible world and makes itself a gaze of the mind, *intuitus mentis* – this is always in virtue of the same fundamental phenomenon of reversibility which sustains both the mute perception and the speech and which manifests itself by an almost carnal existence of the idea, as well as by a sublimation of the flesh.[258]

Language translates no silent pretext; 'language is not a mask over

Being'. Both vision and thought, Merleau-Ponty insisted (with debts to Jacques Lacan's famous description of the unconscious), are 'structured like a language'.[259]

The categories of Saussure's linguistics thus moved beyond the confines of a philosophy of expression to replace the now-evicted categories of the 'philosophy of consciousness'. To appreciate the extent of the rethinking Saussure had provoked, we need only recall the proposals for alterations in the terminology employed by philosophers which we quoted once before in our introduction:

> Replace the notions of concept, idea, representation with the notions of *dimensions*, articulation, level, hinges, pivots, configuration – – The point of departure = the critique of the usual conception of the *thing* and its *properties* → critique of the logical notion of the subject, and of logical inherence → critique of the *positive* signification (differences between significations), signification as a separation [*écart*], theory of predication – founded on this diacritical conception.[260]

He turned to Saussure in hopes of finding the basis for a new philosophy of history. What he wound up taking from Saussure was a new ontology. But, could phenomenology accept this ontology and still remain even remotely related to Husserl's project? It is to this question which we must turn in our conclusion.

5
Conclusion: Between Phenomenology and Structuralism

What, then, are we to make of Merleau-Ponty's reflections on the relation between philosophy and the human sciences, the problem of our knowledge of others, and the implications of the phenomena of speech and expression for the philosophy of history? In wrestling with these and kindred problems, was he deepening Husserl's analyses and applying an existential phenomenology to certain of crucial dimensions of social life? Or was he staking out a position beyond phenomenology, a position whose full implications would become clearer only in the decade after his death? We have seen how he became uncomfortable with such notions as 'lived experience', 'constitution', 'intentionality', and the 'tacit *cogito*'. Yet we have also seen that his reading of Saussure, his use of Lacan, and his response to Lévi-Strauss betray a continued commitment to certain fundamental concerns of the phenomenological project. Where, then, are we to place this most elusive of thinkers?

Merleau-Ponty at the limits of phenomenology

In the last years of Merleau-Ponty's life, a group of new terms comes to the forefront of his writings. The relationship of these terms to the orthodox categories of Husserlian phenomenology is at best ambivalent. Notions like 'chiasm', 'flesh', '*écart*', and 'reversibility' are often introduced and illustrated in the company of certain characteristically Husserlian quandaries: for example, the analysis of the touched hand or the discussion of the way in which the 'other side' of the other's body is 'appresented'.[1] Yet, the account which is given of these Husserlian problems is an account which has been carefully purged of a number of the most basic terms in the phenomenological lexicon. In the working notes for *The Visible and the Invisible*, Merleau-Ponty argued that his philosophy must proceed without recourse to such notions as *'Erlebnis'*,[2] 'concept, idea, mind, and representation',[3] 'consciousness and projections',[4] 'subject',[5] 'intentional act and noema'.[6] These concepts, so crucial for the articulation of Husserl's phenomenology, are dismissed by Merleau-Ponty as 'the bric-a-brac of *positive* psychic so-called "realities" . . . abstractly carved out from the ontological tissue, from "the body of the mind" '.[7] In 1946 Jean Beaufret had asked whether phenomenology, when 'fully developed', might not require 'the abandonment of subjectivity and the vocabulary of subjective idealism'.[8] In 1959, it was clear that Merleau-Ponty was in the process of dispensing with much of the terminology which had struck Beaufret as not 'sufficiently radical'. But it is not clear whether Merleau-Ponty saw what he was doing as a contribution to the continued 'development' of phenomenology.

The discussion of phenomenology in the text of *The Visible and the Invisible* is a good deal more critical than in any of Merleau-Ponty's previous analysis. It is now characterised as a philosophy of the 'pure gaze'.[9] It is chastised for transforming the world into 'ideates, *cogitata*, or noemata subsisting before the pure subject'.[10] It is accused of perpetuating the dichotomies of subject and object and of fact and essence.[11] His 1959 essay, 'The Philosopher and his Shadow', appears, in retrospect, to have been a last attempt, from within the camp, to 'push' Husserl away from subjective idealism. After 1959, he was no longer interested in moving phenomenology from within; he was now taking a measure of its failings from the outside.

Much of what he had to say against phenomenology originated from a dissatisfaction with the concept of intentionality. A note from April 1960 began by discussing the extent to which the Freudian idea of the unconscious challenged the conventional Husserlian understanding of time as a 'series of *Erlebnisse*' and culminated in a sweeping critique of Husserl's entire philosophy:

> The whole Husserlian analysis is blocked by the framework of *acts* which imposes upon it the philosophy of *consciousness*. It is necessary to take up again and develop the *fungierende* or latent intentionality which is the intentionality within being. That is not compatible with 'phenomenology', that is, with an ontology that obliges whatever is not nothing to *present* itself to *consciousness*

across *Abschattung* and as deriving from an originating donation which is an *act*, i.e. one *Erlebnis* among others.[12]

Husserl's analyses made the world into the sum total of the perspectival experiences that consciousness has of it. The world attained unity and coherence only through the synthesising acts of this consciousness. By dissociating the notion of intentionality from consciousness and speaking of an 'intentionality within being', Merleau-Ponty was seeking to wrest the account of the life-world free from the account of transcendental subjectivity. The analysis of the life-world does not lead Merleau-Ponty back to the 'subjective operations' which Husserl saw as the ultimate foundation of this world.[13] Rather, the analysis of the life-world proceeds with no recourse to 'consciousness' whatsoever. What was fundamental for Merleau-Ponty was 'flesh' and the 'chiasm', not 'consciousness facing a noema'.[14]

The concept of intentionality had long been a point of tension in Merleau-Ponty's relationship with phenomenology. Throughout the *Phenomenology of Perception* Merleau-Ponty paid homage to the notion while nevertheless continuing to stress the independence and self-sufficiency of the life-world.[15] He looked 'beneath intentionality related to acts or thetic intentionality' for 'another kind which is the condition of the former's possibility'.[16] In the *Phenomenology of Perception* (unlike *The Visible and the Invisible*) this 'operative intentionality' was alleged to be a fundamental attribute of 'consciousness', although this consciousness was described as an 'incarnate' rather than a 'transcendental' consciousness. Yet, in crucial ways, this incarnate consciousness behaved no differently than a transcendental consciousness. As Gary Brent Madison has aptly observed, 'The substitution of a philosophy of experience for a philosophy of consciousness changes nothing in regard to the basic structure of this philosophy.' Operating with 'all the presuppositions of a philosophy of consciousness', the *Phenomenology of Perception* represents – at best – a 'palace revolution, a revolution within idealism'.[17]

Nowhere do the tensions inherent in Merleau-Ponty's dual commitment to the intentionality of consciousness and the autonomy of the world manifest themselves more forcefully than in his constant recourse to the rhetorical form of the chiasmus whenever he needs to reconcile the conflicting claims of consciousness and world in the *Phenomenology of Perception*. Reading the book, one is constantly confronted with such passages as:

> There is a world for me because I am not unaware of myself; and I am not concealed from myself because I have a world.[18]

> The world is inseparable from the subject, but from a subject who is nothing but a project of the world, and the subject is inseparable from the world, but from a world which it projects itself.[19]

> We choose the world and the world chooses us.[20]

It is as if Merleau-Ponty is torn between two positions and is unable to decide on the one or the other. Whenever he strays too far in the direction of idealism and asserts that subjects are conscious of the world by being self-conscious, or that the world is dependent on the subject, or that subjects choose their world, he must immediately restore an equilibrium by assuring the reader that subjects are self-conscious only by being conscious of the world, that subjects are dependent on the world, and that the world somehow 'chooses' the subject.

His subsequent attempt at curbing some of the idealistic over-tones of Husserl's phenomenology by speaking of an 'instituting' rather than a 'constituting' subject is no more successful. As we have seen, before his summary of his course on 'Institution in Personal and Public History' is over he has managed to reproduce the tensions of the *Phenomenology of Perception* within the new vocabulary. He now speaks of the subject as both 'instituted' and 'instituting'.[21]

All of the problems posed in the *Phenomenology of Perception*, Merleau-Ponty reflected in a note from July 1959, 'are insoluble because I start there from the "consciousness"–"object" distinction'.[22] It was this starting-point that condemned the *Phenomenology of Perception* to playing out that unhappy dialectic which had been the fate of Western philosophy since Descartes:

> Philosophy elects certain beings – 'sensations', 'representations', 'thought', 'consciousness', or even a deceiving being – in order to separate itself from all being. Precisely in order to accomplish its will for radicalism, it would have to take as its theme the umbilical

bond that binds it always to Being, the inalienable horizon with which it is already and henceforth circumvented, the primary initiation which it tries in vain to go back on.[23]

The vacillations in the *Phenomenology of Perception* testified to the inability of a philosophy which had broken the bond of 'perceptual faith' with the overly abstract categories of the philosophy of consciousness, ever to return to that 'umbilical bond' with being which Merleau-Ponty came to see as the authentic concern of ontology. No less than the 'reflective' philosophies criticised in the first chapter of *The Visible and the Invisible*, the analyses of the *Phenomenology of Perception* were marked by the 'original stain' of trying to 'coincide with a constitutive principle already at work in the spectacle of the world', but – as 'reflection, re-turn, re-conquest, or re-covery' – always arriving *post festum.*[24]

The *Phenomenology of Perception*, seeking to reconcile subject and world, wound up weaving them both into a chiasmus. It began from a divergence between subject and object which it could never overcome, however strenuously Merleau-Ponty might seek to uncover a 'pre-reflective' world where all of the entities fathered by reflection were alleged to be at one with each other. With an uncompromising radicalism *The Visible and the Invisible* dispensed with all the positive entities of the *Phenomenology of Perception* and tried to begin thinking again from the starting-point of the chiasm and the *écart*. It attempts to dispense with the inherited notions of 'selves', 'others', and 'things' and instead tries to focus on the reversibility which ties together as obverse and reverse the self and things and the self and others. If the insecure arguments of the *Phenomenology of Perception* remind us of the famous *Gestalt* drawing which can be seen either as a rabbit or a duck – from one perspective the book seems to be a concerted attempt to dismantle the categories of transcendental philosophy; from another, it is an attempt at reconstructing transcendental philosophy on the basis of the incarnate consciousness – *The Visible and the Invisible* has a focus of a most peculiar and challenging sort. It enjoins us to look neither at the duck, nor the rabbit, nor the oscillating series duck-rabbit-duck-rabbit-duck-rabbit . . . Rather, we must learn to look at the pattern of lines which cleave space in such a way as to make a hinge around which ducks and rabbits may pivot.

160 *Maurice Merleau-Ponty*

Some equivocations on the threshold of structuralism

If, by 1959, phenomenology had become problematic for Merleau-Ponty, what can be said about his stance towards structuralism? If he was no longer unequivocally a 'phenomenologist' could he be said, in some sense of the term, to have been a 'structuralist' before the fact?

The question admits of no simple answer. To begin to give an adequate response it would be necessary to find some way of characterising the minimal commitments which define that remarkably heteroclite movement which has been known, for better or worse, as structuralism.[25] But, as Eugenio Donato has noted, 'structuralism', like 'existentialism' before it, possessed such coherence only at the outset:

> Initially the term is used against the established ideologies of the day to mark the presence of something new or different in the works of a certain number of thinkers; the new element being attributed to a new method of analysis . . . Then as the opposition diminishes or disappears and the new term becomes the new ideology, the need to insist on the methodological pretexts which at first seemed so important diminishes and as individual thinkers continue with their distinctive concerns and preoccupations, the differences between them became more and more marked. In the same way that by, say, 1960 it was impossible to speak of Sartre and Merleau-Ponty in the same breath, it has nowadays become, except in the most trivial and superficial way, impossible to put under the same heading, say, Foucault, Lacan, and Lévi-Strauss.[26]

To the extent that 'structuralism' can be talked about as a coherent movement at all, the only way to proceed may be to try to understand what it was that various alleged 'structuralists' were at one in rejecting. What Lévi-Strauss, Roland Barthes, Jacques Lacan, and Michel Foucault (to name only the usual suspects who are rounded up whenever it is necessary to talk about 'structuralism') share is less a common commitment to a set of methodological principles than a common set of antipathies. They all, in one way or another, have rejected the *cogito* as the starting-point for their inquiries, they all view the quest for an ultimate foundation or origin which can 'ground' inquiries with considerable suspicion, and they have all rebelled against the priority given to 'History' in the Hegelianised Marxism articulated by Merleau-Ponty in the late 1940s and taken up again by Jean-Paul Sartre in his *Critique of Dialectical Reason* (1960). Thus, instead of asking 'Was Merleau-Ponty a structuralist?', we might do better to see to what degree he shared the same antipathies as those thinkers who have typically been associated with 'structuralism'.[27]

As we have seen, there is much in Merleau-Ponty's critique of Marx and Husserl that bears a resemblance to what came to pass in French thought in the decade after his death. His 'defenestration of the *cogito*' culminated in an attempt to elaborate an ontology which dispensed with the conventional categories of the 'philosophy of consciousness' and instead sought to develop a new conceptual apparatus which rested on concepts such as 'flesh', 'chiasm', '*écart*' and 'reversibility'. Further, the foundation on which this ontology rested was less a primordial 'ground' than a 'spread' or 'divergence'; what was fundamental for Merleau-Ponty was not a common origin but rather a network of divergences and differences. Finally, his critique of Marx's vision of a universal history moving towards one goal gave rise to an alternative vision of history as a series of multiple, local histories, each defined by their own peculiar symbolic matrix.

We would, however, be doing Merleau-Ponty a considerable disservice if we were to present him merely as anticipating certain positions which were subsequently elaborated, with fewer hesitations, by Lévi-Strauss, Lacan, Barthes, or Foucault. As we have seen, there were dimensions of his work which, even in the last years of his life, continued to draw upon his earlier concerns and thus set him in opposition to many of the positions that came to the fore after his death. However much he embraced Saussure's linguistics, his Saussure remained a very different creature from the thinker to whom Lévi-Strauss, Lacan, Barthes, and – to a much lesser extent – Foucault turned for inspiration.

Saussure's definition of the linguistic sign, as Emile Benveniste pointed out in his classic 1939 article, tended to confuse the 'signified' and the '*object* signified'. Saussure could claim that the relation between signifier and signified was arbitrary, Benveniste argued, only 'by an unconscious and surreptitious recourse to a third term which was not included in the initial definition . . . the thing itself, reality'.[28] The ox 'in its concrete and "substantial" particularity' is indeed connected in an arbitrary and unmotivated fashion with the signifiers '*böf*' and '*oks*', but Saussure claimed, at the outset, to have banished the living and breathing ox from consideration and to be dealing only with the relationship between the 'sound-images' '*Böf*' and '*oks*' and the 'concept' 'ox'. This relation between sound-image and concept is 'arbitrary', in Benveniste's words, 'only under the impassive regard of Sirius or for the person who limits himself to observing from the outside the bond established between an objective reality and human behaviour and condemns himself thus to seeing nothing in it but contingency'.[29]

It is indeed true that there is little of interest to be said about the relation between signifier and signified. But this is *not* because the relation is an arbitrary one. Rather it is because the relationship between sound and meaning is so *necessary* and *unavoidable* for speakers of a language that there is simply nothing that can be said about the language which does not begin by accepting this coupling of sound-image and concept, a coupling which – as Saussure put it in one of his happier analogies – is as indissociable as that between the recto and verso of a piece of paper.[30] Saussure was also right in maintaining that the relation between the act of signification and the object which it signifies is mutable, contingent, and relative to differing temporal or geographical circumstances. But to explore what was involved in the act of signification he would have had to take up those problems of reference which the doctrine of the 'arbitrary nature of the sign' prematurely foreclosed.[31]

Such inquiries, as we have seen, stood at the centre of Merleau-Ponty's account of expression, even in the period when he was most inspired by Saussure. The conceptual mayhem which he wreaked on Saussure's distinctions has its logic. The 'synchronic linguistics of *parole*' made little sense in terms of Saussure's categories, but that may be more a criticism of Saussure than of Merleau-Ponty. What Merleau-Ponty was looking for in Saussure was a way of understanding how subjects polarise a set of instituted signs in ways that enable them to say something new. What he wanted to understand was the way in which a finite number of signs could be put to an infinite number of uses. What he wanted to show was how conventions could produce something unconventional. These are not unreasonable requests to make of an account of language and Merleau-Ponty's obsession with the practical dimension of speech is ample testimony to his ability to sense what was lacking in Saussure's account, even if he tried to convince himself that what he was inventing was in fact already there in Saussure himself.

It is this concern with the problem of *parole* which makes Merleau-Ponty's work of such relevance to contemporary social theory. He was one of the few thinkers of his time to have tried to think seriously about both agency and structure. His account of the subject was never as oblivious of the degree to which institutions place limits on individual freedom as Sartre's was. From his very first writings he was articulating a more convincing account of the nature of human action than that unlimited Cartesian freedom that stood at the centre of Sartre's account. He was drawn to Saussure in hopes of finding a way of better understanding the opacity and thickness of the world of intersubjective meaning. He was well aware that the problem of agency could not be resolved simply by assuming that the Cartesian *cogito*, with suitable modifications, could be resurrected as that 'body-subject' which grounds our grasp of language and supports our interactions with others. A proper consideration of the implications of social action, of expression, and of history requires, he argued, a new ontology which breaks with the prejudices of the Cartesian account of subjectivity.

The question of the unwritten chapter of *The Prose of the World* was only partially answered by *The Visible and the Invisible*. In the latter as in the former he was still trying to determine '*what*, across the successive and simultaneous community of speaking subjects, *wishes*, *speaks*, and finally *thinks*'.[32] His response that what is needed is an account of the 'savage spirit' or the 'subject of praxis' is less an answer than a rubric under which possible answers might be pursued. But the fact that he was *asking* the question is perhaps enough. He recognised that Saussure's linguistics, Lacan's psychoanalysis, and Lévi-Strauss's ethnology spelled the end of the hoped-for *rapprochement* between the human sciences and a phenomenology which still conceived of itself as a philosophy of the *cogito*. But he did not conclude that it was possible for these approaches to neglect completely the problem of agency. What was needed, and what philosophy could conceivably contribute, was an understanding of the peculiar sort of subject which these disciplines seemed to presume – a subject which both shapes and is shaped by the structures it employs.

The party at Durkheim's breaks up

The doctrine of the arbitrary nature of the linguistic sign inspires many of the arguments of those who sought to extend Saussure's approach to the human sciences in the decade after Merleau-Ponty's death. If the relation of signifier to signified is indeed 'arbitrary' and 'unmotivated', then it clearly escapes the intentions of the speaking subject. To understand the way signs are related to one another, it is necessary to turn away from the subject and consider instead the system which is alleged to govern their deployment. As Vincent Descombes has argued:

> Semiology displaces all issues towards the analysis of discourse and gives pride of place to the relationship of emitter to code . . . The result is that the origin of meaning can no longer be located where the phenomenologists had thought to find it, in the author of discourse, the individual who believes he is expressing himself, but rather it lies in language itself . . . *Not man, but structures are decisive! Man is nothing!* Such was the lesson that public opinion drew from the research of structural anthropology; or so we might think, to read the scandalised commentaries of the now-obsolete 'humanists'.[33]

That 'philosophy without a subject' which had presumably been put to rest during the heyday of existentialism and phenomenology reappeared, draped now with the terminology of structural linguistics.[34]

Hence Lévi-Strauss could express a lack of interest in the meaning that the myths he analysed had for those who in fact told them, a lack of interest which was as complete as Durkheim's disdain for the non-social facts of individual psychology. As he stressed in the 'Overture' to *The Raw and the Cooked*:

> I . . . claim to show not how men think in myths, but how myths operate in men's minds without their being aware of the fact. And . . . it would perhaps be better to go further and, disregarding the thinking subject completely, proceeded as if the thinking process were taking place in the myths, in their reflection upon themselves, and their interrelation.[35]

In much the same way, Louis Althusser's reading of Marx argued that the true subject of historical materialism was not 'man' but rather 'relations of production'. 'Man' enters the theoretical universe of *Capital* only under a mask and only in the role of a 'support' (*Träger*) of relations of production.[36] The very notion of 'subject' is itself the product of an ideological discourse which, like Lacan's mirror, 'interpellates' the subject as a subject.[37] And, mustering that sort of apocalyptic prose of which he was a master, Michel Foucault could conclude an 'archaeology' of the 'fundamental arrangements of knowledge' with the observation that, far from being an 'age-old concern', the category of 'man' is 'an invention of recent date' fated to be erased in time 'like a face drawn in the sand at the edge of the sea'.[38]

Such stances may seem a bit excessive, but then patricide is not an affair for the faint-hearted. What mattered was to be rid of a philosophy which appeared to be only a continuation of Cartesianism by other means. As Michel Foucault, the 'structuralist' who was most effective in dodging the label, observed:

Everything that took place in the sixties arose from a dissatisfaction with the phenomenological theory of the subject, and involved different escapades, subterfuges, breakthroughs, according to whether we use a negative or a positive term, in the direction of linguistics, psychoanalysis or Nietzsche.[39]

By the mid-1960s the deed had been done, using whatever lay closest to hand. Against Sartre, against Husserl, and – at the bottom of it all – against *père* Descartes, structure was privileged over the subject, the unconscious over the conscious, constraint over action. Effective as a way of throwing off a philosophical tradition which everywhere saw only consciousness, freedom, and creativity, it is less clear that such strategies have served to liberate social theory from its patriarchs. As Pierre Bourdieu and Jean-Claude Passeron commented in 1967:

All the social sciences now live in the house of Durkheimism, unbeknownst to them, as it were, because they walked into it backwards.[40]

But once inside, they have had a chance to look around, realise where they have wound up, and begin to inch towards the door again.

French social thought since 1968 has been, among other things, the story of repeated attempts at mitigating the abstract formalism and rigid constraint which were the hallmarks of structuralism in its salad days.[41] A kindred movement can be seen in Roland Barthes's shift from a 'semiotics of the message' to a 'semiotics of the interlocuter'.[42] Neither tendency marks a return to a Cartesian or even a Sartrian subject, but both do address one of the more problematic aspects of the early structuralist project. Devoid of any reference to the subject which shapes and is shaped by the structures which the theorist analyses, accounts such as Lévi-Strauss's 'science of myths' run the risk of becoming, at worst, rather pointless exercises in pattern-picking and, at best, quite bizarre attempts to learn the rules of languages which appear to have no native speakers.[43] Saussure's structural linguistics was able to elaborate a coherent and suggestive research programme because the object it studied – unlike the 'languages' of myth, ideology, fashion, or what have you – had a coherence independent of the constructs of the theorist. Languages are spoken by a linguistic community. Their parts belong together, and have been brought together as a result of the actions of subjects who have a practical understanding of what it means to make sense to one another and the requisite competencies to go on and speak the language in ways that, more often than not, do make sense to others.[44] The reconstruction of these competencies and the analysis of this knowledge need not and cannot take the form of an effort at coinciding with the 'lived experience' of any particular subject. But neither can such inquiries be undertaken by an approach which assumes that language can somehow manage to speak itself.

What has come to be called 'post-structuralism' (but not, perhaps, with sufficient embarrassment over how empty the term is) thus faces a problem which is the mirror image of the one which confronted Merleau-Ponty. He was faced with the task of taming an excessively subjectivist theory with a knowledge of the opacity and density of the world of structures. Contemporary social theorists are faced with the task of overcoming an excessively objectivist understanding of structures with the knowledge that structures do not simply constrain agents, they also allow agents to act in ways which frequently lead to the transformation of the structures themselves. It would not be surprising if, sneaking out of Durkheim's house in the dead of night, they should run into a familiar figure, slipping out of Descartes's house. Meeting in that no-man's land where, for better or worse, the human sciences seem condemned to camp out for the foreseeable future, they might well greet one another with a smile of recognition.

Notes and References

Chapter 1: Introduction

1. The characterisation of Merleau-Ponty is that of Paul Ricoeur, 'The Question of the Subject: The Challenge of Semiology', trans. K. McLaughlin, in *The Conflict of Interpretatons* (Evanston: Northwestern University Press, 1974) p.247, ft.7. See also Ricoeur's brief 'Hommage à Merleau-Ponty', *Esprit*, 29 (1961) pp.1115–20. For a general account of Merleau-Ponty's relationship to phenomenology, see Gary Brent Madison, *The Phenomenology of Merleau-Ponty: A Search for the Limits of Consciousness* (Athens, Ohio: Ohio University Press, 1981).
2. For George Lichtheim, the publication of Merleau-Ponty's *Adventures of the Dialectic* marked the moment at which 'the French discussion had recovered the level of the earlier German one': *Marxism in Modern France* (New York: Columbia University Press, 1966) p.80, ft.5. Note also the central role given to Merleau-Ponty's writings in Jürgen Habermas's 1957 literature review on the 'philosophical discussion of Marx and Marxism', reprinted in *Theorie und Praxis* (Frankfurt: Suhrkamp, 1971) pp.425–8.
3. Merleau-Ponty's pioneering role was noted by Roland Barthes in his *Elements of Semiology* (London: Jonathan Cape, 1967) p.24. Maurice Lagueux, 'Merleau-Ponty et la linguistique de Saussure', *Dialogue*, V (1965) pp.351–64, gives the most complete discussion of the idiosyncracies of Merleau-Ponty's interpretation of Saussure.
4. To cite two fairly recent examples, Richard Rorty in *Philosophy and the Mirror of Nature* (Princeton: Princeton University Press, 1979) carries out a penetrating critique of the metaphors of 'mirroring' and 'reflection' which have stood at the heart of western philosophy since Descartes, but gives no indication that he is aware of the similar critique Merleau-Ponty mounted in his discussion of Descartes's *Dioptric* in 'The Eye and the Mind' (*PrP*, pp.169–78). Likewise, the exhaustive *Dictionary of Marxist Thought*, ed. T. Bottomore *et al.* (Cambridge, Mass.: Harvard University Press, 1983) contains no entry for Merleau-Ponty, despite the fact that the use of the term 'Western Marxism' virtually begins with Merleau-Ponty's discussion in *Adventures of the Dialectic*.
5. Marjorie Grene, 'Merleau-Ponty and the Renewal of Ontology', *Review of Metaphysics*, XXIX:4 (1976) p.622.
6. Jean-Paul Sartre, 'Merleau-Ponty', in *Situations*, trans. B. Eisler (Greenwich, Conn.: Fawcett, 1966) p.157. The most detailed biography down to 1945 is in Theodore F. Geraets, *Vers une nouvelle philosophie transcendentale* (The Hague: Martinus Nijhoff, 1971) pp.4–31. Barry Cooper, *Merleau-Ponty and Marxism: From Terror to Reform* (Toronto: University of Toronto Press, 1979) pp.4–16,

covers the same period, with a greater stress on the importance of Kojève's lectures for his abandonment of Catholicism.

7. *SB*, p.199.
8. H. L. Van Breda, 'Maurice Merleau-Ponty et les Archives-Husserl à Louvain', *Revue de métaphysique et de morale*, 67:4 (1962) pp.410–30 gives a detailed account of Merleau-Ponty's use of Husserl's *Nachlass*.
9. The most comprehensive account of Merleaú-Ponty's courses in the late 1940s is Hugh J. Silverman, 'Translator's Preface', in *CAL*, pp.xxxiii–viii.
10. Sartre's account of the break, in 'Merleau-Ponty', pp.188–206, remains the basic source, subjected to different interpretations in Michel-Antoine Burnier, *Choice of Action: The French Existentialists on the Political Front Line*, trans. B. Murchland (New York: Random House, 1968) pp.69–76 (mainly from Sartre's side), and Cooper, pp.102–6 (more sympathetic to Merleau-Ponty).
11. *VI*, p.274.
12. Claude Lévi-Strauss, *The Savage Mind* (Chicago: University of Chicago Press, 1966) pp.245–69; see also Lévi-Strauss's discussion of his friendship with Merleau-Ponty, 'On Merleau-Ponty', trans. C. Gross, *Graduate Faculty Philosophy Journal*, 7:2 (1978) pp.179–88.
13. Vincent Descombes, *Modern French Philosophy*, trans. L. Scott-Fox and J. M. Harding (Cambridge: Cambridge University Press, 1980) pp.71–2.
14. Gilles Deluze, 'Un nouvel archiviste', *Critique*, no.274 (1970) p.195.
15. Michel Foucault, *Language, Counter-Memory, Practice*, trans. D. Bouchard (Ithaca, N.Y.: Cornell University Press, 1977) p.170.
16. See Bernard Pingaud's comment at the close of a special issue of *L'Arc* devoted to Merleau-Ponty on the tenth anniversary of his death: 'a strange silence reigns in so-called "advanced" intellectual milieux: the name Merleau-Ponty is almost never cited by fashionable thinkers although he had posed before them a certain number of the problems they still confront and his reflection – whether it concerns politics or language, psychoanalysis or art – has not entirely lost its actuality': *L'Arc*, no.46 (1971) p.96.
17. *PrP*, p.3.
18. *PrP*, p.7.
19. *PrP*, pp.8–9; the list of authors comes from a résumé of Sartre's *What is Literature?* from 1948 or 1949, cited by Claude Lefort in his preface to *PW*, p.xvi; Valéry is not mentioned on this list, but figures prominently (along with Breton) in a section from Merleau-Ponty's 1951 lecture 'Man and Adversity' (*S*, pp.232–5) which appears to be a sketch of the proposed argument of *The Prose of the World*. Merleau-Ponty had written an essay on Montaigne as early as 1947 (*S*, pp.198–210) and Proust had been discussed at a number of points in *Phenomenology of Perception*.
20. Lefort, 'Preface' to *PW*, p.xvi.
21. *PrP*, p.9.

170 *Notes and References*

22. Ibid; an argument of this sort is developed in 'Man and Adversity', where the section on Breton and Valéry is followed by a discussion of politics and history; see *S*, pp.235–9.
23. *IPP*, p.54.
24. 'The Sensible World and the World of Expression' (1952–3) *TFL*, pp.3–11; 'Studies in the Literary Use of Language' (1952–3) *TFL*, pp.12–18; 'The Problem of Speech' (1953–4) *TFL*, pp.19–26; 'Materials for a Theory of History' (1953–4) *TFL*, pp.27–38; and 'Institution in Personal and Public History' (1954–5) *TFL*, pp.39–45.
25. *AD*, p.3.
26. Claude Lefort, 'Editor's Foreword' to *VI*, pp.xi–xxxiii; cf. Merleau-Ponty's own approach to Husserl, *S*, pp.159–60.
27. Claude Lefort, 'Editor's Foreword', *VI*, p.xxxiv; see also *SNS*, p.94, ft.13.
28. *VI*, pp.168, 183.
29. *VI*, pp.176, 167.
30. Samuel B. Mallin, *Merleau-Ponty's Philosophy* (New Haven: Yale University Press, 1979) attempts to articulate an 'ontology of situations' which rests on this sort of understanding of the relationship between the *Phenomenology of Perception* and *The Visible and the Invisible.* For reasons which will become obvious shortly, this is not an interpretation of the relation between the books that I share. See also my discussion of Mallin in 'Maurice Merleau-Ponty: Politics, Phenomenology, and Ontology', *Human Studies*, VI:3 (1983) pp.301–4.
31. *VI*, p.183.
32. *VI*, p.200.
33. *VI*, p.224.
34. The sudden appearance of these new terms has been noted by Madison, p.97.
35. *PrP*, p.167 (also see *VI*, p.139); *VI*, p.194 (also see *VI*, pp.185, 190).
36. Remy C. Kwant, *From Phenomenology to Metaphysics* (Pittsburgh: Duquesne University Press, 1966).
37. J. F. Bannan, 'The "Later" Thought of Merleau-Ponty', *Dialogue*, V:3 (1966) pp.383–403.
38. Xavier Tilliette, *Merleau-Ponty* (Paris: Seghers, 1970) pp.136–7; Madison, pp.32, 170, 186–7, 240, 273.
39. Claude Lefort, 'Maurice Merleau-Ponty', in R. Klibansky (ed.), *Contemporary Philosophy: A Survey. Vol. III: Metaphysics, Phenomenology, Language, and Structure* (Firenze: La Nuova Italia Editrice, 1969) pp.206–14.
40. Marcel Gauchet, 'Le lieu de la pensée', *L'Arc*, no.46 (1971) pp.19–30.
41. Marc Richir, 'La défenestration', *L'Arc*, no.46 (1971) pp.31–42.
42. Gérard Granel, *Le sense du temps et de la perception chez E. Husserl* (Paris: Gallimard, 1968) p.103.
43. Grene, p.605.
44. Madison's account of the relationship between these three works can

by the time he wrote his thesis on theories of the imagination that Bergson was not radical enough: see Ronald Aronson, *Jean-Paul Sartre: Philosophy in the World* (London: New Left Books, 1980) pp.30–1; 'An Interview with Jean-Paul Sartre', in Paul Arthur Schilpp, ed., *The Philosophy of Jean-Paul Sartre* (La Salle, Indiana: Open court, 1981) p.7; and Jean-Paul Sartre, *Imagination: A Psychological Critique*, trans. F. Williams (Ann Arbor, Michigan: University of Michigan Press, 1962) pp.36–57. Merleau-Ponty's review of Sartre's *L'Imagination*, in *Journal de Psychologie normale et pathologique*, 33 (1936) pp.756–61, was highly critical of Sartre's treatment of Bergson; see esp. p.761.

23. Sartre, *Search for a Method*, pp.19–20; Geraets, pp.11, 16, 51.
24. Cooper, pp.14–22.
25. *PP*, p.viii.
26. Simone de Beauvoir, *The Prime of Life*, trans. P. Green (New York: Harper & Row, 1976) p.112.
27. Jean-Paul Sartre, 'Intentionality: A Fundamental Idea of Husserl's Phenomenology', trans. J. P. Fell, *Journal of the British Society for Phenomenology*, I:2 (1970) p.4.
28. Ibid; see the discussion in Dominick LaCapra, *A Preface to Sartre* (Ithaca, N.Y.: Cornell University Press, 1978) pp.47–51.
29. Geraets, p.7.
30. Merleau-Ponty, 'Projet de travail sur la nature de la perception' (1933) in Geraets, pp.9–10.
31. Ibid, p.10; Geraets argues that Merleau-Ponty is referring here to William James and A. N. Whitehead, both of whom were discussed in Jean Wahl's *Vers le concret*.
32. Herbert Spiegelberg, *The Phenomenological Movement*, 2nd edn, vol.II (The Hague: Martinus Nijhoff, 1971) p.529 (based on a 1953 interview).
33. Spiegelberg suggests (ibid, pp.529–30) that Merleau-Ponty read the *Crisis* as early as 1936. Geraets, pp.28–31, 130–40, sees the publication of 'The Origin of Geometry' in 1939 as the decisive turning-point. For Merleau-Ponty's first visit to the Husserl archives, see the account in Van Breda, pp.411–15 (the fact that Merleau-Ponty seems to have believed that Part II of the *Crisis* was never published, which Van Breda notes on p.415, weighs in favour of the later date). 'The Origin of Geometry' first appeared in *Revue internationale de philosophie*, I:2 (1939) pp.203–25 (it has been translated as an appendix to Edmund Husserl, *The Crisis of European Sciences and Transcendental Phenomenology*, trans. D. Carr (Evanston: Northwestern University Press, 1970) pp.353–78), along with articles on Husserl by Fink and Landgrebe which influenced Merleau-Ponty's own reading. The same journal also contained an essay by H.-J. Pos, 'Phénoménologie et linguistique', which Merleau-Ponty drew upon in his subsequent work on language (see *S*, p.85). *Experience and Judgement* was published in Prague in 1939, immediately before the German occupation, and was seized and

pulped, with the exception of 200 copies which were shipped to England and a hundred which were sent to Louvain.

34. See the discussion in Geraets, pp.182–7. For an early discussion of Scheler, see Merleau-Ponty's first publication, a review entitled 'Christianisme et ressentiment', *La Vie intellectuelle*, 7 (1935) pp.278–306 (note especially the critique of Brunschvicg on p.305 and the frequent references to Husserl's *Ideas*). For Marcel, see Merleau-Ponty's review 'Etre et Avoir', *La Vie intellectuelle*, 8 (1936) pp.98–109 (especially the discussion of Marcel's critique of approaches to the body which take the standpoint of an *'attitude spectaculaire'* and the rejection of the *cogito* in favour of the notion of incarnate consciousness, pp.98–101). Mournier's influence is noted in Merleau-Ponty, 'La Philosophie de l'existence', pp.311–12.

35. For a suggestion of some lines of congruence, see Spiegelberg, vol.II, pp.398–400. Emmanuel Levinas's 1930 study of Husserl's work, *The Theory of Intuition in Husserl's Phenomenology*, trans. A. Orianne (Evanston, Ill.: Northwestern University Press, 1973) shows how fleet-footed a commentator had to be to prevent the distinctiveness of Husserl's thought from being lost. Against Bergson, Levinas stressed that Husserl saw the intellect as 'not foreign to intuition', while, against Brunschvicg, he stressed that truth, for Husserl, lay not with the internal consistency of subjective representations, but rather with 'the presence of life to its objects given "in person" ' (pp.153–4).

36. 'Do not wish to go out; go back into yourself. Truth dwells in the inner man': Husserl, *Paris Lectures*, p.39; see also Edmund Husserl, *Cartesian Meditations*, trans. D. Cairns (The Hague: Martinus Nijhoff, 1970) p. 157.

37. *Cartesian Meditations*, p.1. For general discussions of Husserl's divergences from Descartes, see James Street Fulton, 'The Cartesianism of Phenomenology', *The Philosophical Review*, XLIX:3 (May 1940) pp.285–308, and Gaston Berger, *The Cogito in Husserl's Philosophy*, trans. K. McLaughlin (Evanston, Illinois: Northwestern University Press, 1972) pp.106–10.

38. See, for example, the beautifully ambivalent sentence which marks the climax of Husserl's description of the phenomenological attitude in the first book of the *Ideas*; he claims that with the suspension of the natural attitude 'a central though not fully developed thought of (the quite otherwise oriented) meditation of Descartes comes at last to its own': Edmund Husserl, *Ideas: General Introduction to Pure Phenomenology*, trans. W. R. B. Gibson (New York: Collier, 1962) p.132; for other invocations of Descartes, see Husserl, 'Inaugural Lecture at Freiburg im Breisgau (1917)', trans. R. W. Jordan, in Lester E. Embree, ed., *Life-World and Consciousness: Essays for Aron Gurwitsch* (Evanston, Illinois: Northwestern University Press, 1972) p.13, and Husserl, *The Idea of Phenomenology*, trans. W. P. Alston and G. Nakhnikian (The Hague: Martinus Nijhoff, 1964) p.23.

39. Husserl, 'Philosophy as a Rigorous Science', in *Phenomenology and the Crisis of Philosophy*, trans. Q. Lauer (New York: Harper

Torchbooks, 1965) p.144; Husserl, *Logical Investigations*, trans. J. N. Findlay (New York: Humanities Press, 1970) vol.I, p.252. The parallel to Descartes has been noted in Walter Biemel, 'The Decisive Phases in the Development of Husserl's Philosophy', trans. R. O. Elveton, in Elveton, ed., *The Phenomenology of Husserl* (Chicago: Quadrangle Books, 1970) p.164.

40. *Cartesian Meditations*, p.7.
41. *Crisis*, p.79.
42. Ibid, p.124.
43. *Cartesian Meditations*, p.9.
44. Ibid, p.12.
45. Ibid, pp.12–13, 15–16.
46. Eugen Fink, 'The Phenomenological Philosophy of Edmund Husserl and Contemporary Criticism', in Elveton, ed., *The Phenomenology of Husserl*, p.98.
47. Ibid, p.99.
48. Descartes, *Meditations on First Philosophy*, trans, N. K. Smith, in Descartes, *Philosophical Writings* (New York: Modern Library, 1958) p. 193.
49. *Cartesian Meditations*, p.24.
50. *Ideas*, p.97; see also Erazim Kohák, *Idea and Experience* (Chicago: University of Chicago Press, 1978) pp.37–8.
51. *Ideas*, pp.97–8; Kohák, pp.36–7.
52. Descartes, *Meditations*, p.193.
53. *Cartesian Meditations*, p.20; see Levinas, pp.91–2.
54. *Cartesian Meditations*, p. 33.
55. Ibid, pp.35–6; *Crisis*, p.77.
56. Franz Brentano, *Psychology from an Empirical Standpoint*, trans. D. B. Terrell, in R. M. Chisholm, ed., *Realism and the Background of Phenomenology* (New York: Free Press, 1960) pp.50–51. For a contrast of Brentano and Husserl on this point, see Marvin Farber, *The Foundation of Phenomenology* (Albany, New York: State University of New York Press, 1968) pp.11–15.
57. *Ideas*, p.229.
58. *Cartesian Meditations*, p.33.
59. Maurice Natanson has developed the implications of this point for Sartre's interpretation of Husserl, in 'Phenomenology and Existentialism', *The Modern Schoolman*, 37 (1959) pp.1–10.
60. Sartre, 'Intentionality', p.5.
61. *Crisis*, p.81; cf. Fulton, p.302; 'In the second *Meditation*, Descartes was not in fact interested in pure, transcendental subjectivity, but in a thinking substance distinct from extended substance. And it may be inferred that, had he really discovered transcendental subjectivity, it would have been both astonishing and unwelcome.'
62. *Crisis*, pp.80, 82; *Cartesian Meditations*, p.90, ft.2.
63. *Cartesian Meditations*, p.24.
64. Descartes, *Meditations*, p. 185.
65. *Crisis*, p.81; see also Husserl, 'Phenomenology' (article for the

176   *Notes and References*

Encyclopedia Britannica) trans. R. E. Palmer, *Journal of the British Society for Phenomenology*, 2:2 (May 1971) pp.82–3, and Husserl, *Formal and Transcendental Logic*, trans. D. Cairns (The Hague: Martinus Nijhoff, 1969) pp.227–8.

66. Enzo Paci, *The Function of the Sciences and the Meaning of Man*, trans. P. Piccone and J. E. Hansen (Evanston, Illinois: Northwestern University Press, 1972) pp.148–9; see also Ludwig Landgrebe, 'Husserl's Departure from Cartesianism', in Elveton, *The Phenomenology of Husserl*, pp.275–6.

67. See Farber, pp.25–60, for a summary of the argument of the book and a discussion of the criticisms of Frege and others.

68. See, for example, Victor Delbos, 'Husserl: Sa critique du psychologisme et sa conception d'une logique pure', *Revue de métaphysique et de morale*, XIX:5 (1911) pp.685–98.

69. Berger noted the prevalence of this interpretation of Husserl's development in his *The Cogito in Husserl's Philosophy*, p.6. Heidegger reacted this way upon his first reading of the second volume as well: see 'My Way into Phenomenology', trans. by J. Stambaugh, in *On Time and Being* (New York: Harper & Row, 1972) p. 76. For other examples, see Spiegelberg, *The Phenomenological Movement*, vol.I, pp.101–3.

70. Husserl, *Logical Investigations*, I, pp.262–3.

71. Ibid, p.48 (for a summary of the article, see Farber, pp.170–95).

72. Husserl, ibid, p.261.

73. For an extensive analysis of Dilthey's conception of a 'descriptive psychology', see Husserl, *Phenomenological Psychology*, trans. J. Scanlon (The Hague: Martinus Nijhoff, 1977) pp.1–14.

74. Husserl, *The Idea of Phenomenology*, p.5; 'Inaugural Lecture', p.12; Husserl, *Phenomenology and the Foundations of the Sciences* (*Ideas*, III) trans. T. E. Klein and W. E. Pehl (The Hague: Martinus Nijhoff, 1980) p.59.

75. See, for example, *Crisis*, pp.79–80.

76. Husserl, 'Philosophy as a Rigorous Science', p.116; *Ideas*, pp.39–40, 55, 57, 193.

77. Husserl, ibid, p.193.

78. Husserl, *The Idea of Phenomenology*, p.33; 'Philosophy as a Rigorous Science', p.91; 'Inaugural Lecture', p.12.

79. Husserl, *Ideas*, pp.150–1, 165–6, 194; *Formal and Transcendental Logic*, pp.252–3; *Cartesian Meditations*, pp.25, 32.

80. Husserl, 'Phenomenology', p.77.

81. Husserl, ibid, pp.30–1, 38–41, 81; cf. *Ideas*, pp.38, 206.

82. Husserl, *Phenomenological Psychology*, p.31.

83. Ibid, p.32; Husserl, 'Phenomenology', p.88.

84. Husserl, *Phenomenological Psychology*, pp.40–1; 'Phenomenology', pp.79, 84–6; *Ideas*, pp.7–8; *Formal and Transcendental Logic*, pp.254–5; *Crisis*, pp.205, 236.

85. Husserl, *Ideen zu einer reinen Phänomenologie und phänomenologis-*

chen Philosophie, Zweites Buch (The Hague: Martinus Nijhoff, 1952) p.313.
86. Husserl, 'Phenomenology', p.77.
87. *Ideas*, III, p.22.
88. A chiasmus is a rhetorical form in which, as Fowler explains, 'the terms in the second of two parallel phrases reverse the order of those in the first to which they correspond': *Modern English Usage*, 2nd edn (Oxford: Oxford University Press, 1965) p.86; *vide* Vince Lombardi's immortal 'When the going gets tough, the tough get going', which (of course) Fowler did not quote.
89. *Ideas*, pp.195–6.
90. Ibid, p.9; see also Husserl, *Phenomenological Psychology*, p.32; *Formal and Transcendental Logic*, p.253; *Cartesian Meditations*, pp.32, 131.
91. Husserl, 'Phenomenology', pp.86–7; for a penetrating discussion, see Jacques Derrida, *Speech and Phenomena*, trans. D. B. Allison (Evanston, Illinois: Northwestern University Press, 1973) pp.11–15.
92. *Crisis*, p.137; cf. p.148.
93. For a discussion of the genesis of the *Crisis*, see David Carr, *Phenomenology and the Problem of History* (Evanston: Northwestern University Press, 1974) pp.181–4.
94. *Crisis*, pp.23–59.
95. Ibid, pp.103–89.
96. Husserl, *Paris Lectures*, p.4; *Cartesian Meditations*, p.2.
97. *Crisis*, p.3, ft.1.
98. Ibid, p.52.
99. Ibid, pp.73–4.
100. Ibid, p.3, ft.1.
101. See Paul Ricoeur, 'Objectivity and Subjectivity in History', in *History and Truth*, trans. C. A. Kelbley (Evanston: Northwestern University Press, 1965) pp.21–40: note especially the equating of Husserl's approach to history with Brunschvicg's, pp.33, 35; see also Ricoeur, *Husserl: An Analysis of his Phenomenology*, trans. E. G. Ballard and L. E. Embree (Evanston: Northwestern University Press, 1967) pp.168–70.
102. *Crisis*, p.73.
103. Ibid, p.70.
104. Ibid, pp.49–50.
105. Ibid, pp.47–8.
106. Ludwig Landgrebe, 'The World as a Philosophical Problem', *Philosophy and Phenomenological Research*, I:1 (1940) pp.38–58; Hans-Georg Gadamer, 'The Science of the Life-World', in *Philosophical Hermeneutics*, trans. D. E. Linge (Berkeley, California: University of California Press, 1976) pp.182–96; Carr, pp.134–61.
107. Carr, p.198; cf. Ricoeur, *Husserl*, pp.138–9.
108. *Crisis*, p.172.

178   *Notes and References*

109. Husserl, *Experience and Judgement*, trans. J. S. Churchill and K. Ameriks (Evanston: Northwestern University Press, 1973) p.50.
110. *Crisis*, p.51.
111. Husserl, *Experience and Judgement*, p.47.
112. *Crisis*, p.155.
113. Van Breda, pp.413–5, 424–5; it should also be noted that Merleau-Ponty had a copy of Van Breda's dissertation from 1941 onwards, which included a ninety-page appendix consisting of unpublished texts by Husserl (p.420).
114. Ricoeur, *Husserl*, pp.204–5.
115. *PP*, p.vii.
116. *PP*, p.274, ft.1.
117. Marvin Farber, *Naturalism and Subjectivism* (Springfield, Ill.: Thomas, 1959) pp.356–65, quotes from Husserl's predominantly negative marginal notes to his copy of *Being and Time*.
118. For an evaluation of Merleau-Ponty's reading of Husserl, see Spiegelberg, II, pp.517–18, 531–9.
119. *PrP*, p.72.
120. *S*, p.84.
121. *S*, p.160.
122. Husserl, *Experience and Judgement*, p.50; Merleau-Ponty did, however, note that Husserl himself saw the return to the life-world as 'a preparatory step which should be followed by the properly philosophical task of universal constitution' (*S*, p.110).
123. *PP*, p.viii.
124. *PP*, pp.viii, ix, 23; cf. *VI*, pp.14–16.
125. *PP*, pp.xx, 24, 330; *PrP*, p.17.
126. *PrP*, pp.29, 36–7.
127. *PrP*, p.30.
128. *S*, p.22.
129. *PP*, pp.viii, xxi.
130. *PP*, pp.xi, xiii–xiv; cf. *S*, p.175; Merleau-Ponty here follows the discussion in Fink, pp.95, 101–2, 110, 112–16. Parallels between Merleau-Ponty's position and that of Heidegger in his posthumously published *Fundamental Problems of Phenomenology* have been developed by John D. Caputo, 'The Question of Being and Trans-cendental Phenomenology: Reflections on Heidegger's Relationship to Husserl', *Research in Phenomenology*, VII (1977) pp.87, 91, 104.
131. *PP*, p.60, cf. 96; and *SB*, pp.244–5.
132. *PP*, p.47; for a discussion of the 'constancy hypothesis', see Aron Gurwitsch, 'Some Aspects and Developments of Gestalt Psychology', a 1936 article which acknowledges Merleau-Ponty's aid, trans. R. M. Zaner, in Gurwitsch, *Studies in Phenomenological Psychology* (Evanston: Northwestern University Press, 1966) pp.4–5.
133. *S*, p.164.
134. *PrP*, p.79.
135. Husserl, *Ideas*, p.49.
136. Ibid, pp.50–1.

137. Ibid, pp.56–7.
138. *PrP*, pp.90–2; *S*, pp.107–8; for a critique of Merleau-Ponty's interpretation, see Jacques Derrida, *Edmund Husserl's Origin of Geometry: an Introduction*, trans. J. P. Leavey (Stony Brook, N.Y.: Nicolas Hays, 1978) pp.111–17.
139. *S*, p.108.
140. This understanding of the significance of phenomenology can be found as early as *SB*, pp.171–2, where Scheler's notion of a 'material *a priori*' is discussed.
141. *PP*, p.221.
142. *PP*, p.388.
143. *PP*, p.221; *PrP*, p.68.
144. *PP*, pp.xvi, xiv.
145. *PP*, p.xvii: this interpretation differs markedly from Sartre's discussion of Husserl in 'Intentionality'.
146. *PP*, p.121, ft.5.
147. *PP*, p.243.
148. *Ideas*, pp.226–230; as early as his review of Sartre's *L'Imagination*, Merleau-Ponty expressed reservations about the concept of *hylé* (p.761).
149. *PP*, pp.243, xviii, 428–9.
150. *PP*, pp.ix–x.
151. *PP*, p.x.
152. *PP*, p.xviii.
153. *PP*, p.xiii.
154. *PP*, pp.xiii, 456.
155. *PP*, p.297.
156. *PP*, p.377.
157. *PP*, p.424.
158. *PP*, p.276, ft.1.
159. *PP*, p.129.
160. *PP*, p.383.
161. *PP*, pp.82, 85, 92, 140–1, 181.
162. *PP*, pp.402–4.
163. *PP*, p.404.
164. *PP*, p.406.
165. *PP*, p.xi.
166. 'Reading Montaigne', in *S*, pp.198–210; the essay, which dates from 1947, can be read in part as a response to Brunschvicg's *Descartes et Pascal, lecteurs de Montaigne* (Neuchâtel: Baconnière, 1945), which sees Descartes as the culmination of the reflection initiated by Montaigne.
167. *S*, p.199.
168. *S*, p.200.
169. Descartes, *Meditations*, p.176.
170. *S*, p.202; for a more extended discussion of the importance of Montaigne for Merleau-Ponty, see Thomas Langan, *Merleau-Ponty's Critique of Reason* (New Haven: Yale University Press, 1966) ch.5,

180 *Notes and References*

and John O'Neill, *Perception, Expression, and History* (Evanston: Northwestern University Press, 1970) ch.6.
171. *PrP*, pp.45–6; *S*, pp.98, 110. The English translation of the résumé of the Sorbonne course (*PrP*, pp.43–95) omits the second part, 'The Convergence of Contemporary Psychology and Phenomenology'. To fill that gap, I have employed Alexandre Métraux's German translation, Merleau-Ponty, *Vorlesungen* (Berlin: Walter de Gruyter, 1973) pp.129–226, which includes extensive and helpful notes as well as hitherto unpublished materials from Merleau-Ponty's own lecture notes.
172. *S*, p.102; see also *PrP*, p.73.
173. *S*, p.99.
174. *PrP*, pp.55–9, 78–80, 85–8; *S*, pp.102–4.
175. *PrP*, pp.72, 80–5, 88–92; *S*, pp.104–9.
176. *Crisis*, p.206.
177. Ibid, p.257.
178. Martin Heidegger, *Being and Time*, trans. J. Macquarrie and E. Robinson (New York: Harper & Row, 1962) pp.28–31, 71–7.
179. *PrP*, p.94; see also *VI*, p.266.
180. *PrP*, p.59.
181. *PrP*, p.73; see Sartre, *Imagination*, p.129.
182. Jean-Paul Sartre, *The Emotions: Outline of a Theory*, trans. B. Fretchman (New York: Philosophical Library, 1948) p.20; cf. Peter Winch's distinction between 'conceptual' and 'empirical' inquiries, *The Idea of a Social Science* (London: Routledge & Kegan Paul, 1958) pp.15–18.
183. *PrP*, p.75.
184. Ibid. Merleau-Ponty goes on to note, 'Husserl never explicitly stated this. But at least he was aware of the necessity of defending phenomenology against verbalism', and suggests that Husserl's exchange with Lévy-Bruhl led to a revised notion of eidetic variation (*PrP*, pp.75–6).
185. *SNS*, pp.92–3.
186. *SNS*, pp.83–6; *Vorlesungen*, I, pp.189–226; VI, pp.20–23. For a comprehensive discussion of Merleau-Ponty's use of *Gestalt* psychology, see Embree, 'Merleau-Ponty's Examination of Gestalt Psychology'.
187. *SNS*, p.87.
188. *SNS*, p.89.
189. Ibid.
190. Ibid.
191. *PrP*, p.85; *S*, p.115; cf. Lévi-Strauss, 'French Sociology', in G. Gurvitsch and W. E. Moore, eds, *Twentieth Century Sociology* (New York: Philosophical Library, 1945) p.516.
192. *PrP*, p.86.
193. *SNS*, p.89.
194. *S*, p.114.
195. *SNS*, p.90.
196. Ibid.

197. *SNS*, p.90; cf. *S*, p.115.
198. Marcel Mauss, *The Gift*, trans. I. Cunnison (New York: W. W. Norton, 1967) pp.7–8.
199. *S*, pp.114–25; cf. Lévi-Strauss, 'Introduction à l'oeuvre de Marcel Mauss', in Marcel Mauss, *Sociologie et Anthropologie* (Paris: Presses Universitaires de France, 1950) pp.ix–lii.
200. *S*, p.116; Lévi-Strauss, 'Introduction', pp.xxxvii–xlvii. Merleau-Ponty reverses these categories when he writes that Mauss 'looks for the principle of exchange in *mana*, as he had looked for that of magic in *hau*' (*S*, p.116). '*Mana*' played a central role in Mauss's 1904 study, *A General Theory of Magic*, trans. R. Brain (New York: W. W. Norton, 1975) pp.108–12, 136–8. '*Hau*' was of primary importance in the 1925 *Essai sue le don*; see *The Gift*, pp.8–10. '*Mana*' is mentioned at the start of this discussion of '*hau*' (*The Gift*, p.8), but Merleau-Ponty's way of posing the relationship seems to have been a slip of the pen.
201. *S*, p.116.
202. Lévi-Strauss, 'Introduction', p.xxxix.
203. *S*, p.116.
204. Lévi-Strauss, 'Introduction', p.1.
205. Ibid, p.xliv.
206. In his inaugural lecture at the Collège de France, Lévi-Strauss cited Merleau-Ponty's essay 'The Philosopher and Sociology' approvingly and went on to develop the implications for ethnology; see *Structural Anthropology*, II, p.26.
207. *S*, p.117.
208. *S*, p.118.
209. *S*, p.119.
210. Ibid; Merleau-Ponty's position in this respect resembles Alfred Schutz's requirement that sociological explanation exhibit what Weber termed 'meaning adequacy' as well as 'causal adequacy'; see Schutz, *Collected Papers*, vol.1 (The Hague: Martinus Nijhoff, 1971) pp.59, 24–5, 34–6, 43, and Schutz, *The Phenomenology of the Social World*, trans. G. Walsh and F. Lehnert (Evanston: Northwestern University Press, 1967) pp.234–6. But for a wide-ranging contrast of the more general positions of Schutz and Merleau-Ponty, see Fred R. Dallmayr, 'Genesis and Validation of Social Knowledge: Lessons from Merleau-Ponty', in J. Bein, ed., *Phenomenology and the Social Sciences* (The Hague: Martinus Nijhoff, 1978) pp.74–106.
211. *S*, p.112.
212. *S*, p.101.
213. *Structural Anthropology*, II, p.7.
214. Cf. *SNS*, p.90, with Lévi-Strauss, 'Introduction', p.xxx; 'French Sociology', pp.518–20, 528; and *Structural Anthropology*, trans. C. Jacobson and B. G. Schoepf (New York: Basec, 1963) p.65.
215. *Structural Anthropology*, II, p.38.
216. Lévi-Strauss, *The Naked Man*, trans. J. and D. Weightman (New York: Harper & Row, 1981) p.687.

182   *Notes and References*

217. *Structural Anthropology*, II, p.37.
218. Ibid, p.40.
219. Ibid.
220. Lévi-Strauss, *Structural Anthropology*, pp.56–7; cf. also pp.19, 33; and Lévi-Strauss, *The Raw and the Cooked*, trans. J. and D. Weightman (New York: Harper & Row, 1969) p.11.
221. Lévi-Strauss, *The Savage Mind*, p.252.
222. Lévi-Strauss cited Köhler at the close of his preface to the first edition of *The Elementary Structures of Kinship*, trans. J. H. Bell, J. R. von Sturmer and R. Needham (Boston: Beacon Press, 1969) p.xxvi; for an early reading of the book from the standpoint of existential phenomenology, see Simone de Beauvoir, 'Les structures élémentaires de la parenté, *Temps Modernes*, 5 (1949) pp.943–9. Clarke, pp.65–6, discusses the plausibility of such readings.
223. *Structural Anthropology*, I, p.203.
224. *The Raw and the Cooked*, p.11, citing Paul Ricoeur, 'Structure and Hermeneutics', in *The Conflict of Interpretations*, p.33; Ino Rossi, 'Intellectual Antecedents of Lévi-Strauss' Notion of Unconscious', in Rossi, ed., *The Unconscious in Culture* (New York: E. P. Dutton, 1974) pp.7–30 contrasts Lévi-Strauss's conception with its predecessors.
225. Lévi-Strauss, *Tristes Tropiques*, pp.57–8.
226. Lévi-Strauss, *The Savage Mind*, p.247.
227. *SNS*, p.93; cf. *PrP*, pp.21–2.
228. *VI*, p.182; for even earlier reservations about the notion, see Merleau-Ponty, *Vorlesungen*, p.302: 'the reduction of all experience [*Erfahrung*] to lived experience [*Erleben*] is a bad phenomenology, a phenomenological psychology'.
229. *S*, p.112.
230. *PrP*, p.41.
231. *VI*, p.240.

Chapter 3: Others

1. *SB*, p.221; cf. pp.126, 156.
2. *PP*, pp.346–65.
3. *PrP*, pp.96–155; *CAL*, pp.40–8.
4. *PW*, pp.131–46.
5. *AD*, pp.107, 138, 142, 153, 161–2.
6. See especially the 1958–9 course, 'The Possibility of Philosophy', *TFL*, pp.106–8. I have restored Claude Lefort's title for this course since it is a bit more accurate than the substitute proposed by the English translator.
7. *VI*, p.193.
8. See especially the discussion in *S*, pp.166–72.
9. See, for example, *PP*, p.355; *CAL*, p.48; *SNS*, p.68.

10. See, for example, *PP*, pp.337, 351, 373; *CAL*, p.3; *SNS*, p.201.
11. For other discussions of Merleau-Ponty's critique of Sartre's analysis of the other, see Margaret Whitford, *Merleau-Ponty's Critique of Sartre's Philosophy* (Lexington: French Forum, 1982) pp.98–114, and Francois H. Lapointe, 'The Existence of Alter Egos: Jean-Paul Sartre and Maurice Merleau-Ponty', *Journal of Phenomenological Psychology*, 6 (1975–6) pp.209–16. I should also note my own earlier discussion 'Lordship and Bondage in Merleau-Ponty and Sartre', *Political Theory*, 7:2 (1979) pp.201–27, which has been modified in a number of ways in the chapter which follows.
12. See, for example, the brief sketch in A. J. Ayer, *Philosophy in the Twentieth Century* (New York: Random House, 1982) which comes to the rather surprising conclusion that 'Merleau-Ponty's treatment of freedom adds nothing to Sartre's' (p.232).
13. *SNS*, pp.72, 69. Sartre, it should be noted, was equally disturbed by the *Phenomenology of Perception*. In a 1973 interview he commented, 'We were starting from the same philosophy, namely Husserl and Heidegger, but he did not draw the same conclusions from it that I did. It is impossible for me to get my bearings in the philosophy of perception.': 'An Interview with Jean-Paul Sartre', in Paul Arthur Schilpp (ed.), *The Philosophy of Jean-Paul Sartre* (La Salle, Ill.: Open Court, 1981) pp.43–4.
14. Cf. Jean-Paul Sartre, *Being and Nothingness*, trans. H. E. Barnes (New York: Philosophical Library, 1956) pp.439–85, with *PP*, p.xix; cf. Sartre, 'No Exit', in *No Exit and Three Other Plays*, trans. S. Gilbert (New York: Vintage, 1949) p.47, with *PrP*, p.25.
15. *PP*, pp.434–56.
16. *SNS*, p.73.
17. *SNS*, p.77; cf. *TFL*, pp.48–9 where, in a 1954 course on the 'problem of passivity', Sartre's rejection of Freud's concept of the unconscious is taken to task.
18. *SNS*, p.81.
19. *SNS*, p.73.
20. *PW*, p.62.
21. *AD*, pp.188–9, 153–4.
22. *VI*, pp.69, 170–1, 175–6; for a discussion of the degree to which Merleau-Ponty is criticising himself as well as Sartre, see John Sallis, *Phenomenology and the Return to Beginnings* (Pittsburgh: Duquesne University Press, 1973) pp.64–9.
23. Simone de Beauvoir, 'Merleau-Ponty et le Pseudo-Sartrisme', *Les Temps Modernes*, 10:114–5 (1955) pp.2072–122; for a discussion of the article, largely sympathetic to de Beauvoir and Sartre, see James F. Sheridan, 'On Ontology and Politics: A Polemic', *Dialogue*, 7 (1968) pp.449–60. For a more balanced account, see Whitford, pp.41–51.
24. *S*, p.159.
25. Paul Valéry, *Collected Works*, vol.6: *Monsieur Teste*, trans. J. Mathews (Princeton: Princeton University Press, 1973) p.121.

26. For a concise critique of the argument from analogy, see Norman Malcolm, 'Knowledge of Other Minds', *Journal of Philosophy*, 55 (1958) pp.969–78. For a defence of the argument, see A. J. Ayer, *The Problem of Knowledge* (Harmondsworth: Penguin, 1956) pp.214–22; Ayer has contrasted his own position to that of Merleau-Ponty in *Philosophy in the Twentieth Century*, pp.219–22.
27. *Being and Nothingness*, p.224.
28. *PP*, p.224; cf. *SB*, p.156; *PrP*, pp.115–16.
29. For a slightly different list of the parties involved, see *PrP*, p.115; cf. *VI*, pp.79–80.
30. Descartes, *Meditations*, p.190.
31. Ibid, p.235; the problem of the 'phantom limb' is analysed by Merleau-Ponty in *PP*, pp.76–87.
32. Descartes, *Meditations*, pp.201–4.
33. *CAL*, p.41.
34. Descombes, p.21; the exchange comes from a 1921 colloquy.
35. Ibid.
36. G. W. F. Hegel, *Phenomenology of Spirit*, trans. A. V. Miller (Oxford: Clarendon Press, 1977) pp.111–19.
37. For Kojève's impact, see Descombes, pp.9–16, 27–48; Mark Poster, *Existential Marxism in Modern France* (Princeton: Princeton University Press, 1975) pp.8–18, 32–5; George L. Kline, 'The Existentialist Rediscovery of Hegel and Marx', in E. Lee and M. Mandelbaum (eds), *Phenomenology and Existentialism* (Baltimore: Johns Hopkins Press, 1967) pp.114–21; and Jean Hyppolite, 'La "Phénoménologie" de Hegel et la pensée française contemporaine', in *Figures de la pensée philosophique* (Paris: Presses Universitaires de France, 1971) vol.1, pp.231–41. For a comprehensive discussion of Kojève's writings, see Patrick Riley, 'Introduction to the Reading of Alexandre Kojève', *Political Theory*, 9:1 (1981) pp.5–48.
38. This point is developed in Descombes, pp.20–23.
39. The synopsis in this paragraph and the next is drawn from the article Kojève published in *Mesures* in 1939, reprinted in Alexandre Kojève, *Introduction to the Reading of Hegel*, trans. J. H. Nichols, Jr (New York: Basic Books, 1969) pp.3–30.
40. Ibid, p.20. For a critique of Kojève's account of Hegel's argument, see Mikel Dufrenne, 'Actualitie de Hegel', in *Jalons* (The Hague: Martinus Nijhoff, 1966) pp.72–6; Jean Wahl, 'A Propos de l'introduction a la Phénoménologie de Hegel par A. Kojéve', *Deucalion*, 5 (1955) pp.77–99; Tran-Duc-Thao, 'The Phenomenology of Mind and its Real Content', trans. R. D'Amico, *Telos*, 8 (1971) pp.91–110; George Armstrong Kelly, *Hegel's Retreat from Eleusis* (Princeton: Princeton University Press, 1978) pp.29–54; and my 'Lordship and Bondage in Merleau-Ponty and Sartre', pp.202–5.
41. Despite claims to the contrary by many commentators, Sartre did *not* attend Kojève's lectures; see Kojève's letter to this effect quoted in the paperback edition (1969) of Lee and Mandelbaum, p.vii. This, of course, does not foreclose the possibility that Sartre knew of the

contents of the lectures by word of mouth or through transcripts. For discussions of parallels between Sartre and Kojève, see Descombes, pp.48–54, and Kline, pp.123–31. For the equally compelling argument that Sartre's view of Hegel 'has been formed *ad hoc*, in connection with his phenomenological philosophy' and thus 'not derived from the French Hegelian tradition', see Klaus Hartmann, *Sartre's Ontology* (Evanston: Northwestern University Press, 1966) p.xvi. Hartmann's fine study explores the argument of *Being and Nothingness* in light of Hegel's *Logic* and thus focuses on a dimension of the book which a reading informed only by the *Phenomenology* tends to overlook.

42. *Being and Nothingness*, pp.236–8.
43. Ibid, pp.238–40; cf. pp.231–2, 244.
44. Ibid, pp.240–3.
45. Ibid, p.243 (cf. Hartmann, pp.118–19, for a defence of Hegel against this charge).
46. Ibid, p.243.
47. For discussions of Kojève's influence on Merleau-Ponty, see Rabil, pp.76–84; Barry Cooper, 'Hegel and the Genesis of Merleau-Ponty's Atheism', *Studies in Religion*, 6 (1976–7) pp.665–71; and Cooper, *Merleau-Ponty and Marxism*, pp.14–16, 38–40, 114–15, 136–7. For examples of his use of the motif of Lordship and Bondage in his political writings, see *SNS*, p.142, *S*, p.215, *H&T*, pp.37, 102–3, 109–11, 155.
48. *PP*, p.355; see also *SNS*, p.68. *PrP*, p.142, however, finds something akin to the struggle even within childhood.
49. Husserl, *Paris Lectures*, p.34.
50. Husserl, *Formal and Transcendental Logic*, p.237.
51. Husserl, *Cartesian Meditations*, pp.89–151. The *Cartesian Meditations* were held back from publication by Husserl, at least in part because of dissatisfaction with the account of the other, a dissatisfaction which would seem to post-date the *Formal and Transcendental Logic* which describes the forthcoming discussion of the other in the *Cartesian Meditations* as 'short' (p.243). For commentaries on the Fifth Meditation, see Paul Ricoeur, *Husserl*, pp.115–42; Carr, *Phenomenology and the Problem of History*, pp.84–99; Alfred Schutz, 'The Problem of Transcendental Intersubjectivity in Husserl', *Collected Papers*, vol.III, pp.51–84; and Frederick A. Elliston, 'Husserl's Phenomenology of Empathy', in F. A. Elliston and P. McCormick (eds), *Husserl: Expositions and Appraisals* (Notre Dame: University of Notre Dame Press, 1977) pp.213–31. On the more general problem of the other in Husserl, see Michael Theunissen, *The Other*, trans. C. Macann (Cambridge, Mass.: MIT Press, 1984) pp.13–163.
52. *Cartesian Meditations*, pp.93–4.
53. Ricoeur, *Husserl*, p.118.
54. *Cartesian Meditations*, pp.106, 92–4.
55. Ibid, p.96.

56. Ibid, pp.96–7. The German terms *Körper* and *Leib* allow Husserl to make a distinction between bodies of any sort (*Körper*) and the body of a living person (*Leib*). I will translate the former as simply 'body', the latter as 'lived' or 'living body', and – whenever a misunderstanding might arise – will use the German terms. Dorion Cairns employs 'animate organism' as a translation for *Leib* in his rendering of *Cartesian Meditations*, a choice which strikes me as having neither economy, accuracy, nor grace in its favour.

57. Suzanne Bachelard, *A Study of Husserl's Formal and Transcendental Logic*, trans. L. E. Embree (Evanston: Northwestern University Press, 1968) p.108; *Cartesian Meditations*, p.98. See also Merleau-Ponty's discussion of a parallel argument in *Ideen* II, in *S*, pp.173–4.

58. *Cartesian Meditations*, p.99.

59. Ibid, p.109; following this argument, Merleau-Ponty speaks of a 'lacunary' perception of the other, in *CAL*, p.42.

60. *Cartesian Meditations*, pp.110–11.

61. Ibid, p.114.

62. Ibid, p.115.

63. Ibid, pp.116–19.

64. Sartre, *The Transcendence of the Ego*, trans. F. Williams and R. Kirkpatrick (New York: Noonday Press, 1957) pp.37–8, 41–2.

65. Ibid, p.83.

66. Ibid, p.95.

67. Ibid, p.104.

68. *Being and Nothingness*, p.235.

69. Ibid, pp.234–5.

70. Schutz concedes Sartre's argument; see *Collected Papers*, I, pp.183–4, 197. For a defence of Husserl, see Frederick A. Elliston, 'Sartre and Husserl on Interpersonal Relationships', in H. J. Silverman and F. A. Elliston (eds), *Jean-Paul Sartre: Contemporary Approaches to His Philosophy* (Pittsburgh: Duquesne University Press, 1980) pp.157–67.

71. *Being and Nothingness*, p.233; for a critique of Sartre's characterisation of Husserl's argument, see Maurice Natanson, 'The Problem of Others in *Being and Nothingness*', in Schilpp (ed.), *The Philosophy of Jean-Paul Sartre*, pp.326–44.

72. *Being and Nothingness*, p.235.

73. *CAL*, pp.45–6.

74. *SB*, p.221.

75. *PP*, p.352; see also *PrP*, pp.116–17.

76. *Cartesian Meditations*, p.111; Merleau-Ponty quotes this passage in *CAL*, p.43; see also the discussion of a parallel argument from *Ideen* II, in *S*, pp.168–9.

77. *Cartesian Meditations*, p.111.

78. Ibid.

79. Ibid, p.112.

80. *PP*, pp.346–65.

81. See especially *AD*, pp.142, 153, 155, 161–2.
82. *VI*, pp.50–104.
83. For helpful commentaries on this section, see Marjorie Grene, *Sartre* (New York: New Viewpoints, 1973) pp.140–61; Hartmann, pp.108–25; and Theunissen, pp.199–254.
84. *Being and Nothingness*, p.255.
85. Ibid, p.256.
86. Ibid, pp.259–60.
87. Ibid, pp.257–8.
88. Ibid, p.257.
89. Ibid, pp.261–3, 266.
90. Ibid, p.363.
91. Ibid, pp.364–412.
92. *PP*, p.355.
93. *PP*, p.361.
94. *PP*, p.348.
95. *PP*, p.352.
96. *PP*, p.351.
97. Ibid.
98. *PP*, p.354.
99. *PP*, p.352.
100. *PrP*, p.118; *CAL*, p.43.
101. For a discussion of the courses, see Hugh J. Silverman, 'Translator's Preface', in *CAL*, pp.xxxiii–xxxix.
102. *PrP*, p.119.
103. Wolfgang Köhler, *The Mentality of Apes*, trans. E. Winte (London: Routledge & Kegan Paul, 1925) pp.317–24; Paul Guillaume, *Imitation in Children*, trans. E. P. Halperin (Chicago: University of Chicago Press, 1971) pp.150–4; and Henri Wallon, *Les origines du charactere chez l'enfant* (Paris: Presses Universitaire de France, 1949) pp.218–34 (first published as 'Comment se dévéloppee chez l'enfant la notion du corps proper', *Journal de Psychologie* (1931) pp.705–48).
104. *PrP*, p.135.
105. *PrP*, pp.135–41; for a translation of Lacan's paper, see his *Écrits: A Selection*, trans. A. Sheridan (New York: W. W. Norton, 1977) pp.1–7.
106. *PrP*, p.136.
107. Ibid.
108. *PrP*, p.108.
109. Lacan, *Écrits*, p.6.
110. Ibid; Lacan makes his debts to Kojève most explicit in a lecture from 1946, 'Propos sur la causalité psychique', included in the French edition of *Écrits* (Paris: Seuil, 1966) but not in the English translation; see pp.172, 181. For a discussion of the relationship between Kojève's reading of Hegel and Lacan's discussion of the mirror stage, see Anthony Wilden, 'Lacan and the Discourse of the Other', in

Lacan, *The Language of the Self* (New York: Delta, 1968) pp. 192–6.

111. Jacques Lacan, 'Maurice Merleau-Ponty', *Les Temps Modernes*, 17:184–5 (1961) pp.245–54.

112. Ibid, p.249. Lacan's opinion was not changed by the publication of *The Visible and the Invisible* three years later. He devoted four weeks of his seminar to the book and while he found certain of Merleau-Ponty's formulations to parallel his own use of topological models of the psyche, he concluded that Merleau-Ponty still remained tied to the standpoint of 'the philosophy of the cogito'; see Jacques Lacan, *The Four Fundamental Concepts of Psycho-Analysis*, trans. A. Sheridan (New York: W. W. Norton, 1978) pp.70–119, especially the closing exchange with Jacques-Alain Miller, who questioned, 'if Merleau-Ponty is seeking to subvert Cartesian space, is it in order to open up the transcendental space of the relation to the Other? No, it is in order to accede either to the so-called dimension of inter-subjectivity, or to that so-called pre-objective, savage, primordial world. This leads me to ask you if *Le Visible et l'invisible* has led you to change anything in the article that you published on Merleau-Ponty in a number of *Les Temps Modernes*?' Lacan replied 'Absolutely nothing.' (p.119.)

113. For a differing assessment of the impact of Freud on Merleau-Ponty, see André Green, 'Du Comportement a la chair: itinéraire de Merleau-Ponty', *Critique*, no.211 (1964) pp.1017–46.

114. *PP*, p.166.

115. *S*, p.229. See also, *TFL*, pp.129–30; his exchange with Lacan in *La Psychoanalyse et son enseignement*, *Bulletin de la Société Française de Philosophie*, 52 (1957) pp.98–9; and the summary of his response to papers by Stein, Laplanche and Leclaire in Henry Ey (ed.), *L'Inconscient, VIe Colloque de Bonneval* (Paris: Desclée de Brouwer, 1966) p.143.

116. See Madison, p.164; J.-B. Pontalis, 'Note sur le problème de l'inconscient chez Merleau-Ponty', *Les Temps Modernes*, 17:184–5 (1961) pp.287–303; J.-B. Pontalis, 'Présence, entre les signes, absence', *L'Arc*, no.46 (1971) pp.56–66; and the more general discussion in Paul Ricoeur, *Freud and Philosophy*, trans. D. Savage (New Haven: Yale University Press, 1970) pp.375–418.

117. Lacan, *Écrits*, p.166.

118. Ibid, pp.55–6, 193–5, 264, 269, 312.

119. Pontalis, 'Le problème de l'inconscient', p.303; Pontalis, 'Présence', p.62.

120. Jacques Lacan, 'Discours de Jacques Lacan', *Actes du Congrès de Rome, La Psychanalyse*, I (1956) p.210, as quoted in Anthony Wilden's notes to Jacques Lacan, *The Language of the Self*, p.100 ft; see also *Écrits*, pp.44, 49, 89–90.

121. *Being and Nothingness*, pp.372–4; a more extensive discussion of language had to await the publication of *What is Literature?*

122. *PP*, p.357; Merleau-Ponty had broached the theme as early as *SB*, p.126.

123. *PP*, p.354.
124. *CAL*, pp.31, 50.
125. *PW*, p.135 (ellipses in original).
126. *PW*, p.139.
127. *TFL*, p.40.
128. For a discussion of the events, see Alexander Werth, *France 1940–1955* (New York: Henry Holt & Co., 1956) pp.575–80.
129. Sartre, *Situations*, p.198.
130. Sartre, *The Communists and Peace with A Reply to Claude Lefort*, trans. M. H. Fletcher, J. R. Kleinschmidt, and P. R. Bert (New York: George Braziller, 1968).
131. Sartre, *Situations*, p.198.
132. Ibid, pp.171–3.
133. On this period see Cooper, pp.82–103.
134. *S*, pp.264, 269.
135. *AD*, p.230.
136. Sartre, *Situations*, pp.205–6.
137. Ibid, p.204.
138. Sartre, *The Communists and Peace*, pp.9–13.
139. *Being and Nothingness*, pp.419–20.
140. Ibid, pp. 421–2.
141. Sartre, *The Communists and Peace*, pp.188–94, 199–206.
142. Ibid, pp.59, 129, 283.
143. Ibid, pp.76–7.
144. See also Dick Howard, 'A Marxist Ontology?', *Cultural Hermeneutics*, 1 (1973) pp.251–2. In a 1975 interview Sartre confessed 'what is particularly bad in *L'Etre et le Néant* is the specifically social chapter, on the "we", compared to the chapters on the "you" and "other" ': Schilpp (ed.), *The Philosophy of Jean-Paul Sartre*, p.13.
145. *Being and Nothingness*, pp.423–4.
146. For a parallel argument, see Sartre 'Materialism and Revolution', in *Literary and Philosophical Essays*, trans. A. Michelson (New York: Collier, 1962) pp.238–9.
147. This instalment followed an exchange with Claude Lefort on the question of whether the proletariat was capable of organising itself spontaneously.
148. Sartre, *The Communists and Peace*, pp.207–8.
149. Ibid, p.208.
150. Ibid, p.216. Poster, *Existential Marxism in Postwar France*, pp.170–1, sees Sartre moving closer to Merleau-Ponty with these arguments, an interpretation I find difficult to accept in light of the continued assertion, on Sartre's part, that 'the very essence of the masses forbids them from thinking and acting politically' and that 'one cannot claim, properly speaking that they make the policy, but rather that they are its instruments': *The Communists and Peace*, p.226.
151. See Sheridan, 'Ontology and Politics', pp.453–4.
152. *H&T*, p.102.
153. *H&T*, p.xxxii.

154. *H&T*, p.xl.
155. *S*, p.223; cf. Machiavelli, *The Prince*, VIII, and Sheldon Wolin, *Politics and Vision* (Boston: Little, Brown, 1960) pp.220–24.
156. *H&T*, pp.109–12.
157. Whitford rightly notes that at times Merleau-Ponty blurs the two levels in his comments on Sartre; see pp.109–14. Kruks strikes me as committing a similar error in her discussion of Merleau-Ponty's politics; see my discussion in 'Maurice Merleau-Ponty: Politics, Phenomenology, and Ontology', p.300.
158. *PP*, pp.442–3.
159. *PP*, pp.444–5.
160. *H&T*, pp.113, 119, 146–7.
161. *AD*, p.105.
162. Ibid.
163. *AD*, p.161.
164. *AD*, p.154.
165. *AD*, pp.107–8.
166. *AD*, p.155.
167. *AD*, p.137.
168. *AD*, p.142.
169. *AD*, p.124.
170. *AD*, p.147.
171. *AD*, p.200; Monika Langer, 'Sartre and Merleau-Ponty: A Reappraisal', in Schilpp (ed.), *The Philosophy of Jean-Paul Sartre*, pp.300–25, has argued, like Simone de Beauvoir, that Merleau-Ponty is attacking a pseudo-Sartrism and that in fact Sartre's position can incorporate the 'interworld' Merleau-Ponty claims is lacking. In an interview in the same volume, however, Sartre states emphatically 'I admit neither that I have the same philosophy as Merleau-Ponty nor that there is this element of interworld . . . The entire ontology that emerges from the philosophy of Merleau-Ponty is distinct from mine. It is much more a continuum than mine. I am not much of a continuist; the in-itself, the for-itself, and the intermediary forms . . . that is enough for me' (p.43).
172. For Merleau-Ponty's earliest use of the concept, see *SB*, p.126.
173. *VI*, pp.50–104.
174. *VI*, p.63.
175. *VI*, pp.62–3.
176. *VI*, p.87.
177. 'We see the things themselves; the world is what we see: formulae of this kind express a faith common to the natural man and the philosopher – the moment he opens his eyes.': *VI*, p.3. In a note written opposite the title of the section which begins with these words, Merleau-Ponty added that perceptual faith 'is not faith in the sense of decision but in the sense of what is before any position'. The earliest use of the term occurs in an article from 1947 where Merleau-Ponty states his intention to describe 'the passage of perceptual faith into

explicit truth' in a work to be called 'The Origin of Truth': *SNS*, p.94 ft.
178. *VI*, pp.52, 77.
179. *VI*, p.68.
180. *VI*, p.72.
181. *VI*, pp.64, 69.
182. *VI*, pp.73, 236–7.
183. *VI*, p.75.
184. *VI*, pp.68–9.
185. *VI*, p.78.
186. Paul Valéry, *Analects*, trans. S. Gilbert, *Collected Works*, vol.14 (Princeton: Princeton University Press, 1970) p.26 – I have modified the translation slightly, which renders *'chiasma'* as 'intercrossing'. Merleau-Ponty quoted the passage in *S*, p.231, and *TFL*, p.14.
187. *VI*, pp.193, 215; Valéry, *Analects*, p.26.
188. *AD*, p.204.
189. *VI*, p.91.
190. *VI*, p.199.
191. *VI*, pp.214–5.
192. *VI*, p.266.
193. *VI*, p.199; the theme was pursued in one of the courses Merleau-Ponty was teaching at the time of his death, 'Philosophy and Non-Philosophy Since Hegel', a course which devoted a good deal of time to Heidegger's discussion of the Introduction to Hegel's *Phenomenology of Spirit*.
194. *VI*, p.268.
195. *VI*, p.260.
196. *PP*, p.92.
197. *S*, pp.166–7; *VI*, pp.9, 133, 141, 204, 249, 254–7.
198. *Being and Nothingness*, p.304.
199. *PP*, p.93; Merleau-Ponty is following Husserl's discussion in *Cartesian Meditations*, p.97, which concludes with the following chiasmus: 'I "can" perceive one hand "by means of" the other, and eye by means of a hand, and so forth – a procedure in which *the functioning organ must become an Object and the Object a functioning organ.*'
200. *PP*, p.95.
201. M. C. Dillon, 'Sartre on the Phenomenal Body and Merleau-Ponty's Critique', *Journal of the British Society for Phenomenology*, 5:2 (May 1974) p.154; see also the discussion in Marjorie Grene, 'Merleau-Ponty and the Renewal of Ontology', pp.618–20, and Grene, *Sartre*, pp.167–9.
202. *Being and Nothingness*, p.358.
203. Dillon, p.157.
204. *VI*, p.171.
205. *VI*, pp.220–1.
206. *VI*, p.171.
207. *VI*, p.254; cf. *TFL*, pp.80–1.

208. *VI*, p.254.
209. *VI*, pp.254–5.
210. *VI*, p.136.
211. *VI*, p.148.
212. *VI*, p.262.
213. *VI*, p.264.
214. *VI*, p.263.
215. *VI*, pp.82–3.
216. *VI*, p.141.
217. *VI*, p.142.
218. *VI*, p.269.
219. *VI*, p.142.
220. *VI*, p.193.
221. *VI*, p.99.
222. *VI*, p.75.
223. *VI*, pp.242, 183. One of the courses he was teaching at the time of his death, 'Cartesian Ontology and Contemporary Ontology', was presumably designed to allow him to make an initial exploration of the themes he would be developing in this part of *The Visible and the Invisible*; see the 'reconstruction' based on student notes attempted in Alexandre Métraux, 'Vision and Being in the last Lectures of Maurice Merleau-Ponty', in L. E. Embree (ed.), *Life-World and Consciousness*, pp.323–36.
224. Descartes, *La Dioptrique*, in *Oeuvres de Descartes*, vol.VI, ed. C. Adam and P. Tannery (Paris: Vrin, 1965) pp.79–228. There is a partial English translation by N. K. Smith in his edition of *Descartes: Philosophical Writings*; it will be cited in parentheses after the citation to Adam and Tannery.
225. *SB*, pp.191–201.
226. *PrP*, p.169.
227. *PrP*, p.170; *Dioptrique*, pp.84, 113–14 (*Philosophical Writings*, p.147).
228. *PrP*, p.170.
229. *PrP*, pp.170–1, 176; *Dioptrique*, p.113 (*Philosophical Writings*, p.146).
230. '. . . it is the soul that sees, and not the eyes, and . . . the soul sees immediately only by the intervention of the brain': *Dioptrique*, p.141 (*Philosophical Writings*, p.157). The passage seems to have held a particular fascination for Merleau-Ponty. He quoted it in *SB*, p.192, and in 'Reading Montaigne' he cited Leon Brunschvicg's *Descartes et Pascal lecteurs de Montaigne*: 'It is never the eye which sees itself . . . but clearly the mind, which alone knows . . . the eye and itself' (*S*, p.199). Also, see *PP*, p.309, where he wrote 'the eye is not the mind, but a material organ'. There is a parallel passage in the *Meditations*, quoted above on p.62. Finally, Sartre came close to Descartes's formulation in *Being and Nothingness*, p.277: 'it is never eyes which look at us; it is the Other-as-subject'.

231. See *Dioptrique*, pp.116, 119, 122, 125, 139 (*Philosophical Writings*, p.146).
232. *VI*, p.210.
233. Paul Valéry, 'Descartes', in *Masters and Friends*, trans. M. Turnell, *Collected Works*, vol.9 (Princeton: Princeton University Press, 1968) p.17. Merleau-Ponty drew on this essay in his 1951 lecture 'Man and Adversity'; see *S*, p.228.
234. *VI*, p.210.
235. Ibid.
236. *PrP*, p.186.
237. Marc Richir, 'La défenestration', *L'Arc*, no.46 (1971) pp.31–42.
238. *VI*, p.113.
239. *VI*, pp.100, 113.
240. *VI*, p.138.
241. *VI*, p.139.
242. *VI*, pp.139–40, 259.
243. *VI*, p.139.
244. *SNS*, p.73.
245. Marjorie Grene, 'The Aesthetic Dialogue of Sartre and Merleau-Ponty', *Journal of the British Society for Phenomenology*, I:2 (May 1970) p.72.
246. *SNS*, p.73.

Chapter 4: Speech, Expression

1. *PrP*, p.25.
2. *PrP*, pp.12–13.
3. *PrP*, p.11.
4. *SNS*, p.94, ft.13.
5. *PrP*, pp.7–9,
6. *PrP*, p.9.
7. Husserl's essay was, as noted above, first published in the 1939 issue of the *Revue internationale de philosophie* devoted to Husserl. It has been translated as an appendix to the *Crisis* (pp.353–78).
8. *Crisis*, pp.354–5, 377–8.
9. *PW*, p.xvi.
10. Jean-Paul Sartre, *What is Literature?*, trans. B. Frechtman (New York: Harper & Row, 1965) p.2.
11. Ibid., pp.6–7.
12. Ibid, pp.7, 9, 3–4. For discussions of Sartre's argument, see Joseph P. Fell, *Heidegger and Sartre* (New York: Columbia University Press, 1979) pp. 268–301; Aronson, pp.122–53. and LaCapra, pp.63–91.
13. Kurt Goldstein, 'L'Analyse de l'aphasie et l'etude de l'essence du langage', *Journal de Psychologie Normale et Pathologique*, 30 (1933) pp.430–96; Kurt Goldstein and Adhémar Gelb, 'Uber Farbennamenamnesie', *Psychologische Forschung*, 6 (1924) pp.127–86;

and Roman Jakobson, *Child Language, Aphasia, and Phonological Universals*, trans. A. R. Keiler (The Hague: Mouton, 1968).

14. Wallon, *Les origines*; Guillaume, *Imitation in Children*; and Jean Piaget, *The Language and Thought of the Child*, trans. M. and R. Gabain (London: Routledge & Kegan Paul, 1932). Piaget, it should be mentioned, succeeded Merleau-Ponty at the Sorbonne and has recalled that when he corrected his first set of examinations 'some candidates, not noticing that the professor had changed, explained that Piaget had understood nothing whatever, "as M. Merleau-Ponty has demonstrated" '. See Piaget, *Insights and Illusions of Philosophy*, trans. W. Mays (New York: Meridian, 1971) p.24. For Gustave Guillaume, see *L'architectonique du temps dans les langues classique* (Copenhagen, 1945).

15. Roland Barthes, *Elements of Semiology*, p.24.

16. The most accessible general introduction to Saussure's work is Jonathan Culler, *Ferdinand de Saussure* (Harmondsworth: Penguin, 1977).

17. Stephen H. Watson, 'Merleau-Ponty's Involvement with Saussure', in Hugh J. Silverman (ed.), *Continental Philosophy in America* (Pittsburgh: Duquesne University Press, 1983) suggests that Merleau-Ponty was aware of Saussure's work as early as 1935 when he assisted Aron Gurwitsch on his article 'Psychologie de langage', *Revue Philosophique de la France et de l'Etranger*, LXX (1935) pp.399–439. Gurwitsch makes, however, only a passing reference to Saussure in a discussion of the work of M. K. Bühler (see p.402). Watson further suggests that Merleau-Ponty 'probably' was making reference to Saussure's distinction between *langue* and *parole* in his discussion of expression in the *Phenomenology of Perception* (p.196), but Merleau-Ponty garbles the distinction slightly, producing an opposition of '*parole*' and '*langages*'. Watson does not feel that Merleau-Ponty addresses Saussure's work 'in its specificity' until his 1949–50 course on *Consciousness and the Acquisition of Language*. See Watson, pp.209–12.

18. Watson, p.212.

19. 'The Metaphysical in Man', in *SNS*, esp. pp.86–8; *PW*, pp.22–46 and ff.

20. *IPP*, pp.54–8.

21. *TFL*, pp.5, 19–20.

22. *SNS*, pp.86, 87; *CAL*, p.97; *PW*, p.23.

23. *PW*, p.38.

24. *PW*, p.23.

25. Culler, p.4, quoting Saussure's letter of 4 January 1894 to Meillet.

26. *IPP*, p.55.

27. Ibid.

28. Ferdinand de Saussure, *Course in General Linguistics*, trans. W. Baskin (New York: McGraw-Hill, 1966). The *Course* is a compilation of Saussure's lectures from 1906–7, 1908–9, and 1910–11 edited by his students, Charles Bally and Albert Sechehaye in 1915. Their

choice and ordering of materials has been the subject of much recent discussion. For a critical edition of the *Course*, with helpful notes, see Saussure, *Cours de linguistique générale*, édition critique préparée par Tullio de Mauro (Paris: Payot, 1972).

29. For a discussion of the various ways Saussure posed the distinction and the various ways it can be translated, see de Mauro's note, *Cours*, pp.419–27.

30. *Course*, p.9.

31. *Course*, pp.18–19, 33; see Baskin's note, *Course*, p.32, for a discussion of Saussure's peculiar use of the term 'phonology'.

32. *Course*, p.98.

33. *Course*, p.87.

34. *Course*, p.19.

35. For a discussion of the methodological implications of Saussure's distinction, see Barthes, pp.13–34.

36. *Course*, p.79; de Mauro notes that the discussions Saussure seems to have been alluding to here were those of Menger and Schmoller (*Cours*, p.451). For a critique of Saussure's distinction which takes Marx's critique of political economy as its model, see Jean Baudrillard, *For a Critique of the Political Economy of the Sign*, trans. C. Levin (St Louis: Telos Press, 1981) pp.143–63.

37. *Course*, pp.81, 90.

38. James Edie, for example, offers an intelligent defence of Merleau-Ponty's interpretation which explains everything except how Merleau-Ponty worked himself into a position where he needed such a complex argument to bail him out. Granting that the object of synchronic linguistics is of course 'the "form" or "system" of the present state of a given language and not the speech act itself', Edie goes on to insist that this object, nevertheless, is 'nothing other than the presently given, incubating and changing structure of the sum total of all presently recognized acts of speaking that take place within a given community' and hence that synchronic linguistics might well be said to be 'nothing but the description of the structure of these acts': see James M. Edie, *Speaking and Meaning: The Phenomenology of Language* (Bloomington: Indiana University Press, 1976) p.219, ft.55. But did Saussure in fact see the structure of a community's speech acts as 'incubating and changing'? Wasn't he concerned to stress that while *what* is said in speech acts varies enormously, the basic structure of a language, the social fact which allows speakers to understand one another, varies only gradually over time and never as a result of innovations intentionally introduced by speakers? We might well say that the concern of synchronic linguistics lies with the structure underlying individual speech acts, but that structure is precisely what Saussure denotes as *langue*. Gary Brent Madison's explanation of how Merleau-Ponty came to identify synchrony with *parole* and diachrony with *langue* is a good deal simpler: Merleau-Ponty 'confused' Saussure's arguments with von Watburg's (Madison, p.322, ft.1). It is difficult to believe that

196   Notes and References

Merleau-Ponty would be this confused in the early 1950s after having taught several courses on Saussure. Watson offers a more convincing explanation, suggesting that Merleau-Ponty might have been seeking to follow up on Saussure's own argument that 'everything diachronic in language is diachronic only by virtue of speaking. It is in speaking that the germ of all change is found' (*Course*, p.98). Watson, however, does not develop the argument very far (see Watson, pp.219–20).

39. *TFL*, pp.19–20.
40. *Course*, pp.65–7.
41. *Course*, p.112.
42. Maurice Lagueux, 'Merleau-Ponty et la linguistique de Saussure', pp.357, 361.
43. Ibid, pp.362–3.
44. Roland Barthes, 'The Imagination of the Sign', in Barthes, *Critical Essays*, trans. R. Howard (Evanston: Northwestern University Press, 1972) p.205.
45. Ibid., p.207.
46. Ibid, pp.206–8; for an example of this type of approach, see Paul Ricoeur's contrasting of the work of M.-D. Chenu with that of Lévi-Strauss, in *The Conflict of Interpretations*, pp.54–61.
47. Saussure, pp.67–70; see the critique of Saussure's more extended argument in Emile Benveniste's famous essay 'The Nature of the Linguistic Sign', in Benveniste, *Problems in General Linguistics*, trans. M. E. Meek (Coral Gabels: University of Miami Press, 1971) pp.43–8.
48. Barthes, *Critical Essays*, pp.207–9.
49. Ibid, p.210.
50. Ibid, p.209.
51. Lagueux, p.361.
52. Barthes, *Critical Essays*, p.210.
53. Ibid, p.208.
54. *PP*, p.174.
55. *PP*, pp.193, 136, 157, 168–9.
56. *PP*, p.197.
57. Ibid.
58. *PP*, p.183.
59. *PP*, pp.183, 193.
60. *PP*, p.185.
61. *PP*, p.405.
62. *PP*, p.193.
63. Ibid.
64. *PP*, p.177; see also *PP*, p.212.
65. *PP*, p.430; see also *PP*, p.253, 'the very significance of the object . . . must be linked to its orientation, as indeed is indicated by the double usage of the French word *sens*'.
66. *PP*, p.176.
67. *PP*, p.114.

68. *PP*, p.429.
69. Ibid.
70. *PP*, pp.185–6.
71. For an analysis of gestures which proceeds from a rather different set of assumptions, see Julia Kristeva, *Semiotícé: Recherches pour une sémanalyse* (Paris: Seuil, 1969) pp. 90–112.
72. *PP*, pp.186–7.
73. *PP*, pp.196–7; it should again be noted that Saussure distinguishes between *parole* and *langue* and reserves the term *langage* to refer to the fusion of the two.
74. *PP*, p.197.
75. Ibid.
76. *PP*, p.184.
77. Ibid.
78. See Heidegger, *Being and Time*, pp.211–14.
79. *PP*, pp.187–8.
80. *PP*, p.187; cf. *CAL*, p.81.
81. *PrP*, p.7.
82. Ibid.
83. *SNS*, p.19.
84. Ibid.
85. *SNS*, p.21.
86. *SNS*, p.32.
87. *SNS*, pp.37, 40.
88. *SNS*, pp.3–4.
89. *H&T*, pp.62, 7–12, 15.
90. *H&T*, pp.52, 55, 62–3.
91. *H&T*, p.40.
92. *H&T*, p.100; cf. Koestler, *Darkness at Noon*, trans. D. Hardy (New York: Modern Library, 1941) pp.82–3.
93. *H&T*, p.55.
94. *H&T*, pp.95, 65–6.
95. *H&T*, p.41.
96. *H&T*, pp.61–2.
97. Stephen F. Cohen, *Bukharin and the Bolshevik Revolution* (New York: Vintage, 1975) pp.359–63.
98. See Roy A. Medvedev, *Let History Judge: The Origins and Consequences of Stalinism*, trans. C. Taylor (New York: Vintage, 1973) pp.349–54, 464–5.
99. Cohen, pp.373–4.
100. Cohen, p.377; see also his meticulous analysis of Bukharin's testimony, pp.377–80; for the arrest of Bukharin's wife and his son, see p.375. They were released twenty years after his execution.
101. *PP*, p.448.
102. *PP*, pp.448–9.
103. *PP*, p.450.
104. For an earlier discussion of Marx's philosophy of history, see 'Concerning Marxism', in *SNS*, pp.99–124.

105. *H&T*, p.108.
106. *H&T*, p.110.
107. *H&T*, p.153.
108. *H&T*, pp.129–30.
109. *H&T*, p.153.
110. *H&T*, pp.155–6.
111. *H&T*, p.126.
112. *SNS*, p.121.
113. *SNS*, pp.121–2.
114. *H&T*, pp.118–9.
115. *AD*, pp.230–2.
116. *PP*, p.450.
117. Kojève, *Introduction to the Reading of Hegel*, pp.29–30; Georg Lukács, *History and Class Consciousness*, trans. R. Livingston (Cambridge, Mass.: MIT Press, 1971) pp.121, 142, 147, 159.
118. For a discussion of these tensions, see James Miller, *History and Human Existence: From Marx to Merleau-Ponty* (Berkeley: University of California Press, 1979) pp.207–19.
119. *IPP*, p.50.
120. Ibid.
121. *IPP*, p.51.
122. *IPP*, pp.53–4.
123. *IPP*, pp.55–6.
124. *CAL*, p.102.
125. *IPP*, p.56.
126. *IPP*, p.54.
127. *PrP*, p.9.
128. Lefort, 'Editor's Preface' to *PW*, p.xxiv; see also the anticipations of these discussions in *PW* , pp.83–4, 112–13.
129. *PW*, pp.3–6.
130. *PW*, pp.31–3, 36.
131. *PW*, pp.43, 36.
132. See the discussion of Sartre in *PW*, pp.61–2.
133. The relationship of 'Indirect Language and the Voices of Silence' to *The Prose of the World* is as follows. The essay begins with a long section on signs which is essentially a summary of the second chapter of *The Prose of the World* (cf. *S*, pp.39–44 and *PW*, pp.22–43). This is followed by a discussion of Malraux's writings on painting (*S*, pp.45–76) which is taken, with only a few stylistic modifications, from the book (see *PW*, pp.43–88). This, in turn, is followed by a discussion of the parallels between writing and painting (*S*, pp.76–82) which is taken, with considerable editing, from *PW*, pp.89–113. One section not taken over into 'Indirect Language', a discussion of problems in the writing of histories of philosophy (with particular reference to Descartes), bears a certain resemblance to Merleau-Ponty's later essay on the problem of treating philosophers historically: 'Everywhere and Nowhere' (cf. *PW*, pp.91–9 and *S*, pp.126–33, 147–52).

134. *PW*, pp.123–4; see also the summary in *PrP*, p.8.
135. The most important aspects of this discussion have been analysed above in Chapter 3.
136. *PW*, pp.147–52; Merleau-Ponty had discussed the parallels between drawing and language acquisition in *CAL*, pp.11 and 61.
137. *PW*, p.148.
138. *TFL*, pp.27–38; see Métraux's notes in *Vorlesungen*, pp.284–5, for a discussion of the relationship of the course to Merleau-Ponty's earlier writings.
139. Kruks ignores the book altogether, as does Cooper. Spurling's discussion of language is confined almost exclusively to the *Phenomenology of Perception* (pp.48–75) and Rabil's work was published before *The Prose of the World* was available. There is a suggestive discussion of the relation between Merleau-Ponty's notion of 'instruction' and his philosophy of expression in O'Neill, pp.46–64, which draws on 'Indirect Language and the Voices of Silence'.
140. *PW*, p.31; cf. pp.33, 115 and *CAL*, pp.28–9.
141. *PW*, pp.6–7.
142. *PW*, p.115.
143. Ibid.
144. *PW*, p.32.
145. *PW*, pp.31–2; 116.
146. *S*, p.39.
147. *S*, pp.41–2; cf. *CAL*, p.92.
148. *S*, pp.44–5; *PW*, p.144.
149. *PW*, p.37.
150. *PW*, p.115.
151. *PW*, p.37.
152. *S*, pp.54–5, 75–6; *PW*, pp.60–1, 87–8.
153. *S*, p.55; *PW*, p.61.
154. *S*, p.81; *PW*, p.103.
155. For a discussion of the treatment of questions of reference in structuralist approaches to language, see Paul Ricoeur, 'Structure, Word, Event', in *The Conflict of Interpretations*, pp.84–5.
156. By 'object', Saussure meant the *telos* towards which a science moves, as opposed to the 'material' which a number of sciences can share; see de Mauro's note, *Cours*, pp.414–5.
157. *CAL*, p.101.
158. *PW*, p.83.
159. *AD*, p.19; see the parallel discussion in 'Everywhere and Nowhere', *S*, pp.126–7.
160. *AD*, pp.3–4.
161. *S*, p.73; *PW*, p.85.
162. Barthes, *Elements of Semiology*, pp.23–5 (the discussion, however, misses the point of Merleau-Ponty's use of the concept of 'advent' and presents him as simply reiterating the distinction between structure and event); and Ricoeur, *Conflict of Interpretations*, pp.86–8.

163. Fernand Braudel, *On History*, trans. S. Matthews (Chicago: University of Chicago Press, 1980) pp.27–34, 74–6.
164. *S*, pp.60–2, 68–70; *PW*, pp.71–2, 80–3.
165. Ricoeur, 'Objectivity and Subjectivity in History', in *History and Truth*, pp.33–6. The essay dates from 1952; Merleau-Ponty attributes the notion to Ricoeur in 'Indirect Language and the Voices of Silence' but does not cite the article itself.
166. *Crisis*, p.354.
167. Ibid, pp.354, 359.
168. *S*, p.59; *PW*, p.68. The term is defined (*'fondation ou éstablissement'*) only in 'Indirect Language and the Voices of Silence'. The words 'foundation, institution' which follow the German term in *PW*, p.68, have been added by the translator.
169. *PW*, p.72.
170. *S*, p.60; *PW*, p.72.
171. *PW*, p.23.
172. *PW*, pp.23, 36 (both are marginal notes to the text).
173. *S*, p.61; *PW*, p.71.
174. *S*, p.64.
175. *S*, p.61; *PW*, p.71.
176. *AD*, pp.16–17.
177. Merleau-Ponty's interpretation of Weber's account of rationalisation was guided by Karl Löwith's great 1932 essay, *Max Weber and Karl Marx*, trans. H. Fantel (London: Allen & Unwin, 1982).
178. *AD*, p.17.
179. Ibid.
180. *AD*, p.16.
181. *AD*, p.11; cf. the discussions of Weber in Alfred Schutz, *The Phenomenology of the Social World*, pp.31–8; 234–6.
182. Weber, *Economy and Society*, ed. G. Roth and C. Wittich (Berkeley: University of California Press, 1978) pp.3–26. It is this discussion which serves as the basis for Schutz's analysis.
183. *AD*, pp.13–14.
184. *AD*, p.13; cf. Schutz, *Phenomenology*, pp.224–9.
185. *S*, p.119.
186. Max Weber, *The Protestant Ethic and the Spirit of Capitalism*, trans. T. Parsons (New York: Scribner, 1958) p.175; see *AD*, p.15. Weber's footnote to the Wesley quotation is worth noting as it bears out Merleau-Ponty's reading rather nicely: 'The reading of this passage may be recommended to all those who consider themselves today better informed on these matters than the leaders and contemporaries of the movements themselves. As we see, they knew very well what they were doing and what dangers they faced': Weber, *Protestant Ethic*, p.280. See also Merleau-Ponty's discussion of Lucien Febvre's study of Rabelais in *SNS*, p.92, for a similar argument.
187. *AD*, p.28.
188. *AD*, p.16.

189. *AD*, p.24.
190. *AD*, p.23.
191. *PW*, p.148.
192. *AD*, p.3.
193. Ibid.
194. *AD*, pp.30–31.
195. Paul Breines and Andrew Arato described *Adventures of the Dialectic* as 'the most lucid brief commentary on *History and Class Consciousness*'. See *The Young Lukács and the Origins of Western Marxism* (New York: Seabury, 1979) p.220.
196. The earliest citation of *History and Class Consciousness* comes in an article from 1946 (*SNS*, p.126) but it is likely that he read the book much earlier. In the same year, he and Lukács were present at the Recontre Internationales de Genève, although at this point Lukács had renounced his earlier work and devoted his talk to a critique of 'irrational' and 'aristocratic' doctrines such as the writings of Nietzsche and Spengler, which brought on a series of exchanges with Karl Jaspers; Merleau-Ponty, who had delivered a talk at the meetings which stressed the importance of Husserl's *Crisis of the European Sciences* for a renovation of the concept of reason, responded to the Lukács–Jaspers exchange with an attempt to recall certain of the dimensions of voluntarism and contingency which had stood at the centre of Lukács's 1923 discussion of Marx; see *L'Esprit européen. Recontres internationales de Genève* (Neuchatel: Editions de la Baconniére, 1947) pp.74–7, 252–6. See also Merleau-Ponty's 1949 note on one of Lukács's many self-criticisms and disavowals of his earlier work, reprinted in *S*, pp.261–2.
197. *AD*, p.30; for Lukács's own account, see 'Mein Weg zur Marx', in Lukács, *Schriften zur Ideologie und Politik* (Neuwied: Luchterhand, 1967).
198. *AD*, pp.30, 21.
199. *AD*, p.30.
200. *AD*, pp.30–1.
201. *AD*, p.31.
202. *AD*, p.32.
203. *AD*, pp.35–6; in the passages that follow I have retained Merleau-Ponty's own translation of the German as '*devenir-société de la société*'. Merleau-Ponty's English translator employs a translation based on the German: 'the socialization of society'.
204. *AD*, p.37.
205. Ibid.
206. *AD*, p.38.
207. *AD*, pp.38, 57.
208. *AD*, p.44.
209. Ibid.
210. *AD*, p.45.
211. *AD*, p.47.
212. *AD*, p.50.

213. *AD*, p.51.
214. *AD*, pp.51–3.
215. *AD*, p.57; for a discussion of the fate of the book, see Arato and Breines, pp.163–89.
216. *AD*, p.60.
217. *AD*, pp.61–2.
218. *AD*, p.62.
219. Ibid.
220. *AD*, p.63.
221. *AD*, p.64.
222. For the relation of the two books, see Arato and Breines, pp.170–5.
223. *AD*, p.64.
224. Ibid.
225. *AD*, p.66.
226. *AD*, pp.64–5.
227. *AD*, p.221.
228. *AD*, pp.72–3.
229. *AD*, p.90.
230. *AD*, p.221.
231. *AD*, p.207.
232. See the Introduction to *Signs*: 'Man is hidden, well hidden, and this time we must make no mistake about it: this does not mean that he is there beneath the mask, ready to appear ... there are no faces underneath the masks, historical man has never been human, and yet no man is alone' (*S*, pp.33–4).
233. *AD*, p.227.
234. *AD*, p.226.
235. *S*, p.178.
236. *S*, p.84.
237. *PW*, p.148.
238. *S*, p.70; *PW*, p.83.
239. See the qualifying statements in the text and the marginal note in *PW*, pp.80–1.
240. *S*, p.70.
241. *S*, p.67; *PW*, p.78; *PW*, pp.18, 123.
242. *PP*, p.402.
243. *PP*, p.403.
244. Ibid.
245. See Stephen Watson, 'Pretexts: Language, Perception, and the Cogito in Merleau-Ponty's Thought', in Sallis (ed.), *Merleau-Ponty: Perception, Structure, Language*, pp.149, 153; see also *PP*, p.153.
246. *VI*, p.171.
247. *VI*, p.179.
248. *VI*, pp.171, 179.
249. *VI*, p.179.
250. *VI*, p.176.
251. *VI*, p.201.
252. Ibid.

253. Ibid.
254. *VI*, p.145.
255. *VI*, p.153.
256. *VI*, p.155.
257. Ibid.
258. *VI*, pp.154–5.
259. *VI*, p.126.
260. *VI*, p.224.

Chapter 5: Conclusion

1. Drawing on Merleau-Ponty's continued reliance on certain phrases and examples from Husserl's writings, Jacques Taminiaux has argued that claims that he abandoned phenomenology towards the end of his life are overstated; see 'Phenomenology in Merleau-Ponty's Late Work', in Embree (ed.), *Life-World and Consciousness*, pp.307–22. Frederic L. Bender, 'Merleau-Ponty and Method: Toward a Critique of Husserlian Phenomenology and Reflective Philosophy in General', *Journal of the British Society for Phenomenology*, 14:2 (May 1983) pp.176–95, argues in contrast that the repudiation of the 'philosophy of reflection' in *The Visible and the Invisible* must be read as a critique of Husserl as well.
2. *VI*, pp.181–2.
3. *VI*, p.224.
4. *VI*, p.227.
5. *VI*, p.239.
6. *VI*, p.244.
7. *VI*, p.253.
8. *PrP*, p.42.
9. *VI*, pp.107, 49.
10. *VI*, pp.30, 173, 35, 43.
11. *VI*, pp.35, 107, 112.
12. *VI*, p.244; see also *VI*, p.165.
13. Husserl, *Experience and Judgement*, p.50.
14. *VI*, p.244.
15. For a thoughtful analysis of the ambiguities which plague Merleau-Ponty's handling of the notion of intentionality, see Madison, pp.32, 170–1, 186–7.
16. *PP*, p.429.
17. Madison, p.272; see also p.33.
18. *PP*, p.298.
19. *PP*, p.430.
20. *PP*, p.454.
21. *TFL*, p.40.
22. *VI*, p.200.
23. *VI*, p.107.
24. *VI*, p.45; there is an interesting parallel here to Jacques Derrida's

otherwise quite different discussion of Husserl in his introduction to *The Origin of Geometry*, pp.152–3; see also the discussion of his notion of 'ordinary delay' in Descombes, pp.145–52.

25. Descombes provides a helpful overview and typology of different orientations within 'structuralism'; see pp.75–109. The most rigorous attempt to formulate a coherent sense of what is involved in a 'structuralist' analysis is Philip Pettit's brilliant little book *The Concept of Structuralism: A Critical Analysis* (Berkeley: University of California Press, 1975). For other helpful discussions see the essays in John Sturrock (ed.), *Structuralism and Since: From Lévi-Strauss to Derrida* (Oxford: Oxford University Press, 1979), and Jonathan Culler, *Structuralist Poetics* (Ithaca: Cornell University Press, 1975).

26. Eugenio Donato, 'Structuralism: The Aftermath', *Substance*, no.7 (Fall 1973) pp.9–10.

27. For other discussions of Merleau-Ponty's relationship to structuralism, see James M. Edie, 'Was Merleau-Ponty a Structuralist?, *Semiotica*, 4 (1971) pp.297–323 (subsequently rewritten in Edie, *Speaking and Meaning*, pp.72–123); James M. Edie, 'The Meaning and Development of Merleau-Ponty's Concept of Structure', in Sallis (ed.), *Merleau-Ponty: Perception, Structure, Language*, pp.39–57; Colin Smith, 'Merleau-Ponty and Structuralism', *Journal of the British Society for Phenomenology*, II:3 (October 1971) pp.53–8; William C. Gay, 'Merleau-Ponty on Language and Social Science: The Dialectic of Phenomenology and Structuralism', *Man and World*, 12 (1979) pp.322–38; Jonathan Culler, 'Phenomenology and Structuralism', *The Human Context*, 5 (1973) pp.35–42; and John Mepham, 'The Structuralist Sciences and Philosophy', in David Robey (ed.), *Structuralism: An Introduction* (Oxford: Oxford University Press, 1973) pp.104–37. The Culler and Mepham essays are the best of the lot. There is also a rather esoteric German work on the subject: Klaus Boer, *Maurice Merleau-Ponty: Die Entwicklung seines Strukturdenken* (Bonn: Bouvier Verlag Herbert Grundmann, 1978), which is concerned with interpreting Merleau-Ponty's work in the light of the *Strukturontologie* of Heinrich Rombach.

28. Benveniste, p.44.

29. Ibid; for a discussion of the implications of Benveniste's critique for the social sciences, see Anthony Giddens, *Central Problems in Social Theory* (Berkeley: University of California Press, 1979) pp.14–18.

30. Saussure, *Course*, p.113.

31. This point has been stressed by Giddens, see pp.15–16.

32. *VI*, p.176.

33. Descombes, pp.104–5.

34. For an extremely helpful discussion see Pierre Bourdieu and Jean-Claude Passeron, 'Sociology and Philosophy in France Since 1945: Death and Resurrection of a Philosophy Without a Subject', *Social Research*, 34:1 (Spring 1967) pp.162–212.

35. Lévi-Strauss, *The Raw and the Cooked*, p.12.

36. Louis Althusser and Etienne Balibar, *Reading Capital*, trans. B. Brewster (New York: Pantheon, 1970) pp.63, 112, 252.
37. Louis Althusser, *Lenin and Philosophy and Other Essays*, trans. B. Brewster (New York: Monthly Review, 1971) pp.173–4, 180.
38. Michel Foucault, *The Order of Things: An Archaeology of the Human Sciences* (New York: Vintage, 1973) p.387.
39. Gérard Raulet, 'Structuralism and Post-Structuralism: An Interview with Michel Foucault', *Telos*, no.55 (1983) p.199.
40. Bourdieu and Passeron, p.168.
41. See Charles Lemert's introduction to his collection of essays, *French Sociology: Rupture and Renewal Since 1968* (New York: Columbia University Press, 1981) esp. pp.24–6. One thinker who comes most readily to mind in this context is Pierre Bourdieu. See his *Outline of a Theory of Practice*, trans. R. Nice (Cambridge: Cambridge University Press, 1977) esp. pp.25–7, 72–3, 80, 84. Bourdieu's work has been compared with Merleau-Ponty's by James M. Ostrow, 'Culture as a Fundamental Dimension of Experience: A Discussion of Pierre Bourdieu's Theory of Human Habitus', *Human Studies*, 4 (1981) pp.279–97.
42. See Roland Barthes's inaugural lecture at the Collège de France trans. by R. Howard in S. Sontag (ed.), *A Barthes Reader* (New York: Hill & Wang, 1982) pp.457–78 and his comments in *Prétexte: Roland Barthes* (Colloques de Cerisy, 1979) pp.29–30. The parallels to Merleau-Ponty have been noted in Watson, 'Merleau-Ponty's Involvement with Saussure', p.219.
43. See Pettit, pp.40–2, 70–2, and Culler, *Structuralist Poetics*, pp.45, 47–9, 51. From a different perspective Jacques Derrida has noted the tension in Lévi-Strauss's work between interpretations which could go on without the restraint of a 'center' which limits the 'play' of structures, and his often quite arbitrary recourses to the categories of 'mind' and 'nature' as ways of ending the 'play' of his structures; see 'Structure, Sign, and Play in the Discourse of the Human Sciences', in Derrida, *Writing and Difference*, trans. A. Bass (Chicago: University of Chicago Press, 1978) pp.278–93.
44. This point has been stressed in Culler, 'Phenomenology and Structuralism', and developed in his discussion of literary competence in *Structuralist Poetics*.

Index

of the Dialectic 3, 6, 87–9;
critique of *What is Literature?* in
The Prose of the World 6, 60,
127–8, 132; criticism of Sartre's
view of phenomenological
psychology 47; initial
evaluation of *Being and
Nothingness* 59–60; and
Sartre's critique of the
transcendental ego 69–70;
critique of *Being and
Nothingness* in *The Visible and
the Invisible* 89–92, 96–7;
Sartre's evaluation of
Phenomenology of Perception
183n13

works: *The Emotions* 47; *Being and
Nothingness* 58–60, 61–2,
64–5, 68, 78, 83–5, 87, 89–92,
92–4, 100–1; *The Communists
and Peace* 60, 81–3, 84–5; *The
Transcendence of the Ego* 67–8;
What is Literature? 104, 127–8;
Critique of Dialectical Reason
161

Saussure, Ferdinand de: distinction
between 'speech' (*parole*) and
'language' (*langue*) 105–7, 134;
synchrony v. diachrony in 105–7,
195n38; on history 107; on the
sign 108, 109–10, 161–2; neglect
of the problem of reference 162

Merleau-Ponty on: importance of
Saussure's linguistics 1, 47,
141; peculiarities in
Merleau-Ponty's interpretation
11, 105–9, 114, 132–3, 161–3,
194n17, 195n38; significance for
the philosophy of history 105,
127, 133–4, 137, 147; on
diacritical conception of
meaning in 130–2; implications
for 'new ontology' 152–4

Science: relation to philosophy 14,
21–2, 52, 54–5; in Descartes 21;
in Husserl 21, 32; Merleau-Ponty
on 37, 52

Schutz, Alfred 181n210

Sign, the: Sartre on 104, 132;
'arbitrary' relation of signifier and
signified in 108–10, 114–16, 129,
161–2, 164; Saussure on 108,
109–10, 161–2; Merleau-Ponty

on 108, 115, 130–3; Barthes on
109–11; 'symbolic' conception of
109, 129–30, 141; 'paradigmatic'
conception of 110–11, 130–1,
141; 'syntagmatic' conception of
110–11; Benveniste on 161–2

Signification: as imposition of meaning
113; as *Gestalt* 113–14

Signifier: 'floating' 50–1; and
signified 108–10, 114–16, 129,
161–2, 164

Situation 60, 101

Social facts 48–9

Social theory: Merleau-Ponty and 2,
10, 11–12, 163; and structuralism
165; contemporary problems of
166

Society: in Merleau-Ponty 48; in
Mauss 49–50

Sociology, explanations in 51–4, 139

Sorbonne: Merleau-Ponty's courses at
2, 11, 58, 73, 74–6, 78, 105;
Husserl's lectures at 18

Speech *see* Language

Stalin, Josef 119–20

Structuralism: Merleau-Ponty and 4,
9–10, 160; and language 53;
Lévi-Strauss on 53; and the
cogito 160; and disdain for
origins 160; and history 161; and
the subject 164; and Durkheim
165; and social theory 165

Structure: Merleau-Ponty on 51, 52;
Lévi-Strauss on 53; in Saussure
134, 195n38; and event 133; in
language 136; and agency 163;
and the subject 163

Subject: in Husserl 24–5, 27–8, 33, 42;
in Lévi-Strauss 54; Lacan on 75,
76; in Sartre 88; in Lukács 124,
144; and structuralism 164; in
Althusser 165; in Foucault 165;
in post-structuralism 166

in Merleau-Ponty: incarnate 7, 8,
41–4; speaking 46–7, 105, 111,
152; constituting v. instituting
79–80; expressive 79, 128, 141,
149–51, 153; historical 124;
perceiving 124, 151, 152–3;
and his critique of
phenomenology 156;
instituting/instituted 158;
practical 163